BENEATH THE SUN

Portrait of a Strapper by Sir William Dobell (by courtesy of the Newcastle City Art Gallery).

Contents

HESBA BRINSMEAD

The Hijacked Bathtub

Illustrations by Astra Lacis

EMILY had a large number of relatives who lived in the mountains. There was Aunt Gertrude, who lived in a cottage with seven cats, a lazy dog, and Uncle Henry. There was Uncle George, who lived by himself in a bungalow in Grandmother's big garden. There were Great-Aunt Abbie and Uncle Beresford, with whom Aunt Gertrude was not on speaking terms. There were Aunt Rose and Uncle John, who were not on speaking terms with Aunt Gertrude. And there was Grandmother. In summer Emily's mother took her, along with Bill, to stay in Grandmother's house. Bill, unlike Emily, had not yet reached years of discretion. In fact he was scarcely two years old. It was on the very first day, when it came to Bill's bedtime, that the Great Bathtub Affair began.

"Where," asked Emily's mother, whose name was Nell, "is that nice old hip bath that used to hang on the wall in the storeroom?"

"Hip bath?" said Grandmother.

"Yes, you remember the hip bath! Why, I used to be bathed in it when I was Bill's age. There's a snapshot of me being bathed in it! It's in your album!"

Emily remembered the faded picture of a young child in a queerly-shaped bathtub, that was in the album on Grandmother's bookshelf. So that was Mother! Well! Grandmother was saying:

"You were all bathed in it, in your time. You and Gertrude and Rose and even George. That tub belonged to your great-aunt Ruby, if you remember her."

"Certainly I remember her. But where's the tub?"

"I don't really know now, that you mention it. I don't seem to have seen it about lately."

Mother had to bath Bill in a large dish and pour water over him with a dipper. He considered it a terrible indignity. When he was finally put to bed, cross but clean, Mother said:

"I shouldn't be surprised if Gertrude has taken that tub. It would be just like Gertrude. You must tell her to give it back!"

"Well, it isn't as if it belonged to anyone in particular," said Grandmother. "It isn't as if it's a valuable antique. Aunt Ruby didn't mention it in her will."

"I was very fond of that bathtub," said Mother. "Emily was the last child to be bathed in it. Now, here's Bill in need of it. It should be mine."

"Oh dear!" sighed Grandmother. "You know Gertrude."

"In the morning," said Mother with determination, "I shall go to Gertrude and demand that bathtub."

So when morning came Mother and Emily set off for Aunt Gertrude's, with Bill riding in the wheelbarrow. They soon arrived at the open door of the cottage, the morning sun streaming through it. Aunt Gertrude came forward to meet them. She wore flannelette pyjamas with gumboots and a red parka on top.

"I've been picking plums," said Aunt Gertrude. "Have some."

While they ate plums Emily noted two cats, a white and a marmalade, asleep on the couch. They began to uncurl, then jumped lightly to the floor and stretched themselves. From the corner of her eye Emily caught another movement and a flash of white, as a cat jumped down from the top of the television set. The fruitbowl on the refrigerator contained a pretty, half-grown cat who sat in the bowl like a king on a throne, proudly washing himself.

"Shoo!" said Mother suddenly.

Emily was just in time to see another cat jump down from the table. It was as though everything she looked at turned itself into a cat. She had quite given up trying to count them. Then something stirred in the old leather armchair under the window. To her surprise it was not a cat this time, but Uncle Henry.

"Hello, little girl," he whispered hoarsely. "You must be Emily."

"Yes, I am," she whispered back. She remembered that Uncle Henry always spoke in a whisper, but Aunt Gertrude always shouted at the top of her voice. She was doing it now, as she rushed around making tea.

"There are no biscuits," she yelled. Emily thought she must

be furious—but then she bellowed, "Anyway, there's plenty of bread and jam."

Mother uttered a distracted cry and salvaged Bill from a large bowl of cat's food on the floor by the table. He was slapping his hands in it, then licking them with relish. Attention turned to Bill; and a large white cat standing on a chair with his forepaws on the table delicately licked at the contents of the cream-bowl. Aunt Gertrude poured cups of tea, and Mother drank hers as if it were medicine, saying that it was too soon after breakfast and plums to eat anything more. Then——

"Gertrude," said Mother, "do you know anything about that nice old hip bath that used to hang in Mother's storeroom?"

"Yes. I've got it."

Ah-ha! Mother's flashing eyes seemed to say; but she knew that tact was needed. "I *would* like that tub," she said sweetly. "I need it for bathing Bill. And anyway, I've always had a sentimental attachment to that tub. You don't use it, do you?"

"Yes, I do," said Aunt Gertrude. She took a bit of bread and jam and snapped her mouth shut on it.

"Why, whatever do you use it for?"

"I keep cat's food in it."

There was a pause while Mother took herself in hand. Then——"Isn't Bill more important——?" she began. But Aunt Gertrude chopped off her protest.

"You can bathe him in a dish," she said, "and pour water over him with a dipper."

So they took their departure. They had hoped to wheel the tub away in the wheelbarrow, but it still contained only Bill. As they went through the gate they had to detour round the dog, which lay on the path asleep.

When they got back, Grandmother said, "Well, Nell, you must have known what Gertrude would be like."

Uncle George was there, and heard their story with sympathy. "The only thing," he told Mother, "will be to hijack that bathtub."

"You mean—steal it back?"

"That's a nasty word for it! It won't be stealing, because the tub doesn't belong to anyone. We'll just—hijack it. If they can hijack aeroplanes, surely we can hijack a bathtub."

"She'd know I'd taken it," said Mother. "She'd simply come and take it back."

"But you wouldn't have taken it!" Uncle George was full of cunning. "I'll take it! And it won't be here! I'll take it to Great-Aunt Abbie's place. Gertrude isn't speaking to her, so she never goes there."

The more he thought of it, the better Uncle George liked his idea. He decided that the best time for hijacking would be that same afternoon; for then Aunt Gertrude and Uncle Henry would be driving all the way to the nearest town, to go shopping. Emily's mother must play no part in the hijacking; but Uncle George agreed to take Emily along as an assistant.

After lunch, Uncle George came sidling into Grandmother's kitchen. His straw hat was pulled low over his eyes; even in his droopy shorts and blue singlet, he could easily have been a secret agent in disguise. He was quite a young uncle.

"They've gone," he said. "I saw the car drive away. Come on, Emily."

It was hot work, pushing the wheelbarrow up the hill to Aunt Gertrude's cottage. At Grandmother's, wherever one went it was uphill or downhill. Nothing was on the level.

"Where will we *look* for the bathtub?" Emily asked.

"It's probably under the house."

Aunt Gertrude's house was on a steep hillside, with the garage and storage space underneath. They went through the open gate, stepped over the dog, and made their way to the back. Here, among the piles that the cottage was built on, were all sorts of things—broken chairs, tins of paint, an old trunk— and the bathtub. It had a high back, beautifully curved sides, and a delightful curly handle at each end. Mother had said she would paint it white with blue trimmings, and Emily could easily see that it would be the most charming bathtub in the world. She and Uncle George loaded it on to the wheelbarrow.

"What are you doing?"

It was a sudden hoarse whisper behind them. Emily almost

jumped into the wheelbarrow with fright, and Uncle George's eyes popped wildly.

"You shouldn't *do* that!" he gasped. "Creeping up on a bloke! Why aren't you off in the car with Gertrude?"

"Ah——" Uncle Henry cleared his throat to whisper better. "I was real sorry this morning, about this bathtub. I was going to slip it down to Nell while Gertrude does the messages."

Kind Uncle Henry! He helped them load the wheelbarrow, and cleared several cats from their way. "Gertrude won't even notice that it's gone," he said. "I always put away the cats' food. It can go in the trunk just as well."

They said goodbye and set off for Great-Aunt Abbie's house. Emily had to steady the tub all the way down the hill. By the time they reached Great-Aunt Abbie's, Uncle George's arms refused to bend at the elbows and his back refused to straighten. He came into Aunt Abbie's house all bent, still pushing a phantom wheelbarrow.

"And what are you doing with the old hip bath?" asked Great-Aunt Abbie as she poured them a cold drink. "Why don't you leave it outside in the wheelbarrow?" For they had carried it in with them.

They explained that it was being hijacked, and that they expected her to shelter it for a week or two, just until Aunt Gertrude had finished looking for it at Grandmother's house.

"The only thing," said Great-Aunt Abbie, "is that Gertrude and I have ironed out our little misunderstanding. We're really the best of friends. Gertrude was going to call in with some shopping that she was doing for me. I believe this is her now."

Indeed, they heard a car pull into the driveway and stop.

"What will we *do?*" cried Emily.

But Great-Aunt Abbie was always resourceful. Quickly she dragged the tub into a corner of the hall and put a chair in front of it. Then she scooped up a large bunch of hydrangeas from a big vase in front of the fireplace and dropped them into the tub. They still did not fill it adequately, so she ran to the kitchen and came back with a bunch of rhubarb and one of spinach. She added them to the flowers, dropping them well over the sides and back of the tub. It made a magnificent decoration. Hardly had she given an artistic twitch to a rhubarb leaf than Aunt Gertrude walked in.

"Hullo!" she yelled. "Hullo, George—Emily. Having a nice

holiday? Abbie, I couldn't get veal, so here are lamb chops instead——" Luckily, none of the others were expected to say anything, and she was too busy talking to notice their guilty expressions. At last—"I'll be over this evening for a game of Scrabble," she shouted. "Of course Henry won't come. Well, I'd better be on my way——"

As soon as her car pulled out of the driveway, the hijackers conferred.

"You can't leave that bathtub here," said Great-Aunt Abbie. "Gertrude would notice it this evening. And I want to cook the spinach."

It was decided that as soon as it was dark Uncle George and Emily would bring the wheelbarrow and transport the tub to Aunt Rose's house.

"After all," said Uncle George, "if Rose and John are not speaking to Gertrude, she's hardly likely to visit them."

But Mother, on hearing their tale, was so eager to see her favourite bathtub again that she wanted short cuts.

"If Gertrude is going to Abbie's," she said, "she won't come here, surely. It would be *so* marvellous to be able to bath Bill in it this evening. Couldn't you bring it here, after dark? I'll let Bill stay up later than usual, so that he can use it."

She persuaded Uncle George, against his better judgment. At dusk, he might have been seen wheeling the fine old bathtub along the rutted lane by the apple orchard. Emily steadied the bathtub. They had to turn on to the highway for the last few hundred yards. In the poor light a car nearly ran them down. It stopped just ahead of them, and a figure got out. For an awful moment Emily thought it was Aunt Gertrude—but it was only a policeman, trembling with the fright they had given him.

"What in the name——" he bellowed, quite like Aunt Gertrude, "——have you got there?"

"A bathtub," said Uncle George.

"Well, it hasn't got a tail light. See to it, or next time I'll book you!" The policeman seemed all to pieces. Muttering something about bathtubs wandering all over the country, and about no one being safe these days, he got back into his car and drove off. They turned into Grandmother's gate. Mother was waiting with Bill and a bucket of hot water.

What a party it was, when Bill was installed in the vintage

tub on Grandmother's kitchen hearth! Bill laughed and splashed with glee.

"Doesn't he look an angel?" cooed Mother. "I must get my camera. Fortunately I brought a flash-bulb!"

She had hardly left the room when Grandmother rushed in, twisting her hands in agitation. "The worst, the worst!" she cried. "Gertrude has arrived! I suppose she's bringing my plums. George, you must do something!"

Uncle George, calling on all his strength, lifted up bathtub, soapsuds and baby, rushed them outside, and dropped them into the wheelbarrow. Before Emily could even groan, he was wheeling it off at a great rate towards Aunt Rose's house. Emily ran after him, and after her came Mother.

"Emily? George? What on earth——?" She caught up with Emily, camera in hand.

"*Sshh!* We have to take it to Aunt Rose's house!"

Soon it was clear that on the rough, steep track it was no longer Uncle George pushing the bathtub; the bathtub was pulling Uncle George. They could hear him running faster and faster, muttering abuse at the wheelbarrow.

"You—you—cussed—contraption——"

"My baby!" cried Mother. "If they hit a stone, Bill will go into orbit!"

"He might——" panted Emily, "——be the first—space baby!"

Actually, Bill was enjoying the ride. His laughter floated back under the apple boughs.

At last the wild ride was over. The wheelbarrow stopped of its own accord at Aunt Rose's back door. Uncle George leaned over the handles, gasping for breath. Bill stood up in the tub and waved, and the whole thing would have toppled over if Emily had not steadied it. Aunt Rose and Uncle John had come out, wondering. Mother explained their plight, and they were all brought into the kitchen except the wheelbarrow. They propped Uncle George in a chair and found towels for Bill, and also a pink frilly nightgown that had once belonged to Emily's Cousin Joan. The bathwater had almost all splashed out of the tub.

Suddenly a familiar voice shouted from the front of the house. "Anyone home?"

"*It's Gertrude!*" hissed Mother. "Doesn't she *ever* go where she says she's going?"

They crowded to the sitting room, leaving the tub alone and guilty in the kitchen. Uncle John shut the door and turned the key. Aunt Gertrude came sailing in through the front door.

"Nell, you're here? And Emily? And even Bill! Why is he wearing that pink garment?"

"We were—just—trying it on," gasped Mother.

"As it fits him," said Aunt Rose bravely, "I can give Nell the pattern."

"I've brought you some plums," said Aunt Gertrude to Aunt Rose. She seemed to have forgotten that Aunt Rose and Uncle John were not on speaking terms with her since she had backed her car into their letterbox and refused to replace it. She was carrying a bucket of plums. "I'll put them in the kitchen." She lunged past Uncle John and tried to open the door.

"I was just—working—on that door," said Uncle John. "Leave the plums here and we can deal with them later."

Aunt Gertrude chucked Bill under the chin and he giggled, holding his arms to her. "Tude," he said. "Tude."

"He *knows* me! He knows my name!" Aunt Gertrude grabbed him up and gave him a great hug, while he crowed with delight and pulled her nose. "Oh, Nell, do you really think this gorgeous child would like the old hip bath? I'll send Henry down with it first thing in the morning."

"Oh—Gertrude—thank you!" said Mother, and burst into tears.

Aunt Gertrude viewed her with concern. "Well, if it's all *that* important to you," she said, "keep it. I can't stay. I'm on my way to Abbie's for a game of Scrabble. Goodnight, all."

When the sound of her car receded, Mother turned to Uncle George.

"I feel such a *criminal*. George, you'll have to take the bathtub back."

"I can't," croaked George. "I'm done for." He did seem to have set into a peculiar attitude.

"I'll take it," said Uncle John. "In the car. And I'll have a word with Henry while I'm there."

Mother had Emily put Bill up on her shoulders. Poor, bent Uncle George going ahead with a broom to lean on, they made their way back to Grandmother's house.

JEAN GALBRAITH

The Sea, the Shore and the Pool

THE TIDE is going out at Flat Rocks. The sparkling blue of the sea has hardly a whitecap on it, although two hours ago, before the tide turned, it was all flecked with little waves. Twice every day the tide goes out, leaving a bare stretch of sand and rocks and pools where the seagulls fish; and twice every day it comes in, covering the beach right up to the dry edge of sand where the seaweed and shells lie amongst clumps of pink Sea Rocket in flower.

It is a long way out now. When it turns, beginning to go back down the shore, we can't see any difference between one wave and the next, but after a while the waves do not run quite up to the edge of the wet sand. Then we can see the stretch of sand getting wider and wider between the Sea Rocket and the edge of the waves. You can see the patterns the waves make as they run up the sand in lovely curves, one overlapping another. There is foam on the edge of each wave, and some is left behind like a necklace of bubbles that burst one by one until all you can see is the faint pattern of curved lines where the bubbles were.

The shallow wave-edges look as clear as crystal, with nothing in them but stray bits of seaweed, yet they are full of living things, of tiny beautiful plants made of glass—or at least covered with it, in a thousand beautiful shapes which we can see only when they are magnified, and of animals, just as varied, and just as small. They float this way and that at the edge of the waves and are called plankton, the drifting life which is food for the larger creatures of the sea, even whales, just as the plants and animals of the earth are our food.

Although without a microscope we cannot see the plankton, we can see many of the creatures that feed on it. Amongst the wave patterns there are little holes in the sand where shellfish have buried themselves. They are amongst the plankton feeders. We call them shellfish or molluscs because they live in

Look into a rock pool and at first it seems empty but a closer look shows many living creatures. Around this pool are worm tubes and barnacles.

The Sea Star (on right) lies flat on the rock while the Brittle Star (left) lives at the bottom of the pool and if touched is likely to throw off one of its arms.

The 'petals' of the Red Waratah Anemone will close together if touched and then it looks like a dark lump of jelly.

The Feather Duster Worm adds beauty to some rock pools.

A common Lined Bubble Shell photographed alive in all its beauty.

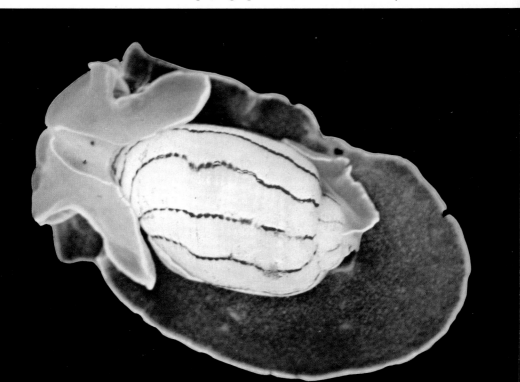

The Blue-ringed Octopus is very venomous and should never be touched.

The Puffer or Toad Fish is very common but highly poisonous to eat.

the water as fish do, and most of them have shells; but they are not really fish, but soft-bodied creatures with no bones. Though they are water-creatures they are related to snails. Like snails they have one strong muscular foot underneath their bodies. With it they drag themselves along without coming out of their shells and with it they dig themselves into the sand when they want to hide.

Like snails they have eyes on stalks, and instead of bones to make their bodies strong they have shells outside to protect them, and just inside the edge of the shell is a mantle, a fold of muscle which can build more layers on the edge of the shell to make it larger as they grow. Like snails, too, they do not have separate teeth, but a strip or ribbon of teeth like a small file to break up their food.

They hatch from eggs which are sometimes in rings of jelly, sometimes in a ribbon beautifully twisted or coiled so that it looks almost like flowers, and sometimes in clusters like tiny white raspberries joined together into a necklace so fine that until it is magnified it looks like white cotton with knots in it.

Snails have one shell which grow bigger and bigger as the snail grows because the snail keeps adding to the open end until a very small curl becomes a big curl. Many shellfish are like that; but many others have two shells, one on each side and fitting together like two soup bowls, with the creature that built them—a soft-bodied mollusc called a bivalve—living in the hollow between them. Sometimes the waves leave the two halves of the shell, joined by a muscle so they look like a butterfly's wings, on the edge of the water, but that is only when the mollusc is dead. When it is alive the shell is closed, unless the mollusc is feeding, and it is usually buried in wet sand. More often the 'butterfly' is broken at the hinge and you find only half of it.

These double, or two-valved shells (called bivalves because *bi* means two) are of every colour you can think of, though they are usually delicate colours that seem to fit in with the colours of the seaweed and sand. They are of many shapes also; long and narrow, round or oval, crinkled or smooth.

Shells of another big group, the snail, or one-valved group (called univalves because *uni* means one) are even more varied than the bivalves. Some are coiled in spirals or circles, or rolled almost into cylinders. Some are long and thin, others short and broad, with patterns of horns or spines or most beautiful curves. Some are not even curled. They are simple little pointed caps which grow wider and wider toward the base, as their mollusc grows and builds on new rings of shell round the bottom of the cap.

But if we stay to look at any more shells with their beautiful colours and strange shapes, and their strange ways, we shall not have time to look in the pool and see the creatures that live there.

Look in a pool well out on the rocks. It is as clear as if there was no plankton in it, but of course there is. Its rock walls are hung with delicate seaweed, green and brown and red, moving softly when the water moves. Many living creatures have homes in crevices and amongst the seaweed. Others live on the floor of the pool, on rocks or sand.

There are sea-stars on the rocks. We often call them starfish although, like the molluscs, they are not fish at all. They lie flat on the rocks and they are the shape of stars with rather blunt points. There are small ones, half an inch across; others are one, two, even four or five inches across, and their colours are beautiful. One is green with a chocolate pattern, some are soft pink and grey; one big one is scarlet; others are green and red; many are blue, soft blue, sky blue, dark blue.

Some of the stars are five-pointed; some eight, some six-pointed, but they all live in much the same way. They have no heads and no eyes, and we can't see their mouths unless we turn them over, and then they do not look much like mouths.

Turn one over. Perhaps you can't. That is because you were not quick enough. When the sea-star felt your touch it held on to the rock with all its feet. You must flick it over quickly before it has time to hold on. In grooves on the under-side of each arm of the star there are rows of strong little sucker feet, like short tubes with a cushion on the edge of each. Once they suck on to the rock you might break the sea-star before you could move it. Leave the first one, and try another—quickly. Now it is over, and you can see its rows of suckers, and, in the middle of the star, a star-shaped hole. That is the sea-star's mouth. It eats the molluscs that live on the plankton. With one of its arms—or we might call them points of the star—it takes hold of one shell of a bivalve, holding it with its row of suckers, and with another it takes hold of the other shell and pulls the two apart. There between them is the bivalve, just ready to be eaten. The sea-star cannot pick it up and put it in its mouth, because its points are not long enough! What does it do? Watch.

Something is coming out of its mouth and folding round the bivalve. It is not a tongue. Sea-stars do not need tongues. Instead the sea-star has pushed out its stomach and taken the food into it. Then it can lie still and digest it. It would not do to leave the star upside down though. A bird might see it and want it for dinner. It can turn itself over, very slowly—but not in the middle of a meal. Turn it right way up, so its useful push-out stomach is safe underneath it, then we can look at the other living things in the pool.

On a stone under the seaweed is a quite different star. If we lift the stone out into the open pool we can see it. It has long thin points, spreading like beautifully coloured spider legs from the button-like centre. Its mouth is under the 'button'. It is a brittle star, and it does not eat molluscs as the sea-stars do. It does not eat live things at all, but the rubbish that lies in the bottom of the pool—the dead plants and animals that would spoil the clean sand. It takes them all into its mouth, then spits out the sand. It is the cleaner of pools.

Brittle Star is a good name for it. It *is* brittle. If you touch one of its long arms (which look rather like a tightly threaded row of small beads, beautifully coloured and often fringed, and usually with cross bands of two colours), it is quite likely to throw one of them off, as a lizard sometimes throws off its tail. The brittle star in our pool has two very short arms—the others are long. It has thrown off two of its arms and has just begun to grow new ones in place of them. They are too narrow to have grooves with many sucker legs in them. The brittle star has small suckers but it doesn't use them for walking. It really walks with what we have called its arms. It would be just as true to call them legs. It uses them as either. They seem like arms when it puts food into its mouth with them, but like legs when it walks with them.

Brittle stars do not like light. Since we have turned its stone over and taken it from under the seaweed it has begun to walk away. We must turn its stone over again and put it back, as we must always do when we move stones in pools, or we may leave the creatures that live under them without a roof, and the ones that live on them without a floor.

Most sea-stars and brittle stars lay eggs, which form part of the plankton until they are eaten or hatch into baby stars which settle down in pools and on rock ledges; but sometimes brittle stars increase in another way. They simply break themselves in half—just as easy for them as throwing off an arm—and each half grows into a whole new star.

But there are more living things than stars and molluscs in the pool, many many more. Small fish often come in with the tide, feeding on plankton in the water, and often going out again on the next high tide. They are hiding under the seaweed now, but every now and then they swim out—tiny things half an inch long, some beautifully coloured, shining blue or green, or pink; some coloured just like the sand or the foam shadows under the water, so you cannot see them unless they move. Once they floated as eggs in the plankton, but those that grew up can swim from place to place instead of drifting wherever the tides and currents carry them.

The tiny beautifully coloured shells that are mixed with the sand under the pool are empty now, but once they were homes of molluscs, built out of layer after layer of lime by the molluscs which lived on the plankton as so many creatures do. Sometimes larger fish come in on the high tides and eat some of the sea-stars, but there always seem to be plenty left.

There is a beautiful Red Waratah Anemone on a rock just under the water. It looks like a red flower, perhaps a very fluffy double chrysanthemum an inch across, but it is not a flower but a sea anemone. If you touch it all the red fluffiness folds together and it looks like a dark lump of jelly. How does it live, clinging to the rock?

The 'petals' of the anemone are little tubes and the centre is its mouth. The thin tube-like petals suck food (usually plankton) from the water and sweep it into the anemone's mouth and it is swallowed and digested in the hollow inside which is partly divided into little open rooms or sections. The Red Waratah Anemone stores its eggs there so they are safe from rough waves and hungry birds while they grow into tiny perfect little anemones which eventually hatch and swim out through the parent's mouth. They swim about for a while then settle down on the rocks of the pool—you can see whole families close together, feeding and growing larger with time, but never swimming away, though occasionally one moves slowly, as sea-stars do, across the rock. Sea-stars store their eggs safely too, but they keep them between their rows of sucker feet until they hatch and can look after themselves.

Now the tide has left whole rocks bare we can see living molluscs which spend most of their time clustered tightly on the rocks. Most of them are univalves. There are hundreds of periwinkles which look like snails with dark green and white shells, cap-shaped limpets, and barnacles of many kinds.

Limpets are amongst the molluscs which build a ring round the base of the shell as they grow, making it into a larger and larger cap. They fit so tightly on the rock that they look almost like part of it. Thousands of them sit side by side on the rocks, 'clinging like limpets' as the low tide uncovers them. You could not possibly move one, but they move themselves easily, often travelling several feet over the rock, each on its single foot.

Look at them all. There are so many of them, and they walk over the rock at night, yet each one comes back to its own spot, the place it left when it began to wander, and settles down in it for the day. How does it know its way back? How does it know its own place amongst the thousands of other limpets on the rock? We cannot tell, but they know, just as each bird knows how to build its own kind of nest, and each penguin, after travelling across the world, comes back to its own burrow amongst the hundreds in the sand.

Barnacles, which are a little, but not quite, the same shape as limpets, are often found rather lower down the rocks than limpets. Some can move about but some cement their shells to the rock and stay in one place all their lives. Instead of going to look for food the food has to come to them as the waves come in with their floating invisible plankton. Barnacles are not molluscs: they are related to shrimps. The creature inside the shell is very like a tiny prawn or shrimp with twelve fringed arms—it is not much use calling them legs as the barnacle does not walk on them—instead of one strong foot.

One of the commonest kinds of fixed barnacles is the Acorn Barnacle, which really does suggest an acorn sitting in its acorn cup. The bottom ring of its shell, the 'acorn-cup' is a ring like a collar, with another rounded shell, the 'acorn' pushing up through it, and marked with a line across the top. As the bottom part is cemented to the rock the top part must have an opening so the fringed arms can reach out to catch food.

It actually has 'doors' in the top. The lines are the edges of the doors, or valves, when they are closed. To open they lift up, as some bridges lift up to let ships go through, and out come the arms to catch plankton.

Chitons are often found on the shady parts of the rocks. They are oval, one or two inches long and usually covered with an algae like dull grey moss, but the mollusc inside is bright orange. They are not bivalves or univalves. Their shell is made of eight overlapping plates, each curved to fit over the mollusc and to closely overlap the one next to it. Because of its many-jointed overlapping armour a chiton can easily curl up into a ball, and usually does if you lift it from the rock. The strips of shell, especially the ones at each end, are bent almost to a butterfly shape (but without a joining muscle in the middle as bivalves have) and when separate bits are found on the shore they are called butterfly shells. Inside they are smooth and a shining blue or blue-green. Chitons walk over the rocks as a snail would do, and they do not like light, so they usually live under rocks or in hollows.

The tide is far out now. As we walk across rocks toward the edge of the waves we walk on a lumpy but soft and tough yellow-brown carpet, rather velvety to look at, but rough if we put our hands on it. It is not seaweed. It is not ribbony or loose and feathery as seaweed is, except where tufts of seaweed grow in it. It isn't a plant at all. It is an animal, that once swam about in the sea but has now settled down to live on the rocks and look rather like bits of doormat. The large patches are not one animal, but a whole colony of animals that swam there and anchored themselves together on the rock and changed their shape and grew until they were all pressed together like a carpet. The very small bits are single animals.

They are cunjevoi or sea-squirts, one of the strangest sea creatures of them all. Look at cunjevoi where it lies in shallow water. The flat uneven cushions and curtains of it are dotted with star-shaped holes, four-pointed stars this time, and you can see through some of them, down into the red inside.

All things change as they grow, but few change as much as the cunjevoi. Once it was an egg, or rather millions of eggs in the plankton. The eggs that hatched became little creatures like tadpoles with (though you could hardly see them) little suckers on their heads. They swam and fed in the plankton for a while, as so many creatures do, but soon each found a place on the rocks and fastened itself there by the suckers on its head. If others were close to it they grew into one big mat of cunjevoi, but where they were far apart each animal remained separate even when it was full-grown.

You know how tadpoles' tails disappear when they turn into frogs. The baby cunjevoi absorb their tails in the same way, but they do not grow legs as tadpoles do. Instead, while the head clings to the rock the inside parts of the cunjevoi turn until the mouth is at the tail end, which is now bent round close to the head so the whole animal is like a tough balloon, but you cannot see that unless it is separate from its neighbours. When many are close together each little cunjevoi spreads until it presses against its neighbour and they become one lump. Each one has two star-shaped openings which look like a cross when they are closed, and inside the cunjevoi, between the openings, there is a strainer of narrow fringed slits. When the waves rush in across the rocks the water pours in one opening and out of the other, and the strainer strains out plankton for food and oxygen for breathing. That is all the cunjevoi does. It strains out food as the water runs through it, digests the food, uses the oxygen, and from time to time lays eggs which float away while it lies still, not even feeling, as we know feeling, because it has so few nerves.

While we have looked at the cunjevoi the tide has gone out to the far edge of the rocks and turned to come in again over the rocks and little pools and seaweedy hollows. Now and then a big wave creams over the big rocks and spills down into the pools.

There are white crests on the blue sea now, and instead of ripples that whispered on the sand the long waves curl and break like far-off thunder. The first wave has poured over the rock into our pool. It is time to go back to the dry sand above the highest tide-mark. Then we can look back over the sea, knowing there is a whole teeming world of life hidden by the waves and fed by them as they bring fresh plankton to the creatures in the pools, to the cunjevoi and sea anemones, the sea-stars and brittle stars, the barnacles and limpets—'things creeping, innumerable, both small and great beasts'.

Spike

Cap This !

TALL TALES FROM *The Bulletin* NEWSPAPER

Illustrations by Will Mahoney

I was drawing water for a Mallee cocky, and was headed for a steep cutting on the Murray bank when both traces snapped. I hopped over to the homestead, borrowed a length of greenhide, and used it for traces.

It was a hard pull up the slope when I had filled the tanker. My vocabulary was just about exhausted when we topped the rise, and so was the mare—but not because she had been hauling the dray up the bank. That blanky greenhide had stretched all the way from the dray at the bottom. It was raining, and for a while those greenhide traces looked like staying stretched; but the cows needed watering, so I thought hard.

I unhitched the greenhide traces from the harness and hitched the ends around a stump. Then I made a row of little fires all down the slope. The little fires grew into a long line of flame, the heat rose to the greenhide, and, as the curlew softly sang his evening dirge, the dray and water-tank gently crawled up the hill.

'Pompoota' *20th November 1929*

Three years ago I was fishing for eels in a creek-hole in the Dungog (N.S.W.) district. I saw a four-footer, but he was not to be tempted—he would swim round the bait, breaking the surface every now and then. Fed up, I fired at him with my shotgun, using my last cartridge, and missed!

I found a blank in my bag—rats had chewed the casing and

let out the shot. I managed to stuff in some small stones, a sinker, and two nails, and tried again. There was a commotion in the water. The mud settled. Beside a log was the eel, wriggling his body gently and moving his gills, unharmed.

I had to return to Sydney then, but recently went back to the same pool. There he was, bigger than ever, and when my bait fell past his nose he grabbed it. I tugged, and he was well hooked; I pulled, and with him came the log that had been embedded in the mud. He was nailed by the tail to the log. I recognised the nail.

'D.G.S.' *26 June 1935*

A cat that came to our camp at Surat (Queensland) had a family of four, hardy little chaps who were soon running around. One day a yell from my mate brought me to the back of the tent.

There I saw a huge goanna that had apparently gone mad. It looped the loop, did its best to turn itself inside out, and performed many other gymnastic feats, stopping every now and again to contort its tummy. It was clearly trying to get rid of something it had swallowed.

The circus came to an end when the goanna ejected one of the kittens. Looking maliciously at his tormentor, the youngster humped his back and spat, and then fled to the scrub. Except for some scars on his head and hips, Puss is none the worse for his Jonah act.

'F.W.' *5 March 1930*

Best Bib and Tucker

Illustrations by Edwina Bell

First-year girls at Fort Street Girls' High School, Sydney, pass on some ideas to make a party swing.

A PARTY WITH A THEME

KAREN MEWETT writes: Successful parties don't just 'happen'; they are the result of hard work and planning. It is often helpful to have a theme that runs through the whole party. A Pirate Party is one idea for a theme. The party could take place inside or out.

The scene could be set with flags and models of sailing ships. On arrival guests could be handed eye-patches (cheaply made from dark cardboard and hat elastic), crêpe-paper head-scarves, and even cardboard cutlasses. Prepared for any danger, they now embark upon a series of pirate or ship games.

Of course there must be a treasure hunt, but instead of the usual clues, charts might be issued. They could be made by scorching sketch-pad paper with the iron, then inscribing them with black or blue ink and burning the edges with a match. The 'treasure' could be found in an imitation treasure-chest, and could be wrapped in gold or silver foil.

Another suggestion is an obstacle course using things likely to be found on a sailing ship. A tree could have a rope hung over it for climbing the rigging. A barrel or tea-chest could be labelled AMMUNITION. Buckets, mops, and even anchor-chains could be used, and the race could end with 'walking the plank'—resting the plank on two chairs.

Next the guests could be divided into two 'crews', wearing a length of wool tied round their left arms; one team all red and the other all blue. Two members of each crew could have 'special messages'—small pieces of paper to hide in their shoes, pockets, etc. Each crew would have a 'treasure chest' which they would be given a few minutes to hide. The crews would try, by ambush or open combat, to rip off opposing arm-bands, checking each captive for 'special messages'. Anyone without an arm-band is out of the game. At the end of the game you could tally the scores: ten points for every arm-band, fifty points for a 'special message', and a hundred points for stealing the opponents' treasure-chest.

Now to the galley! As well as the usual party food there could be Pirate Pete biscuits and toffee bullets. Perhaps chocolate crackles in large slabs could be called 'ship's biscuits'. Cordial could be 'rum'—or red cordial 'blood'. If there is a birthday cake, of course it should bear the symbol of piracy—the skull and crossbones.

This is one example of a party with a theme, and with a little initiative you can stage others.

GAMES FOR A PARTY

DIANA COUTTS suggests a jig-saw treasure hunt: Each person must collect his or her jig-saw pieces and try to complete the jig-saw first.

You need enough pictures for each person, approximately 10″ × 12″ or 18″ × 20″; preferably those commonly seen in advertisements, or pictures of famous people from magazines. Paste the pictures on stiff sheets of cardboard the same size, and cut into jig-saw shapes (five or six pieces should be sufficient). Keep one key piece for each person, one that gives an easy clue to the whole picture, and mix the remaining pieces together. Distribute them in piles of five or six pieces in hiding places in the house or garden.

The players must go from pile to pile trying to find all their pieces.

DEBBIE FUREY suggests Chalk Races: The equipment needed is two blackboards, or large sheets of paper fixed on the wall, and sufficient chalk for each person.

The guests are divided into two groups, each group in a straight line about ten feet from the blackboards. Someone is near the blackboards to clap his hands. At the first clap, the first in each line runs to the blackboard and starts drawing a house. At the next clap, the drawer stops and the next in line runs up to carry on the drawing. At the end, the picture that looks most like a house wins the prize.

Instead of a house, it can be a horse, or a room, or anything.

MARGARET SIVAK tells how to play Questions and Answers: Have two sets of cards of different colours. One set is, for example, blue, and you write something on each card ending with the question, 'What shall I do?'—'I have a toothache, what shall I do?'

The other set of cards, for example red, has a silly answer on each, like 'Hit it' or 'Throw it out'. These are scattered on the table, and the blue cards divided among the players. One person asks another the question on his card; this person picks up a red card and gives the answer. The used cards go to the side. You get quite a few laughs from it.

SERVING THE FOOD

JOY HERRON writes: This is an important feature of any party. The Cobweb Tangle is a way which may appeal to you.

For this you will need a simple menu (sandwiches, cakes, biscuits, sweets) which can be placed on a paper plate, wrapped in plastic sheet wrapping, and hidden. One room would need to be set apart for the Tangle.

You will need as many balls of string as you have guests. Take the end of one ball and fasten it to some place near a wall with the name of a guest. Unwinding the string, walk around the room twisting the string around projections like doorknobs, and winding it around available objects like chair and table legs. You can also employ such tactics as going out of one window and in another, behind tables, and threading through bookshelves. The string wanders all over the room, but you must remember to keep it taut. When the ball of string ends, fasten a paper to it saying where the guest is to go to find his plate of goodies. As each plate is hidden in a different place, it will not be a case of follow-the-leader to where the food is.

Each guest finds his name-tag and follows the string, having to step over other strings and probably meeting other guests who have strings crossing at some point. The more confusion, the greater the fun. When each has found his instructions, and then his plate, he can take it to the party table and enjoy it 'party fashion'. The paper plates cut down on washing up, though there will be some for dessert bowls, if dessert is served later.

The Tangle could be in the garden, with shrubs and trees as obstacles, but not as successfully. There is too much open space in a garden, and if there are not enough twists and corners this can become boring.

Happy party planning!

SCRAMBLES

MARGOT HARROD says you might like to end your party with a Maypole Lolly-scramble at the clothes hoist: Materials. As many pieces of string as guests; as many balloons as guests; lots of little lollies; large ribbons; a cover under the clothes hoist.

Fill milk-bottles with lollies, then stretch lips of balloons over tops of milk-bottles and fill balloons with lollies. Fix strings in slip loops round balloons and attach to clothes hoist. Put bows on clothes line, or over strings—thus 'maypole'.

When guests run round the hoist with their strings it will be like a maypole. When they pull the string hard enough the lollies will fall to the cover and end the party with a scramble.

Lynette Lennard suggests a similar idea using a paper balloon to be torn open with sticks. There could be one large balloon for all the guests to attack, or three or four balloons with guests attacking in a sort of relay race: To make the balloon cut out three crêpe-paper circles with a diameter of 30″ or more. Place them one on top of another. Join them by tacking around the circumference with strong cotton or wool, about half an inch in from the edge. Pull the wool until there is only a small opening left. Fill the balloon with lollies and pull the string until it is closed properly. Tie a knot round the neck of the balloon. Then tie the balloon to something high up, preferably somewhere in the garden. Lay a rug or cloth underneath so when it breaks the lollies will fall on the rug and not get lost in the grass.

Next, sharp sticks are needed. There can be as many sticks as guests so that all the guests can hit at the balloon together; or there may be as many sticks as balloons, so that the guests are lined up in teams behind the balloons. Then each is given a go of three or four hits, and the team which breaks the balloon first wins some little extra prize. Then there is a grab for the contents of the balloon.

Mother and Son by Michael Kmit (in a private collection).

Ming 1963 by Sali Herman (in a private collection).

DENNIS HALL

Cats on a Houseboat

Illustrations by Edwina Bell

I AM NOT in the habit of shooting cats. Cats are so very human, although naturally more intelligent and more resourceful; and only a rare human has a good cat's capacity for affection and trust. Having affection for humans should earn a black mark on the feline intelligence test. It doesn't, simply because the human has to earn that affection instead of assuming it as a right. Anyway, cats are rather special animals, and no one but a mindless moron would destroy one willingly.

I was not willing. I didn't like being down in the echoing, cavernous blackness of the old engine-room, with what seemed like a whole ferocity of felines whirling about my head. When you have only the feeble glow of an old kerosene lantern to intensify the blackness and to turn the crowding shadows into leaping demons, when the old-ship smell of rusting iron and oily bilge water is your only comfort—under such Stygian conditions wild cats about your unprotected ears are no fun.

The cat was the usual fierce offspring of domestic fummies gone wild. She had tried to live, or had been dumped by the floodwaters of that year, on the hungry side of the river. In the nights when the old ship still possessed a gangplank she had made a habit of stealing aboard to hunt for scraps of food. Now her tortoiseshell head was jammed in one of those tall cylindrical fish-tins, and she was exploding mad with fear.

I suppose I could have caught her. After all, sahibs with hundreds of native servants, all eager to be eaten, and a young fortune in nets and traps, have caught tigers. I didn't have any faithful servants, native or otherwise. And in only a pair of pyjama pants, without even a pith helmet or a bottle of Scotch, I felt most un-sahiblike.

Anyway, I'd have backed that cat against a whole jungleful of Bengal tigers.

So, being scared, I shot her, once and mercifully, and went back to bed feeling like a Lilliputian who had shrunk in the wash. In the morning, when I found that the corpse had been a mother cat, and in milk, I felt just the right size for putting under an electron microscope.

This disgraceful scene occurred on the old paddle-steamer *Decoy*. At least, she had been a paddle-steamer. Her career was much the same as that of a smart bird who begins as a glamour model and ends up with bunions and six school lunches to cut.

In her youth, after exploring various opportunities in Melbourne and in South Australian ports, she had steamed— all the 113 feet of her—across the tempestuous Bight to Fremantle. Here she had her first big break in the glamour game, for the Westralians rigged her out regardless as a pleasure craft, giving her a balconied upper deck and fancy railings and all the trimmings.

Her career as a pleasure steamer on the Swan was not a success, financially, so she sailed back meekly to Port Adelaide in tow. Then, as tough as Don Marquis's cat Mehitabel, she steamed into the death-trap of Encounter Bay. Encounter Bay is a permanent lee shore, wide open to the great southwesterly gales which rage up from the Antarctic. And this was before the days of accurate weather information.

To cap it all, she steamed into the Murray Mouth, from which even Charles Sturt turned back.

Her engagement as a pleasure steamer on Lake Alexandrina failed, as ventures in show business often do. The failure was natural, though, because in those days of her youth it was a long, hard journey from Adelaide, over the ranges and across the mallee plains, to the Lake port of Milang. The hardy types who tackled that trip by horse and buggy were more interested in beer and duck-shooting than in fancy cruising.

So she settled down to work for her living on the Murray. The upper deck with all its fancy work came off. She shipped a stumpy mast up forward, with a derrick to sway bales of wool into her holds. She was dressed up with a hardwood sheathing below the waterline, for iron plates puncture like paper when a big engine drives them against red gum snags. With her sleeves rolled up she went to work, and she failed.

She failed because her comparatively deep draught, unlike that of the little wooden paddle-steamers which just sat on the water, allowed her to work only occasionally, on a very high river.

So she was sold. An enterprising and ingenious river-man turned her into a houseboat. Later I rented the old girl.

At that time she was a hull of grey-painted iron, high in the bows and with a shapely counter stern. Amidships her deck was about five feet above the water, and she had iron bulwarks all around. Her engines had gone, but the old pilot-house with its tall wheel stood high above the gaping fore-hatch. Behind the wheelhouse, looking at her from the port hand, you saw a plain wall with two windows and a central door under a gabled roof of galvanised iron.

Under that roof, from forward aft, were first a big bedroom, the full 18 feet of her beam, then a large living-room, followed by another bedroom. Behind these was the open stretch of after-deck.

On the starboard side the outboard paddle platform, of enormously strong hardwood beams, supported a bathroom, laundry and kitchen. The bathroom was a needless luxury: it was easier to ablute by diving from the laundry door.

The tortoiseshell cat died down below, in the disused engine-room with its six-foot-six headroom, from which the ship's carpet snake escaped later by ungratefully climbing up to a porthole.

That cat was as unlucky as the swagman who caught pneumonia after falling into a mirage. For *Decoy* had suffered shipwreck, held fast by fierce westerly winds on a terraced bank just when floodwaters were dropping a foot a day. When the paddle-steamer *Pevensey* got her off and towed her to a safer berth across the river the poor cat was an unwilling stowaway.

This happened on the Murray, east of Sturt's Northwest Bend, in an area where the old river has cut a great valley a mile or so wide through arid plains of red sand and glaring limestone. Today the river is usually between 100 and 200 yards wide, and it uses only one side of its bed. There its waters of green and brown and gold sleep comfortably against a back-rest of apricot-coloured cliffs, sheer walls full of marine fossils. The rest of the bed is wilderness.

We moored *Decoy* in a sandy bay of deep water in the edge of that wilderness. From the laundry door or the kitchen window you looked across the quiet water to the great red-gold cliffs, a hundred feet in height. From the 'front' door you looked up at a canopy of red-gum foliage, part of the line of great gums which march along the water's edge for a hundred miles, and out to the wilderness.

You saw a clearing, floored with grey sand, clumps of rushes and rabbit scratchings, beyond the red-gums. Then there were blue-grey tangles of a tall acacia known as 'Broughton willow', and flats of brown-barked box-trees full of bees' nests, and lignum swamps. (Lignum bushes look like great untidy dark-green haystacks.) It was a pleasant wilderness, full of rabbits and mosquitoes and water-birds and tiger snakes. There was always bird-song, there, and the warm contentment of bees.

But if you crossed the river and climbed the cliffs you left behind the pleasant shade, the cool waters and the water scents, the eye-soothing greens of the reedbeds. Instead, from the rim of the cliffs, you looked across endless plains from which the semi-desert vegetation—mallee and mulga, needlebush, hop-bush and the rest—had been largely cleared away.

The cat had been living somewhere in the cliffs below that red desert. I knew she must have left a family of starving kittens somewhere among the golden rocks.

Two days after the cat was shot I came back from work, clambering down a rock-fall on the cliff-face to where the dinghy tugged lazily at its painter. Halfway down I heard a thin wailing, the crying of a famished kitten, afraid and despairing.

After a bit of climbing that would have surprised Sir Edmund Hilary, I located the kitten, and the two companions from which it had become separated, in what must have seemed to it a vast wilderness of crags and canyons.

Those kittens were tiny and pitifully thin, but their courage was stout. A hand reached towards them acquired an instant tracery of red lace. And for cats so small their language was shocking.

In the end, hanging on by toenails and teeth, I shed my shirt and used it to drop over each furious catlet. Then I tied

it as well as the perpendicular circumstances permitted into a sort of bag in which the kittens were furiously tangled, but no doubt comforted by each other's company.

At least they were quiet enough while I took the oars and sent the dinghy spinning across the river to the old ship. I emptied them out on the after-deck and, by the time I had gone inside and mixed powdered milk and shredded a little raw meat, they were calm enough to be inspected from a distance determined by mutual agreement.

The biggest and the boldest was a black-and-white, who later grew into the name of Pie-cat. The smallest and most pathetic, all great eyes in staring black fur, became Golly. The silver-tabby was Sixpence.

Like all cats who live with people, instead of existing as bits of interior decoration, their characters emerged quickly. Of course they had a cat life of their own, and in mild weather they spent most of the days alternating between wild chasing games round the roomy deck and luxurious sleeping, tumbled in a friendly tangle in the scuppers, lying on the smooth deck planks against the sun-warmed iron of the bulwarks. But in their relations with people each was very different.

Sixpence was the loner, a pale silver shadow who tolerated people but never shared his life with them. Golly, on the other hand, delighted in human company and in the opportunities of domestic life. As she grew up she found for herself every bed, every openable cupboard or inviting box, and played houses in them. When the nights turned cold, as they do in that arid stretch, her delight was a human lap by the blazing fire in the living-room. She was everyone's idea of 'a dear little cat'.

Pie was the bold one. He claimed human company as his right; he liked to be with people and he believed in sharing all they had. Smacks with a rolled-up newspaper quite failed to convince Pie that table-tops were out of bounds and that milk jugs were not for him. It took a baptism in river water to convert Pie to propriety.

All three were like most cats in that they wanted to accompany people on walks, and this was disastrous. My walks were usually far-ranging through the box flats and the lignum tangles in search of food. Cats can walk long distances (in another time and place I knew a tiny tortoiseshell female who left the camp and crossed 14 miles of fox-haunted sandhill and mulga to have her kittens in the boundary riders' hut she regarded as home) but they must do so at their own cat pace.

But humans walk too fast for cats, and in hot weather their efforts to keep up can end in calamity. Although they knew this, nothing could stop those cats from following, if they managed to get ashore. Then one after another would get overheated and dash frantically about in a fit. Golly, in one such seizure, flew up a box-tree and then, from a height of 30 feet, fell. Her broken hip eventually healed, but she was never a strong little cat after that experience.

All three, of course, became mighty hunters. This calls for some explanation because, even at that time when I had to depend on the rifle for much of my meat, I was a conservationist. And cats are supposed to be among the great destroyers of wildlife.

But in those days before myxomatosis the river flats swarmed with rabbits. When Pie and Golly and Sixpence were kittens, I supplied the rabbits. As they grew up, and even without a mother to teach them the tricks, each learned to catch its own underground mutton. Even Golly would come slowly across the clearing beyond the red-gums, dragging a rabbit bigger than herself between her thin legs.

Rabbiting cats usually despise smaller game. They may pounce on a ground bird which appears before their noses, or smack down a cheeky mouse. But their hunting, their regular and systematic early morning and evening rounds of the nearby warrens, is for rabbits. Cats are intelligent and practical; they know that a rabbit is a lot of meat, a worthwhile return for the work of stalking and the patience of waiting. A bird, on the other hand, is just a mouthful.

So the Willy-wagtails flirted on the cap-rails of the bulwarks, and the butcher birds flew down to the hatch coaming outside the kitchen door, where fish cleanings were laid out for them. The drowsy cats, in their sunning places in the scuppers, blinked at them—if they could be bothered.

Dawn and dusk were the hunting times; their days were for resting and companionship and play. As the summer advanced Pie and Golly spent most of the daylight hours in the living-room, or up in the wheelhouse where an occasional breeze fluttered through the glassless windows. But Sixpence walked alone on shore.

When the thermometer aspired towards 120 degrees in the shade, and managed to reach 110 or 115 on most days, Sixpence suffered badly. Being Sixpence, he didn't take his troubles to humans; he made his own arrangements instead.

Not far from the bows of *Decoy* there was a small sandspit, shaded by the big red-gums, where about an inch of clear water covered the white sand. This became Sixpence's refuge. Any hot day would find him there, lying flat on his furry belly in the water, legs spread-eagled, enjoying his private cooling system.

The other two never took to the water, but both took me into it.

With her engines removed, and riding high, *Decoy* was a

restless ship. She was moored fore and aft to gum-trees, but there was no money for expensive steel cables to serve as springs and breast-lines. She was kept off the steep sandy bank by 'spuds', spars 10 or 12 feet long, hanging vertically down her port side from chain lashings. Apart from these simple contrivances she was free to move as she liked, and she did.

When a gusty west wind howled through the trees she would sweep out to the length of her moorings, roll ponderously, and recoil to the bank until the groaning spuds took her weight. On one such a night her gangplank went adrift, and was never replaced.

It seemed to me that a ship ought to have a rope ladder, and that this would provide an easy, appropriate and even romantic way of going ashore. So I made one, and it looked very nautical with its upper end secured to the bitts alongside the wheelhouse and the lower lashed to the arching roots of a big red-gum. It worked, too, for I went ashore to prove it. But while I was standing on the bank admiring the effect, Golly cried out in one of her bouts of pain.

Well, it would be easy to go aboard and comfort her. The rope ladder stretched up tautly at a steep angle, and I started up it hand over hand, like a Cape Horn shellback tackling the weather shrouds in a southerly gale.

But then *Decoy* yawned, shook herself, and decided to rub an itch against the bank. I was just halfway up when that ladder sagged into a beautiful curve, and immediately turned over.

I didn't know rope ladders did things like that, so I took an instant bath.

The second plunge was Pie-cat's fault. Pie had developed a passion for riding in the dinghy. The little twelve-footer, of clinker-built spruce, was the only means of going to work and getting supplies; it was the utility vehicle, in fact. To save its frail sides the dinghy had to be moored where it couldn't smash against *Decoy's* iron plating or hardwood sheathing. The land side was out of the question; the first wind would have used *Decoy* and the bank as a nut-cracker.

But on the starboard side, aft of the kitchen, there was a triangular, unbuilt-on remnant of the old paddle platform. From a scupper hole fourteen or fifteen feet forward of this I rigged out a spar to act as a boom. The dinghy's forward line, suitably bridled, was tied to the end of the boom, and the stern line to the timbers of the paddle platform. The drill was to heave a leg over the bulwarks, go out on the grating of the platform, and jump. After which you untied the stern line and then went forward to cast off from the boom.

Pie knew all about this. He also knew that he wasn't a welcome passenger, simply because, as soon as you rowed round a bend out of sight of the ship, Pie would leap to the bows and yell crimson slaughter to be taken home again. His usual tactics were to leap after me, over the bulwarks and on to the grating. Then, if he was discouraged sufficiently, he would bound back again and out of sight.

I'd go through the unmooring drill, push off and pick up the oars.

The moment I turned my back on the dinghy's bows Pie would shoot through the scupper hole, race out along the boom and make a magnificent flying leap across the water to land in the receding dinghy.

Now, *Decoy* was moored in the lee of the inner angle of a ninety-degree bend. When the river was high, paddle-steamers working upstream would cut the corner, passing almost within hand-shaking distance of *Decoy's* kitchen. Being so close, the surge from the paddles, confined between the steamer and *Decoy's* high sides, formed a perfect succession of symmetrical waves four feet or so high and only about ten feet between crests. It was a favourite game, in idle moments, to jump down into the dinghy and ride this very steep and glassy switchback.

One morning I came out on the after-deck full of breakfast and with my pipe alight. A pipe in a bad mood tastes like old socks stewed with cabbage and seasoned with a spoonful of gall. But nothing tastes so good as a pipe in a good mood, and of all its moods the after-breakfast one is the best. This means that I was really enjoying that daddy's dummy when I looked around and saw the paddle-steamer *Renmark* a few yards downstream, coming fast and very close.

This was too good to miss. I jumped over the bulwarks and down to the dinghy's stern, and I was casting off the hitches as I landed. As the line came clear Pie pounced over the bulwarks. I leaned to shoo him back—and the first swell tossed the stern high in the air.

Caught off balance, over I went. I went down feet first,

down and down until I wondered whether I'd ever rise again. And if I did, whether my head would bash into *Decoy's* bottom or that of the dinghy.

I shot up at last like a breaching whale, clear of the dinghy which was performing acrobatics at the end of its bowline. I trod water; all was well. But it wasn't: my beautiful early-morning pipe, still clasped between my teeth, was sodden and dead.

Pie was couched on the bulwarks, all comfortable with his paws tucked under his snowy chest. His expression was as

interested and gratified as that of someone who has managed to get into a circus without paying.

Pie-cat was clever enough as a boarding party—he'd have earned double rum rations in Nelson's day—but in other ways he was pretty dumb. Rowing back one day with the week's bread supply I was puzzled to see Pie marching along the bank a few yards astern of *Decoy*.

He was marching in a perfectly straight line, a dozen feet above the water's edge, and at every pace one of his forepaws would pat at something I couldn't see.

A few strokes of the oars and I did see. The 'something' was five feet of tiger snake. Pie was following serenely behind it, patting at its tail.

Tiger snakes are notoriously bad tempered. I grabbed the rifle, stood up and shot it.

Pie was very upset. He met the dinghy as soon as it came to the bank, loud with complaints about being deprived of his plaything.

All the cats were landlubbers in one respect: they despised fish in any form. This was unfortunate, because fish were plentiful in the clear-water summer a year after the big flood.

I was helping a neighbouring farmer with his harvest at the time, and the hot and dusty work went on till dusk. Then I'd

walk across paddocks spiteful with bindi-eye for the mile and a half to the river. It would be black dark by then, but the lines had to be run before turning home for a meal.

Confirmed anglers are going to do some nose-turning-up at the mention of set-lines, but a fat lot they know about fishing. I'd push off silently and row smoothly across a black mirror jewelled with stars, in a silence made perfect rather than broken by the chorus of frogs, the occasional sleepy honk of a waterbird, and the liquid gurgle at the bows. Silence instead of the snarl of the tractor; water scents instead of its stink; cool damp air after the parched aridity and the choking dust.

The unpleasant part came first. Round the bend, upstream from *Decoy*, the sandy banks had caved steeply. There in the dense blackness beneath the overhang, deep among the roots of Broughton willows, I had to haul up the shrimp buckets. Old kerosene tins, well punctured and with very dead meat wired inside, were a discord in the harmony of the river night. But each would yield a handful of the glassy freshwater prawns locally called 'shrimps'.

With the shrimps kicking freely in the bait tin, there was another silent row diagonally across the river upstream. You rowed without splashes, for no one would willingly break that perfect peace.

The lines were long lengths of heavy cotton cord, one end tied to a root or a stump, the other far out and anchored with some old iron or a rock. There were drops, each with its hook, every ten feet or so, and intermediate weights to keep the whole on the bottom. You shipped oars and let the light boat glide to the land end of a line. Then, kneeling on a thwart, you pulled yourself along the heavily weighted line, hand over hand. Almost at once the line would come alive, and there was the thrill of *something*, unseen beneath the black water ahead, fighting against being taken.

Presently the thick cord would strain out in a curve, swishing to and fro in the dark water, slicing the mirror, making the stars dance tipsily, pulling the gunwale down till water lipped in, cutting deep into wet palm and fingers.

Then the fish, something heavy and unseen, pounding wildly on the floor boards. It might be a catfish, all slime and poisonous spines. It might be a 3-pound callop, heavy-shouldered and juicy, the sweetest of the river fish. It was often a cod of anything from 5 to 10 pounds, or even more. You knew it only by feel, as you freed the hook for re-baiting.

And so on, along all the lines.

Then the row home to *Decoy*; and when I got there, fishy and wet and too tired to be hungry, the cats would be waiting, crouched on the bulwark cap-rail against the starry sky.

I'd heave the heavy bag up to the grating. There would be a collective feline sniff of disapproval: fish again; just fish. And off they'd go to their rabbit rounds.

All except one. He'd wait, but not for fish.

He was a second-generation ship's cat, for Pie had had kittens. He was just the sort of cat who would. And one of his kittens was Bit-o'-String.

That *was* his name; and that was part of his nature.

For Bit-o'-String was a male cat—well, originally, anyway. He was a big, rangy, dark-tabby; what a horseman would call a 'strong' colour. Like so many male cats he had the capacity to attach himself completely and permanently to one person, as long as that person earned the attachment and did not assume it as a right.

He liked a lot of affection, and he liked vigorous, no-holds-barred boxing-on. He insisted on his own rules: that his human sparring partner must kneel, sit or lie, thus coming down to String's own level; and that the human must use only one hand. Feinting with your left to get an opening for your right fingers to poke his furry tummy was a foul. If you did that, String would leap up and stalk away, his whole bearing showing his contempt for such unfairness.

Like most male cats, he liked to be picked up and stroked or roughed up, according to his mood of the moment, but not to be held. Some he-cats will sit on your shoulder, or on a forearm braced across your chest. String liked to be thrown over a shoulder. He'd hang there, head far down your back, tail brushing your belt buckle. He'd make himself completely limp, so that he felt, and looked, like a fathom of wet grey string.

He was the perfect companion for all times and moods: a critical spectator when you were cutting firewood, a close and silent presence if you sat down to read, a chest-warmer on bitter nights. You dared not touch a rifle in his presence unless you intended to let him come along. If you did he acted as a pointer, standing up on his hind legs to his full and considerable height to see over tussocky grass or reeds. He loved to be allowed to retrieve a dead rabbit.

Of course he had his own regular hunting times, and he often kept the other cats in rabbit. But unlike the others he fancied bird meat, of one special kind. Many times, after dark, a thump at the front door indicated that String wanted to come in. You opened the door, and he came in: soaked with water, dripping all over the carpet, and dragging a dead teal or black duck by its neck.

Right at the point of the bend, astern of *Decoy*, there was a reedy shallow where wild duck often camped for the night. Being ducks, they thought they were safe because they were on water. But the low reeds and the dead timber that sheltered them from the wind made perfect stalking cover for Bit-o'-String.

When he was close enough to an unfortunate duck he sprang, seized it, held on in the thrashing commotion of feathers and water until it was dead. Then he carried it home, managed to get it across to a spud, climbed the vertical spar with the weight in his mouth until he reached the cap-rail of the bulwarks.

He brought rabbits home by the same arduous way, but these were always taken to the kitchen door. The front door was reserved for special occasions.

The regularity of String's hunting schedule presented him with a problem. He liked to begin his rounds of the rabbit warrens in the late afternoon, but this meant that he was away when I came home from work—when I wasn't harvesting and fishing—and String hated to miss his daily opportunity to be a welcoming party.

In calm weather, with the cliffs acting as a sounding board, he could hear the grunting of the dinghy's rowlocks and be home in time. But in a blow, with the trees surfing and groaning in the westerly gale, he had no chance of hearing. So we worked out a ritual for such occasions.

I'd row home against the bullying wind, make fast, and go inside out of it. Then I'd reach for the banjo and play the rowdiest tunes I knew. I seldom played for more than two or three minutes before String was at the living-room door. Never at the kitchen door, please note.

Now, those westerly winds were bitterly cold, chill with a bite they seldom attain in the softer winters of districts humid with rain. They blew hard, and *Decoy* was high above the water, with a house added to her own freeboard and bulwarks. A steady westerly drove the old ship out to the full extent of her lines, and held her there. That meant that there were several yards of cold green water between the bank and the ship.

Neither the cold nor the water worried String. I know, for I sat out in the wind many times, just to watch him.

He'd emerge from the forest of Broughton willows with a rush, race through the reedy tussocks on the clear sand, and so down to the water.

In that bitter wind he never hesitated. One spring took him well out from the bank; a few moments of strong swimming brought him to the spud. He'd race up the vertical spar and dash, sopping wet, into the living-room, the smilingest cat in the world.

Someday, I suppose, I'll forget those burning summers and icy winters, the smoky metal mirror of evening waters, the sway of the riding dinghy, the feel of heavy fish fighting a cotton line. But one thing I will not forget. For me, the old river of the paddle-steamers and the big cod means Bit-o'-String.

And if ever Charon gets round to ferrying me over the Styx, I know who'll swim out to meet the boat.

Winter Stock Route

Here where red dust rose
To raddle sheep and men
And the kelpie tongued at noon,
Silence has come again.
The great-boled gumtrees bow
Beneath their load of snow.

The drover and his dray
Have gone; and on this hill
I find myself alone
And Time standing still.
Printless the white road lies
Before my quiet skis.

But where my skis trace
Their transient snow furrow,
For generations both
Man and beast will follow.
Now in this winter passage
I cross the deserted stage.

DAVID CAMPBELL

Two Thoughts About Waves

If sound
Is only waves that break upon my ear,
Then if I were not here,
And they must just rebound
From rock, and tree, and wall
With no one listening near,
Would there be sound at all?

Sometimes it seems to me,
Hearing the ocean waves along the shore,
That I must stay awake
For each succeeding roar,
Lest it should fail to break;
As if the sea
Could somehow feel a need
That I take heed,
Or surge no more.

LYDIA PENDER

RICHARD PARKER

The Fire Curse

Illustrations by Astra Lacis

THERE was once an old lady called Mrs Mell who lived quite
alone. Her little stone house was at the end of a track a long
way from the nearest township. She liked living alone. She was
a very independent old lady.

One morning she was trying to light her fire so that she
could cook herself some breakfast; but, for some odd reason, the
fire refused to light. There she was, her eyes watering from the
smoke and her back aching, for ten minutes or more, and still
there was no fire. In the end she lost her temper. She threw
down the matches and stamped her foot.

"Never have I known you to be so awkward!" she told the
fire that would not burn. "You're nothing but a wretched,
miserable, no-good . . ."

Just as she said this the door opened and a man came in.
He was an extraordinary man—no taller than the leg of a
chair, and his bright red hair came out from under his hat like
flames from under a kettle, while his long grey beard blew to
one side like smoke from a chimney.

"Mrs Mell!" he said sternly, in a voice that crackled like
fire in a dry scrub. "Mrs Mell—you have cursed the fire!"

Mrs Mell put her hands on her hips and stared at him.
"And what if I have?" she said. She had never been afraid of
anything in her whole life, and she was not going to start now—
although this was a very extraordinary little man indeed.
"What's it to you, may I ask?"

The little man did not answer. Instead he walked solemnly
across to the fireplace and stared down at the sulky, smoking
sticks. "Now then!" he said sharply.

Straight away the sticks crackled and burst into flame, and
the flames roared up the chimney with such a noise that Mrs
Mell could hardly hear herself speak.

"Well," she said, "I don't know who you are, but you can
certainly make a fire burn. Thank you."

"Better not thank me, Mrs Mell," he said. "I haven't finished yet. You cursed the fire, you see, and for that you must be punished. Please stand quite still for a moment."

Mrs Mell was just going to tell him not to be silly, when she felt a cold shiver go down her back. She stood quite still with her mouth open—not because he had told her to, but because she could not help herself. And the old man pointed one finger at her as he chanted:

> "May fire desert you,
> Fire forsake you,
> Wherever you may go.
> May leaves and twigs,
> Wood, coal and paper
> Behave like ice and snow."

Then he nodded his head sharply and said, "Now, try it out for me before I go, if you please."

"Try it out?" said Mrs Mell. The cold shiver in her back had gone, and she began to feel cross with herself for having listened to the strange little man.

"Yes," he said. "Just walk up to the fire as if you were going to start cooking your breakfast."

"And that's just what I am going to do," said Mrs Mell. She picked up her frying-pan and walked across the room towards the blazing fire.

At the first step the flames roared and crackled as before. At the second step the roaring suddenly stopped, and the flames went pale and yellow like straw. At the third step the fire flickered, spluttered, and went out. It was as if someone had poured a bucket of water over it. In the fireplace lay a heap of black, smoking sticks, and the room seemed suddenly cold.

The strange little man shivered and heaved a deep sigh.

"Ah," he said. "A sad sight. I'm sorry for you, Mrs Mell."

And with a quick nod of his head he disappeared.

At first Mrs Mell refused to believe it. She spent the next hour trying to light her fire again, but although she tried butter, mutton-fat, candle-ends, kerosene and castor sugar, nothing was of any use. At last she put on her shoes, took an old iron saucepan in her hand, and went off along the track to walk the two miles to her nearest neighbour.

"Mrs Moon!" she cried as soon as she reached her neighbour's door. "Oh, Mrs Moon—a terrible thing has happened to me." Then she went on to tell of the visit of the extraordinary little man, and ended by asking if she might borrow a little fire to carry away in her saucepan.

Mrs Moon looked at Mrs Mell in an odd way, but all she said was, "Give me the saucepan, then."

She came back directly with it full of glowing embers. But as soon as Mrs Mell took it from her the glow disappeared and the burning sticks turned black and cold.

"Here," said Mrs Moon. "I don't like this. You'd better come in and get the fire yourself."

So Mrs Mell went inside and saw the fine fire blazing and the pots hanging over it bubbling and steaming. But when she had taken three steps towards it, the fire was dead. Mrs Mell dropped the saucepan on the floor with a clatter, and ran outside.

"Come back!" called Mrs Moon. But Mrs Mell made off along the track as fast as her legs would carry her until she reached her own cold, fireless house.

Mrs Mell was lucky that all this happened in the spring. It was a nuisance not being able to cook, but she went over to her neighbour every third or fourth day, and Mrs Moon would give her some hard-boiled eggs. She grew very tired of living on hard-boiled eggs and bread and butter, and she missed her good hot cups of tea; but she was in no danger of starving.

But slowly the winter came, and a very bad winter it was. Poor Mrs Mell had no way of keeping warm. Sometimes at night she had to get up and stamp up and down her room to bring the feeling back into her legs. She longed deeply, then, for a blazing wood fire, with a cheerful bubbling kettle over the flames.

Then one morning, when the cold seemed to be creeping

right into her bones, she said to herself, "Why, Mell, what a silly old woman you are. You're always reading in the paper about how warm it is in Queensland, even in July. What are you waiting for?"

So, without stopping to consider, she set off that very morning. She had a loaf of brown bread wrapped in brown paper under her arm, and half a dozen hard-boiled eggs knotted in a red spotted handkerchief in her hand. When she reached the road she turned north.

The first night she slept under a haystack. The second night she slept in an old barn with a hole in the roof, shaped rather like a map of Tasmania. The next morning she came on to a wide highway with a white line running down the middle of it.

She had not walked very far before she was very nearly run over by a large red fire-engine. The driver blew his horn at Mrs Mell and then shouted, "Where do you think you're going, Granny?"

"It's none of your business," snapped Mrs Mell. "But if you must know, I'm trying to find somewhere warm."

This made the firemen laugh. "You'd better come with us," they said. "We're on our way to a fire."

"Is it a good big one?" asked Mrs Mell.

"It's big, but it's not good," they said. "We're going to put it out."

"I could do that for you," said Mrs Mell, which made the men laugh even more. But they took her up on the fire-engine with them and drove on.

In a short time Mrs Mell and the firemen came to a farmhouse which was burning fiercely. Flames were pouring out of the windows and doors, and the sparks from the burning building had just set light to a haystack not far away.

"You sit here and watch," the firemen said, and then rushed off.

Mrs Mell watched them for some time. They pumped water over the fire until they had emptied the farmer's water tanks. Then they tried with their foam hoses, but still the fire roared. After a while they came back to the fire-engine with their faces black, their eyebrows burnt off, and their hands blistered.

"It's no good," said one of them. "She's too big for us. And there are two more haystacks just round the back."

"We'll never put it out and that's for sure," said another.

Mrs Mell got down off the fire-engine and started to walk towards the burning house.

"Where are you going?" cried the firemen.

"I'm going to put the fire out," said Mrs Mell.

"Is that supposed to be a joke?" asked the men.

"Joke?" said Mrs Mell. "I'll soon show you!" And before they could stop her she walked straight across the yard towards the very hottest part of the fire, which was the haystack. Flames were shooting high into the air. Their roaring sounded like thunder, and great clouds of heavy black smoke rolled across the yard.

When Mrs Mell was ten yards from the fire she stopped. It would be odd, she thought suddenly, if the curse didn't work. . . . Then she clenched her fists and stepped forward again. At the first step the flames roared as loudly as ever. At the second step the roaring suddenly stopped and the flames turned pale and yellow like straw. She quickly took the third step, and the flames flickered out like candles when the door is opened. A thin curl of smoke rose from the centre of the blackened haystack, and from inside the house came the sound of dripping water. The fire was out.

Mrs Mell did not go to Queensland. The firemen took her back with them to town, and in no time at all Mrs Mell was famous. Within a week she had a letter from the Fire Department in Sydney, asking her if she would come and work for them, and offering her an all-electric house and a hundred dollars a week.

Mrs Mell was not much interested in money, but she had always wanted to see Sydney Harbour Bridge, so she said she would take the job. She moved into a neat and shining little modern cottage at Coogee, with the smell of the sea coming in at all the windows. The house had an electric fire set in the wall of every room, an electric stove that Mrs Mell soon grew used to, and every other kind of comfort she could want. There was also a brass plate on the front door which said:

MRS MELL
FIRE DEPARTMENT

Six months later she had a letter from the Fire Department of New York, offering her a thousand dollars a week if she would work for them. Mrs Mell said she was not much interested in the money, but as she had always wanted to have a look at the Statue of Liberty she would take the job.

And so it went on for the next three or four years. Every few months Mrs Mell was offered another job somewhere new, and more often than not she went. And all the time she put out fires.

At the end of seven years Mrs Mell was tired of travelling round the world, so she decided to come back to Australia and retire. She wrote to a famous architect in Brisbane and told him she wanted a beautiful little modern house just outside that city. So the architect designed it and had it built, and when it was ready Mrs Mell came home.

You would have thought that Mrs Mell would now be happy. Sometimes she was—but then, all at once, she would feel miserable, and would mope around the house not knowing what to do with herself, for days and weeks on end.

The truth of the matter was that the curse worried her.

Deep down inside herself she was longing to be able to sit down in front of a fine blazing fire, listening to the cheerful crackle of the flames and smelling the rich scent of burning gum leaves. And that was the one thing she could not do.

At last this longing became so strong that she decided she must do something about it, and the only way she could do something about it was to get hold of that extraordinary little man and ask him to take the curse off again. But where did he live? That was the question.

Mrs Mell sat and thought about this for days and weeks, and still didn't get any nearer to an answer. Then one night, just as she was dropping off to sleep, she had an idea. She remembered flying over Hawaii a few years ago and seeing a red glare in the sky. This glare had come from the volcano Kilauea, which had been belching flame and smoke and melted rock into the air. "That's just the sort of place that queer little man would like," she thought to herself. "Maybe he even lives down there. Anyway, it's worth a try."

So the next day she got in touch with a young aviator, and told him that she wanted to be flown to Hawaii and dropped down the crater of a volcano.

"You're crazy," he said. "Next thing you'll be wanting to be flown to the sun so that you can put that out."

"I don't want to put the volcano out," said Mrs Mell. "I just want to visit an acquaintance of mine who probably lives at the bottom of it."

"You know some very strange people," said the aviator, but he prepared to make the flight without any more argument.

When they reached Kilauea and circled round it, Mrs Mell began to feel a little doubtful. Perhaps she would be burnt to a cinder if she ventured down there. Perhaps the extraordinary little man didn't live there after all. But, having come so far, she decided to go on with it.

"Oh, well——" she said, and began to lower herself down on a rope while the aviator kept the machine steady, right over the centre of the volcano.

The smoke stopped as soon as she got to the crater, and then down, down she went for a very long way. It was extremely dark and smelly—but at least she was not being burnt to a cinder. She had almost come to the end of her rope when she reached the bottom of the pit. The sky was just a small hole

over her head, and the aeroplane was no bigger than a seagull. Mrs Mell stood and looked around.

In one direction there was a kind of tunnel, and at the end of it there was the red glow of fire. Mrs Mell walked towards the glow, and soon came into a huge cave that must have been at least a mile wide. In every direction there were flames of all shapes and colours; the whole cave was filled with fire. It took Mrs Mell some time to get used to the glare, and then she saw that right across the middle of the flames was a long bridge made of white-hot iron. And, standing at the highest point of the bridge, right over the hottest part of the fire, was the extraordinary little man with green and orange flames licking around his feet like playful puppies.

"What are you doing here, Mrs Mell?" he shouted at her.

"I'm looking for you," shouted Mrs Mell. "You must take that curse off me."

"*Must?*" said the little old man. "*Must?* Who are you to tell me what I must do?"

"You'll soon find out who I am," said Mrs Mell grimly, and put her foot on the bridge. As she touched the iron it went cold and rusty, and the flames all round went pale and yellow like straw. For a moment the little man glared at her. Mrs Mell put both feet on the bridge and started to walk towards him. His eyes flashed fire. Then he turned and ran.

Mrs Mell followed him, and wherever she trod the fires of the great volcano went out. At last all the fires had gone except one flickering yellow flame in a corner of the cave. The little man stood in front of it with his arms spread out as though to protect it from Mrs Mell.

"Go away!" he whispered. "Don't you see I can't live without fire?"

"Neither can I," said Mrs Mell firmly, and took a step towards him.

"If you come any closer," he called, "the last fire will go out, and the volcano will die."

"Take off the curse, then," said Mrs Mell sternly.

He hesitated, then glanced over his shoulder and saw that the last flame of Kilauea was hardly hot enough to boil a kettle. "It'll take me years to get all these fires going properly again," he muttered. "Oh—very well! I'll take off the curse."

"And get me home safely?" said Mrs Mell quickly.

"Yes, yes. All right. Are you ready? I shall have to say it backwards. It will sound odd—but it's the only way."

"I'm ready," said Mrs Mell.

And he began to chant: "Og uoy erehwyreve, Uoy ekasrof erif, Uoy tresed erif yam."

The darkness whirled around Mrs Mell, and then suddenly the sky opened over her head like an umbrella and she was standing in her own front garden.

Quickly she picked up some sticks and ran indoors. She laid paper and wood in the fireplace where no fire had ever burned yet, and struck a match. The flame caught the paper and spread. The sticks began to crackle as the red flames licked them. Smoke curled up the chimney, and happiness crept back into Mrs Mell's heart.

"Bless you, fire," she said, still on her knees in front of it. "Never will I say a hard word to you again."

ELLA McFADYEN

Living with Lizards

LIZARDS are such pleasant people that I count myself fortunate to have known so many; but to become close friends with them you must learn their language, and it is a silent one.

Beside a dried creek one hot day, we met a family group of two parents and half a dozen youngsters, the smallest a baby about six inches long. A bush boy with us called them Mugga Muggas, but the books call them Cunningham Skinks. They are dark and rough-skinned, where most skinks are sleek and glossy. As their legs do not grow any longer after the first year the older ones are the slowest, so the baby was the hero of this adventure.

Thirst had drawn them to a deep pothole, with a little stagnant water that they could smell but not reach. *We* had come to the creek for a picnic lunch. As I drew out dripping lettuce leaves to lay on our plates, that little desperado dashed out and snatched a leaf. He carried it back to the family; it was grabbed, torn up, and swallowed in a twinkling. Bravely he came back for another leaf. Soon, with growing trust, the whole family drew near and gobbled up our tomatoes and cucumbers as fast as we could slice them. They may have been thirsty for many days. Later we came on a running creek some way off, and returned with full billycans to fill a dry pothole. We left a stick in it, to help out if anyone fell in.

We had a favourite summer camp called Windy Knoll. Climbing out of the hot, hill-locked gully, we would meet a rush of air rising from Middle Harbour Creek. Once a sudden gust overturned our plates, tossing out such a feast that currawongs, magpies and kookaburras all instantly claimed us as rich relations with whom they were on dining terms. There is always someone watching hungrily—like the crickets at dusk, humbly wishing for a morsel of our wonderful bread. Or like the little brown Egernie lizard who, maddened by the smell of bananas baking in ashes, threw off all fear and came to my feet while

I was peeling off the burnt paper, and snapped up warm fruit-pulp till he could barely waddle.

At Windy Knoll we were tolerated by old King Varanus, who would tramp loudly down from his rocky castle, his heavy tail swishing through the dead leaves. He was not interested in any food we offered, but seemed to like our company. Lizards are full of curiosity about people. This one would climb to his bough overhanging the water and glance down from time to time. In bushfire weather you will often see the wise goannas gather towards the water.

On a western station along the Castlereagh was a goanna who could read my mind, as animals often do. An alarm from the young turkeys' yard had brought us running, to find a goanna halfway through the netting. Caught in the act, he swiftly inflated his sides and dropped his arms helplessly. A trick, of course; but clever enough to deceive the man of the house, who cried, "Fix him with your eyes while I get a gun!"

A big stick would have been quicker, but we both knew a gentleman would prefer a gun.

I fixed him with my eyes—but the goanna knew I was on his side. With a deliberate wink he deflated, restored his arms to action, backed out and made off. I knew I ought to do something; but after all, we would be eating those turkeys ourselves later on.

One spring day I watched two kookaburras battling a goanna on a red gum tree, below one of those swellings that show where termites have made a nest. Kookaburras often break the nest, eat the termites, and clean out a place to lay their own eggs. The goanna, in his turn, was after the kookaburras' eggs. He was dodging on the underside of the bough, where the birds could not strike at him with their great king-fisher beaks. When two more kookaburras joined the battle, he seemed to lose heart and dropped into the ferns below. I waited and waited. At last, sure enough, a scaly head appeared. The kookaburras had left. Stealthily, the old scamp crept up the tree, on the side opposite the direction the birds had taken. He spent some minutes inside the nest and came out looking satisfied. Of course I knew he had found only eggs and not fledglings, or the parents would not have left. In my own garden, where birds are taught to be tame, I always fight nest-robbers; but out in the bush, nature strikes its own balance. The kookaburras would lay again. Besides, they eat all the young lizards they can get.

Speaking of the tenants of termite nests: one day in the city an agitated voice called over the telephone.

"You're a lizard woman, aren't you? I'm a bird man, and I can't handle this. Come quick!"

A friend of his in Queensland had found some large eggs in one of these termite hollows, and had packed them in a box and sent them down by post. The eggs hatched on the way, and the girls on his staff refused to stay in the office another minute with the monsters. There, in the box, I found the thick, wrinkled egg-skins and three of the loveliest little lace monitors I ever saw. Their pale yellow bodies seemed to be sheathed in glove-tight black lace, beautifully patterned. Their little wrists and ankles were circled with ribbon-like bands of sky-blue. These brilliant colours fade after a while, but the lace pattern remains, and gives these aristocrats of the goanna family their delicate air of high fashion.

Pretty colours play a part in the courtship dance of the big water-dragons, and that is something that not many people have been lucky enough to see. It was in a Blue Mountains gully that one pair of lovers found an ideal dancing-log such as lyrebirds sometimes use—a tall, smooth trunk fallen in the ferns beside a creek. The water-dragons love creeksides and are clever swimmers. This pair had lately sloughed off their old skins, and their wedding suits were silvery grey like old gum-leaves. Under the throat each had an attractive colour patch, the one creamy-pale and the other rose-pink. Their long, tapering tails swished to and fro. Facing in different directions, the dancers passed and re-passed each other, casting sideways glances, and popping their heads up and down to show off their beautiful cravats.

On the hillside above, an elderly water-dragon whom I knew well was sitting on his usual stump. I greeted him, and he lifted his right hand, pointing with extended thumb at the courting pair as something too frivolous for either of us. I was grateful that he drew me into the circle of life in this glen. I loved everyone and everything in it, from the first pale daylight when the golden robin piped in the dawn, to the gentle dusk that brought the glowworms' green lanterns.

A fascinating chapter in lizard friendships began when a big box arrived unexpectedly from away beyond Alice Springs. My exploring hand drew forth a little creature about seven inches long, horny-headed and thorny like a pocket-sized dinosaur. This strange little being, dusty brown with rock-red back, looked up and caught my eyes. Then it turned its gaze to the box, to show me there was something else there. (Many birds and animals have this pointing trick.)

The second little dinosaur was about an inch shorter, and of a yellowish shade. They were tired and frightened, hungry and thirsty, and utterly desolate, for they had lost touch with all they ever knew.

Naiaris, the dark tribes along the Condamine call them; but in their wanderings from the corner of Queensland and all the way across the Centre to the goldfields of Western Australia, they have been given many names. They came not only from far, far away but from long, long ago; that Once-Upon-A-Time that the native people call the Dreaming. Their little bodies were very primitive in build. They had survived all these centuries, I found, because they were clever to respond and to adapt themselves to change. I was only beginning to find it out when I lifted them from their box that day.

First I washed my hands very thoroughly to remove all strange scents. Then I breathed upon them to warm them—just as you should dip your hand into cold water to greet a frog. Gently and very slowly, I got these little Horned Dragons to step onto my palms. I knew that a shadow from above, or being lifted through the air with nothing beneath them, would seem like an attack from a big bird, such as all little lizards fear.

The bath I got them was only tap-water which tastes of metal pipes, so they could not drink it through their mouths. But they could take some in through their skins, as frogs do. When they had taken water, I stroked them slowly upwards from throat to jaw, where the skin is thin and sensitive; and then I remembered that we have something about us that talks the language of life itself. I lifted the little fellows to my throat, one each side, where they could feel the warm, rhythmical beat of a pulse. They clung close, and we were friends.

But there were many problems still to be faced, problems of food and housing and water. The small size of their bath troubled them—for where they came from, such a little water-hole would have dried up in an hour. I brought a jug of water and filled the bath before their eyes, and sprinkled them. So I began the habit of making a pantomime to show them things. On picnic days (to which the little dragons travelled in their open box, with rugs and pillows and every comfort) they saw me draw the little black ants towards them by rubbing a piece of meat across a rock. This was good, but better were the hours by the rock-bottomed creek, in shallow pools of sunlit water. One dragon learnt to swim. The other sat wetly in an inch of water, one tiny paw curved over the tip of my finger, timidly holding hands.

Their home was built of rocks in a big wooden tub, with little caves set at angles to catch morning and afternoon sun. There were low-growing succulents to hide in, and a bath in a flowerpot saucer of earthy red. Lizards know that in white vessels they are too easily seen by their enemies.

Now my friend Jean also got two little dragons. We appointed each other to be aunts. If one of us had to go away, the other took over both little groups; and now they had two gardens to feed in.

The bigger of my two dragons we called Wendy, after the little girl who kept house for Peter Pan and the Lost Boys. Indeed, Lost Boys soon began to arrive: from zoo collections where they could not thrive, or from soldiers who brought them back from the Northern Territory. Some we saved; and some, alas, came to us too late.

Wendy's mate was called Marco Polo Junior, after that famous traveller. Every morning the garden paths looked like new roads for him to explore. He used to visit schools in Kindness to Animals Week, making his swaying corroboree dance along the desks. He was always a huge success. Those shy little goblins of the caves and shadows, the Geckos, would have swooned and lost their tails at all the clamouring voices. Yet I have known Geckos to sleep contentedly, head down, in my shirt pocket all day, after being dug gently out of bush fireplaces. They crawl into the warm ashes when they return from hunting in the still of morning—or into campers' beds. I remember little grey hands scratching at my pillow, and glowing golden eyes like the lamps of a tiny coach, creeping into my blankets where I waked on the brink above the old Joadja shale mine, years ago.

After Marco and Wendy, all the little dragons who came to me were strays. I would not be responsible for taking them from their homes to live in gardens where the ants suffer from so many poison sprays. After all the others had passed away to their corroboree grounds in the Land on Top (as the lubras say in telling their old tales) the last of my pocket dinosaurs was Chips, the little Overlander.

Chips loved company. From the first he was quite tame, and would not go to bed until I nursed him off to sleep. Wherever I put him down he stayed till I took him up again. This made it all the more terrifying the day I returned to the verandah after having been called away, and Chips was gone.

The sun was almost spent, and shadows covered the lawn. Only a few sunbeams came through the trees and stippled the lawn, as if someone had walked there in golden sandals. I searched till dark. Chips was not used to finding his way afoot, but usually travelled on my shoulder.

This was not my home garden, but a big overgrown place traversed by other tenants, not all friendly. The garden ran down to the railway fence, where thickets of blackberries took over, and a steep bank dropped to the line below. It was dry weather, too. The danger was that lizards, like tortoises, go downhill in dry weather, seeking water. How could I call a little lost Chips, wandering down towards the railway line?

An anxious week followed, a week of dry days. Every few hours I made a water signal, pouring out a bucket of water below the verandah step; for to one from the desert, water calls the loudest.

There are some moments too keen ever to be forgotten. It was a moment like that when a rattling of leaves summoned me, beaten by a thorny tail. An eager little faced looked up from below the step that he could never climb. Chips was home.

A Thorny Devil.

A Green Gecko of the rainforest.

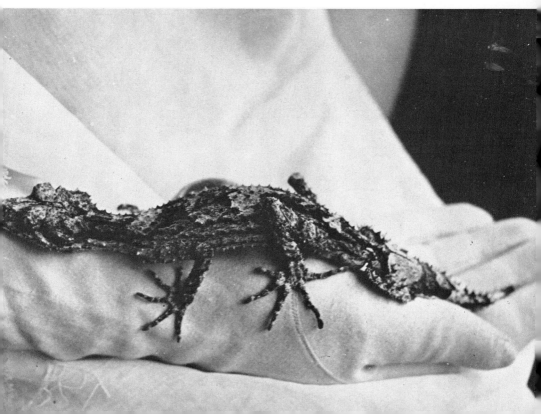

'Wendy' and 'Marko' basking in their armchairs.

Baby Lace Monitors.

N. L. RAY

A Promise is a Promise

Illustrations by Margaret Senior

"But I *must* be in Sydney for the Show."

Bill's boss pushed his hat back on his head. "Well, you just can't be and that's flat. I can't spare you."

"I promised."

"So what? That's your affair. If you go, Bill, and I hate to say it, you don't come back to this job. Right?"

"Right," said Bill. "I'm sorry, but—Goodbye."

"Camels are stubborn and mules are stubborn, but they're sweetly reasonable creatures compared with you, Bill. Good-bye." The boss watched Bill walk across the yard towards his hut. "And there goes the best engine doctor on the place," he added slowly.

Bill loved machinery. He treated his engines like friends and they ran for him like angels. But now he was leaving the northwest Queensland construction camp where he had been in charge of the machinery—and why? Because he had promised to be in Sydney for the Show. Throwing up a good job for a promise like that! The boss snorted.

An hour later Bill stood in the shade of a tree and waited for a truck, because the plane had gone and there would not be another till Friday. The flies crawled over his face, and tried to get into his eyes and up his nose. Bill brushed them away. When he heard a truck coming, he stepped out into the road. The truck stopped and the driver leaned out.

"Want a lift?"

"South?"

"South for a start. Hop in."

Bill tossed his belongings up on the truck and hopped in beside the driver. Time passed. The miles slid by. Bill and the driver talked.

"Where you heading?"

"Sydney."

"Sydney, eh? What's in Sydney?"

"I promised to be there for the Show."

"A promise is a promise," said the driver.

Bill nodded. "You've got a bit of a knock in that engine," he said.

"Yes. Can't seem to place it, either."

"Like me to look at her?"

The driver said nothing for a couple of miles. Bill sat quietly beside him. The driver looked at him carefully when he thought Bill was not watching. He saw Bill's stubby fingers with the grease under the fingernails, and he thought about the tool-kit that Bill had slung in with his bag. "Gunta stop here for a spell," he said at last. "We might have a look at her then."

Bill nodded.

They stopped in the shade of some trees and the driver brought out his tucker-box. "We'll eat first," he said, "and let her cool down a bit." They ate in friendly silence. Then the driver pushed up the bonnet and Bill came and perched beside him on the big mud-guard.

"It isn't this and it isn't that, and I've cleaned every other thing that might be making her cranky. She's just downright cantankerous. Eh?"

Bill nodded as the driver pointed and poked and undid things and did them up again, and then Bill undid things and blew on them or wiped them with the rag he carried for wiping things, and he muttered under his breath as he worked and the driver muttered with him, and they really crooned over that engine, for they were both engine men.

"Try her now," Bill said at last.

"Right." The driver pushed the starter and the great truck engine roared at them while Bill fiddled, making it roar louder and louder, then softer and softer, till it settled down to a steady purr. "That's got her all right," said the driver. "Thanks, mate."

"Pleasure," said Bill, wiping his hands. "She sounds fine now."

A dusty utility drew up alongside. "Want any help?" asked the man in the utility.

"No, thanks," said the truck driver, "we're right now. Hot enough for you?"

"Hot enough. Where are you heading?"

"I'm heading for Townsville, but me mate here wants to get to Sydney."

"Sydney, eh? Perhaps I could help you there. A couple of hundred miles, anyway. Be glad of the company."

"Sure?" Bill asked.

"Sure sure. Townsville's a bit east for a man who wants to get to Sydney. Got any bags? Sling them in the back."

So Bill said goodbye to the truck driver and climbed into the utility. This driver talked all the time; and he drove very fast, so that Bill began to feel happier about getting to Sydney. The pink hills flew by and the trees were a blur and the miles of gibbers were a blur. The road stretched ahead of them for miles without a bend in it, and they could see something some way ahead that didn't look right.

"What's going on up there?" said the driver, slowing down a bit.

"Can't quite see," replied Bill, screwing up his eyes against the glare. "Looks to be a tank there, and a mill, isn't it?"

"A mob of cattle! Of all the luck! Did you ever know anything as muddle-headed as cattle on a road? They can never decide where they want to go till you're right on top of them, and then they decide to go the other way."

Bill laughed. "Poor things. Listen to them, though."

"Kicking up a row, aren't they? There's a truck there. Wonder what gives?" He slowed down and stopped. The cattle, which had moved aside as the utility approached, milled round them.

A man came towards them, slapping the beasts on their backs with his old felt hat to make them move. He was dusty and sweaty and hot. "G'day," he said.

The driver nodded. "Having trouble?"

"Pump's bust. No water. The mob is crazy for a drink."

"Tough luck. Sorry we can't help. So long."

"I might be able to help," said Bill, his hand on the door handle.

The driver looked at him, amazed. "Thought you wanted to get to Sydney?"

"I do, very much, but you can't leave beasts dying of thirst."

"Well, thanks for the company. I'm not waiting."

"Thanks for the lift," said Bill stiffly. "Just a sec till I get my things out of the back. So long."

The utility moved off, hooting through the mob.

An hour later, after Bill had fixed the pump with a bit of

fencing wire and some washers cut from an old boot, his companion squatted on his haunches and rolled a cigarette. The water was flowing into the troughs, the thirsty cattle were pushing and shouldering each other aside to get to it. "Soon be sundown. What'll you do, Bill?"

"Camp by the road. Maybe someone will come past who'll give me a lift."

"You can come back with me. Get some tucker and a bed. You've earned it."

Bill was tired. "Sounds good," he said, "but I've got to get to Sydney for the Show."

"Is the Show that important?"

"I promised."

"Like that, is it? You'll be better for a spell, though. Come on, I'll put you on the track in the morning."

Bill yawned. "Well, thanks, I will. It's been a day."

It was a while before Bill got his rest. When they reached the station, the lighting plant was playing up. "This bloke'll fix it," said the cattle-man, pushing Bill forward.

So Bill got his tool-box and someone held a lamp for him and he talked to that engine. It was very dirty, so Bill took his rag and cleaned this and he cleaned that and he scraped the grease off the other; and then he put them all back and picked up the old tin with the lip bent into it and poured oil in here and oil in there and checked the fuel. Then he kicked her over and she went like a charm and lights came on all over the place.

Next day Bill was up at dawn, anxious to get back to the road to see if he could pick up another lift; but the station manager called to him as he went across the yard.

"I believe you're in a hurry. I've got to fly to Cunnamulla this morning. Would that be any help?"

"It *would*," said Bill. "Thanks very much. It wouldn't be imposing . . . ?"

"Not at all. You've earned it. Oh, and by the way—could you have a look at the missus's sewing machine? She was a bit shy about asking you. She says it sews like a drunk emu in a string factory."

Bill grinned. "Good-oh. A bit out of my line, but I'll have a look."

He fiddled with the sewing machine while the station manager's wife watched and the children all but got stitched up trying to see how he did things, and finally the machine was sewing like a machine again, whirring up and down a straight line with even stitches. Then they all had a cup of tea, and Bill and the manager went flying off to Cunnamulla.

When they arrived they had to have another cup of tea, and the manager told his host about Bill's prowess with machines. "Well," said the host, "if you're not in a hurry you can stay here for a day and see what you can do with a couple of mine."

"I *am* in a bit of a hurry," said Bill, rather desperate now. "I *must* get to Sydney for the Show. I promised."

"Don't worry about that. I'm flying down myself on Thursday in a transport, taking cattle down. You can come with me. O.K.?"

Bill could hardly believe his ears.

"Come and see the cranky lot I've got for you to fix," said the host.

So Bill stayed, and he went over all the engines on the place and had them all going sweetly.

"My word, you're a bobbydazzler with an engine," said the owner. "You wouldn't like to come and help me with the beasts at the Showground, would you?"

Bill shook his head. "No, thanks, I'll be busy at the Showground myself."

When they reached Sydney Bill shook hands with the man from Cunnamulla, picked up his bag and his box of tools and caught a bus, thinking how many friends he'd made on his way down from the north. Next day he was up early, shaved, showered, and in his city clothes. He went along a road and up a quiet street till he came to a big old building.

He went in at the gate, through the big front door, down the tiled hall to the Matron's office. From there he was taken to a bright ward. There was a shriek from the far corner.

"Billie! You *did* come! I knew you would, I told them. You promised."

"Hello there, young Ted. Of course I came. A promise is a promise. How are all you kids? See you later."

Very gently Bill picked up his young brother with the plaster on his legs and together they went out to the Showground. Ted sat on Bill's shoulders, his hands in his brother's curly hair, and saw the people and heard the shouts. He saw the stalls of fairy floss, ice-cream, drinks, hot dogs and waffles; he saw the balloons, the monkeys on sticks, the curly spiders on the end of rubber tubes; he sniffed the smell that goes with the Show and thought he would die of happiness. He tugged at Bill's hair.

"What's up? Leave me some hair now, Ted. I'm attached to it."

"Can we go now, Bill? You know—where you said?"

"Right this minute?"

"Please, Bill."

"Hang on, then. Here we go."

They didn't go to look at the horses. They didn't see the cows, the pigs, the dogs or the Agricultural Hall. They didn't even stop to look at the wood-chopping or the Police Exhibit. Bill knew where they were going, and Ted knew too.

They went right past everything—the sample bags and sideshows, the merry-go-rounds and ferris wheels. They stopped only once because Bill said he needed an ice-cream and didn't Ted? Ted thought he did, so they licked together and went on.

They stopped at last. Ted forgot his poor legs and Bill forgot his lost job, and they stayed very happily among the machinery exhibits and tried everything they were allowed to try. Bill looked at engines, Ted stayed on a tractor the size of a house and pretended he was driving it, and they were very happy.

PETER WRIGHTSON

Coils, Condensers and Crystals

WHEN I was about ten, all I knew about radio was how to switch on the set and how to tune in the station I wanted to hear. I was quite fascinated by the array of glass tubes, metal cylinders, and all the funny little bits and pieces, intricately interconnected, that went into the workings; but, though I *wanted* to know how it worked, I didn't have the foggiest idea.

When I was eleven I read several old articles on the subject, but I was no better off; all the technical jargon and abstract ideas meant nothing to me.

It wasn't until I went away to boarding school at the age of twelve, and saw someone fiddling with a crystal set, that I got to know something about radio.

The first set I saw consisted of a large coil of copper wire wound on a cardboard tube that looked as if it had come from the centre of a toilet roll, a large device made of metal plates mounted close together but not quite touching, and one or two other small things as well as a pair of large headphones.

After closely questioning its owner and examining the set I at last discovered, in a hazy sort of way, how the thing worked. Here, I decided, was a radio that I could build for myself. "Of course," I was told, "crystal sets have very limited power and range"—but they had the great advantage that they were well within my technical and financial capacity. And because they used no external power source, they could be used almost anywhere.

The first set I built for myself gave me a great thrill—even though it was very large and unsightly. I used it for about six months, until I discovered from a friend how to build a better one. Using more modern miniaturised components, I found I could make a set that was much smaller and more compact. In fact, when I'd saved up the necessary sum (my salary was twenty cents a week in those days) I managed quite easily to fit it into a toothbrush case. The advantage of this was that

I could keep it in the dormitory and use it after 'lights out' without arousing the suspicions of either the housemaster or the prefects. Radios were not allowed in the dorm. and there was a constant underground war to get them in and use them. The toothbrush case looked quite innocent when seen in my locker, and it slipped under the pillow neatly when in use.

The aerial and earth were the biggest problem, and both were necessary since the power of the set depends on both being as efficient as possible. Wires hanging out of windows, or looped round the room or hooked up to water pipes, tend to be a bit obvious; but with the help of some friends I managed to conceal mine effectively. A handy lightning conductor makes a perfect earth, and the lead-in wires can be slipped behind skirting boards and rendered invisible. The aerial we rigged right round the building, high up under the eaves.

On a Saturday afternoon when the building was empty (everybody was at the football) we hung out of adjacent windows heaving, from one to another, a length of string with an old bolt tied to the end. The aerial was tied to the other end of the string. By this means, from window to window, we passed the wire right round the building. We then tied the wire to the rafters above each window and pulled it up tight so that it did not sag down where it could be seen. The system requires at least three people (one to heave the line, one to catch it, and one on sentry duty) and is not recommended for extremely high buildings unless the three people are steeplejacks or something.

The lead-in from the aerial we hid behind picture rails and door frames. It worked very well and was never discovered while I was at school. It's probably still there now, come to that.

Since leaving school I have learnt a little more about radio in general and have been surprised to find that crystal sets are not just simple radios; rather that modern transistor radios are complex crystal sets. Crystal sets—or diode receivers, to give them their more correct title—convert the energy of radio waves into electrical energy. Then, by discarding the unwanted parts, they produce a signal which can be converted to sound waves and heard through an earplug or headphone.

Your modern three-band twelve-transistor portable radio does this too, but adds the ability to amplify the signal to operate a loudspeaker. It can also obtain a signal of sufficient strength from a much weaker radio wave, which increases the effective range over which the set can be used.

Crystal sets can still be bought in some shops, but when I bought one it was so inferior that I went back to building my own. The following diagram is a design for a crystal set that is easy to build and gives a much better performance than the two-dollar touch that I bought.

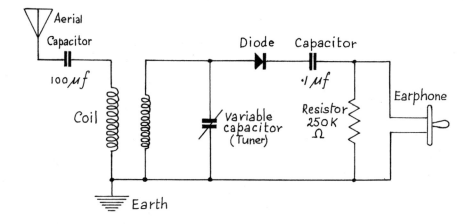

The lines in the diagram represent the wires joining the components, and the symbols represent the components themselves. Where the wires cross, they should be joined only if the crossing is marked with a dot. The symbols are used universally as a form of shorthand, so that circuit diagrams can be quickly and easily drawn and read. The labels are used here only to identify them for you.

All the components can be bought in any radio shop with the exception of the coil, which you had better wind yourself. Ready-made coils can be bought, but for the purpose of this circuit that isn't really necessary. The one you wind yourself may take longer and be a little larger, but it is cheaper, and I'm all for saving money.

To produce your coil you will need to buy some 34 SWG lacquered copper wire (thirty to forty yards should be plenty) and find a cylinder, or former, to wind it on. The former should be 5 centimetres long by 1.6 centimetres in diameter, and made of a non-magnetic substance. Cardboard, wood or plastic will do. If your half-inch plastic garden hose is new and still firm, pinch a few inches of that. A tubular former is better than a solid one like wooden dowel, because it is easier to fix the ends of your coil. I drilled small holes in pairs through the ends of my piece of hose, and fixed the ends of the coil by lacing the wire through them. When you fix your wire to one end, leave four or five inches hanging free.

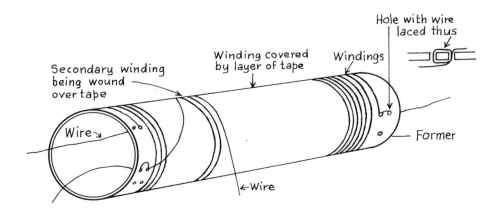

Start winding (in either direction) about an eighth of an inch from the end of the former. Make your turns as firm as possible (but don't break the wire) and wind them so that each turn touches the preceding one. This is called close winding, and the idea is to have all the turns touching with no gaps—to give maximum induction (I'll explain that word later). When you have wound 160 turns stop winding, cut the wire, and fix it through another pair of holes so that it won't unwind. Leave a few inches hanging free so that you can connect it into the circuit later. You have now completed the primary winding of your coil, and if you've wound it properly it should be very close to 4 centimetres long. The next thing to do is to cover the winding with a single layer of adhesive tape (masking tape does very well). This makes it easier to wind the next layer.

Now fix your wire again at the same end that you began last time and, starting about an eighth of an inch in from the edge of the primary, wind on another 120 turns—close wound and in the same direction as the primary. When you have done that, don't break the wire but anchor it with a piece of tape, lay it back across the winding and cover the lot with a single layer of tape.

Starting about an eighth of an inch in from the edge of the previous layer, wind as before another 40 turns. Then continue winding, spacing the turns about an eighth of an inch apart, until you have cleared the primary winding. Tie off with another pair of those holes.

You now have an induction coil; so called because current from the aerial, flowing through the primary winding, will *induce* a current to flow in the secondary winding. Because the secondary (two layers of it) is longer than the primary, the voltage in it is higher, which is one of the reasons we use the coil in our circuit. The coil affects the current in other ways too, but to explain them would take a chapter or two and probably be rather dull.

Having made your coil and collected the other components, you'd best look around for something to put them in. The set can be assembled in any container you choose provided, of course, that they will fit. The container should not be made of metal. I built mine in a small plastic box from which I first removed the cuff-links.

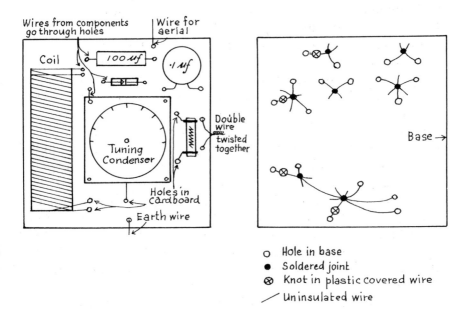

o   Hole in base
●   Soldered joint
⊗   Knot in plastic covered wire
╱   Uninsulated wire

To assemble the set, solder the component wires together according to the diagram—taking care not to use more heat than you need, as this will damage the components. A useful tip is to assemble the components on a piece of cardboard or plastic cut to fit your container. Drill small holes in it, and mount the components on one side with their wires poking through to the other. You then solder the wires together as shown, and your set is complete. The piece of cardboard or plastic, as well as making assembly easier, prevents the components from moving and causing a short circuit.

Once complete, fit the set into its case; but don't forget to make holes in it for the aerial, earth and earphone wires, as well as for the tuning knob.

Your new set should work quite well provided, of course, that you are within about eighty miles of a transmitter, and that you use a good aerial and earth. The big question is *how* it works. I haven't the space to go into any great detail, but basically the theory is quite simple.

The radio waves, which are electromagnetic waves, induce a current to flow in the aerial as they flow round it. This current oscillates at the same frequency as the radio waves which generated it, and is known as an RF (radio frequency) signal. From the aerial it passes through the first capacitor to the coil, where it is stored until required. In our set the coil is used in conjunction with the tuning condenser to set the frequency of the stored signal. This means that only one frequency can be stored, but by tuning the variable condenser this can be changed, so that we can tune to any frequency or station we wish.

From the coil the signal is passed to the crystal or diode which, being a semiconductor, allows only part of the signal through. The crystal is called a semiconductor because it allows current to pass in one direction only. In one direction it is a conductor, and in the other it is an insulator. It's rather like a one-way valve. This is important since the signal oscillates at such a high frequency that the vibrator of the earphone (which operates on magnetism) cannot react to the change. By allowing only half the signal through as a series of impulses, the frequency is halved.

From the crystal the signal, which is now called an AM (audio-modulated) signal, is passed to the earphone, where it causes the thin metal plate to vibrate and give off audible sounds. The capacitor in this part of the circuit controls the frequency of the AM signal; and the resistor bleeds a little of the signal past the earphone, to remove distortion from the sound produced.

The signal is then passed off to earth, together with those parts which were rejected by the coil and crystal.

A good aerial is very important, because the set operates only on the power generated within the aerial. It should be as long as possible and as high as possible, and should be insulated from the ground and from its supports. That way, it collects as much signal as possible and forces it all to pass through the set, without any escape to the ground.

Likewise, the earth is important, to get rid of the signal as quickly as possible once it has done its job. Your earth wire should be soldered to a metal rod and driven into moist ground, or attached to a piece of iron and buried. There are other methods that I'm sure you can think of; but it is important to make sure that the electrical connections are good, the soil is moist, and the shortest path to the ground is used.

If you live in a flat or units, don't use the water-pipes for an earth as they are not very efficient. Use instead the finger-stop of your telephone. It makes a perfect earth, even if it is a little inconvenient for callers. Aerials too can be a bit of a problem in a flat. But, since you are probably fairly close to at least one transmitter, one of those wire screens for the window, or better still a wire-screen door, makes an adequate aerial.

Crystal sets were the earliest form of receiver in common use, but they were by no means the first receivers. People like Marconi had never heard of them while doing their early experiments. The apparatus Marconi first used consisted of an induction coil (called a Ramhkorf coil after its inventor), a condenser (called a Leyden jar), a spark gap, and a battery. That was the transmitter. The receiver consisted of a coherer, a buzzer, and a battery. Later Marconi added an aerial and earth, and found they increased the performance remarkably.

A coherer, for those who aren't in the know, consisted of a glass tube filled with metal filings, and with a wire hanging out of each end. When connected in circuit with the battery and buzzer it would resist the passage of electric current. When a high frequency AC current was generated in the circuit by radio waves (provided by the transmitter) the metal particles would cohere and provide a path for the battery's power—and the buzzer would sound. The apparatus was non-selective; it could not be tuned to transmit or receive on a single frequency but would only operate over a wide frequency range.

In 1900 Marconi tuned his circuits by regulating the frequency of the spark across the spark gap. Later, as techniques developed, the crystal receiver began to replace the earlier types, but was itself replaced by the thermionic valve.

The valve provided amplification, as well as rectifying the signal. But at first it had three big drawbacks: its size, the power it needed, and the heat it generated. One valve, installed in Schenectady, U.S.A., stood $7\frac{1}{2}$ feet high, weighed 100 lbs, and had to be water-cooled. This monster was rated at 100 kilowatts, but most valves were limited to about 25 kilowatts. As techniques of production and operation improved, the crystal vanished from the scene for a time. It made a comeback in the 1930's, when it was used in radar and sonar transmitters.

Then the transistor arrived, and almost made the valve obsolete. The transistor rectifies and amplifies a signal as the valve does, but does it with a fraction of the power and size. A valve requires an electric current in the order of hundreds of volts; a transistor needs power in the order of tens of volts. This means that the other components in the circuit do not have to carry high power loads, and so can be made smaller. Combine this with the small size of the transistor itself, and you have the reason why radios now are so much smaller than their fathers of fifteen years ago.

To make a transistor you simply take our old friend the crystal or diode. You attach one more wire to it, and through this feed a weak current, say from a small battery. Now the diode is receiving current from two separate sources—from the aerial, as in your crystal set, and from the battery. It rectifies the first, as your crystal does; and this RF signal, though it is much the weaker of the two, modulates the DC current from the battery. It is almost as though you used the first as a mould, and poured the second into it. Today there are many types of transistor but they are all of this basic design, though the theory of their operation depends on complex theories of crystaline structure.

I have given a diagram of the circuit of a one-transistor radio to compare with that of your crystal set. You can see that it is almost the same circuit, with the addition of a power

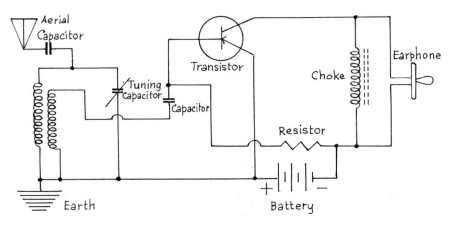

source—the battery. The additional coil is a choke, to bleed the DC part of the AM signal past the earphone. (This is another property of some coils. They offer an easy path to DC current but tend to resist the passage of AC current.)

You see? Crystal sets are not really antique oddities at all. I still use mine occasionally, when I get sick of that twelve-transistor thing on the bookcase.

The Great Australian Game

Bob Skilton won Melbourne football's highest individual honour, the Brownlow Medal, twice in five years—in 1958 and 1963. He is a rover and plays for South Melbourne. Skilton, born November 8th 1938, is not a big man physically, 5 ft 7 in tall, 11 st 13 lb, but he is big in spirit, a physical fitness crank who bounces around foorball fields with zest, unfailing pluck and a desire for victory remarkable in one who plays for a moderately successful club. He is fast, a splendid kick, especially dangerous clear of the pack.

THIS IS A game of soaring high marks, a game of terrific pace in which the ball is driven back and forth across an entire oval by long kicks and handpasses. There's jarring physical contact in which the participants expect hard bumps and it must be one of the most spectacular games ever invented by man, a game full of high-fliers and dramatic clashes between tough, fit men, a game full of doubt and surprise. It can never become stereotyped.

Australian football is the main winter game in four of Australia's six States. From its rough-and-tumble beginnings on the goldfields in the 1850s, it has become a highly organised game. I read that in a poll taken in 1963, the game attracts one out of every two adults in southern Australia sometime or other during an average winter. The main League matches in South Australia, Victoria, Western Australia and Tasmania pull in an aggregate of around half a million spectators every Saturday afternoon.

Australian football is unique, the only sport Australians invented, the most fanatically followed game in a nation internationally famous for its sporting prowess. Lately people have been saying it is dirtier and rougher than it's ever been and that it's deteriorating through punching and fouls and the like. But talk to oldtimers who played it as boys and you soon work out that it's no worse than it's ever been.

State Savings Bank Little League: South Melbourne player punches the ball away from his Melbourne opponent.

South Melbourne *v* Melbourne

Melbourne *v* St Kilda.

Aggregate attendances in Melbourne, main stronghold of the game, run over three million year after year, with crowds up to 100,000 packing in for the Melbourne Cricket Ground grand finals. Only the lack of accommodation at suburban grounds keeps the figures within those limits. Since the first postwar VFL grand final in 1946 the grand final crowd has never been below 80,000 and eleven times it has soared past 100,000, including a record 115,802 in 1956. The VFA, too, has made remarkable progress. The VFA, oldest Australian Rules body in Australia, now comprises 10 teams in each of two divisions.

In this dizzy postwar growth of Australian football, I have frequently heard visitors from overseas or the northern Australian States of Queensland and New South Wales—where Rugby and Soccer predominate—express amazement at the interest in Australian football's club matches. Here newspaper sellers can rub shoulders with company directors, lawyers can argue about rulings with shopkeepers, and housewives can debate the merits of players with architects. And they do just that!

They are not just football fans. They are barrackers. They don't just go to the games, they 'barrack for South', or they 'barrack for the Demons'. Impartial spectators who don't yell encouragement for half the 36 players on view are rare. From the former Prime Minister, Sir Robert Menzies, an ardent supporter of 'The Blues'—Carlton—to ex-Opposition Leader Arthur Calwell who barracks for North Melbourne, the game creates unashamed partisanship. South have never been in the four since I've been with them but my love for the club is as deep as our fans and I would never dream of leaving them for a side likely to make the four every year.

Admittedly, Australian football is a hard game. Rule 15 clearly says a player with the ball can be fairly met by an opponent and brought down by use of the hip, shoulder, chest, arms or open hands. But your son need not be a giant to play it well and if he is destined to be of short or stocky frame he can soon adjust his game to suit his build. Since I started in the game in 1948 as a Port Melbourne schoolboy, the only injuries I have suffered have been a broken wrist (twice) and a broken elbow.

Jack Dyer, one of football's greatest, was stoned from football fields, escorted home by police, kicked and punched un-mercifully by other players. After one match he had to draw a police pistol to keep back a threatening mob. But he managed to keep these incidents in perspective, remembering more often the big lift the game gave him, actions like that of the RAAF ace who named his fighter plane 'Captain Blood'.

The physical clashes, the time off for treating stunned players are dramatised by publicity mediums, but taken overall, few bad injuries come out of Australian football. In 1963, there was a tremendous fuss about an incident in the South Australia versus Victoria match in Adelaide. Television viewers in every State watched enthralled as Victorian ruckman John Peck, who was on the ground, rose and in the act of turning started to throw a right swing. As he regained his feet, he took a step and crashed his fist on to the jaw of SA half-forward Brian Sawley, who was standing with his hands at his side. Sawley dropped unconscious to the turf and lay motionless on his back. The players had to restrain a spectator who jumped the fence to get at Peck.

This punch repeated in slow motion closeups in capital city sports shows throughout Australia, was labelled "one of the most blatant attacks ever made on a player on the football field." In my view it is natural in a game of hard physical contact to get a few knockouts and this affair was blown up beyond all proportion until the VFL tribunal brought the thing into perspective by suspending Peck for only two matches. This kind of incident, exaggerated by TV, is far from typical in 100 minutes of play. In fact, it is rare. TV creates a great deal of extra pressure on every senior player.

One thing I thought the 1963 Victoria-SA matches did emphasise was how the standards of play in all the Australian football States is levelling up. Years ago Interstate football was a joke, with Victoria sure winners every time. But now the other States have a different mental approach. There is no cream puff approach in their play now and they go straight up and bump Victorians hard the way they should.

This has created a marked increase in enthusiasm for Interstate football and I am tipping that before long we will see an Australian Cup competition designed to find the champion club side in all the Rules States.

I have always said there are no deadbeats in top class

Australian football. It's a sport which plays a terrific part in character development of a boy. The only mystery is why such a spectacular code did not spread through every Australian State years ago when it was first developed before codes like Rugby and Soccer had consolidated in NSW and Queensland.

In southern Australia, the game is spreading very quickly in schools of all grades and denominations and each winter more than 100,000 boys play inter-school Rules. The code is studded with good players who are doctors, dentists, architects or are in other professions. Headmasters swear by it as a factor in producing well-rounded youngsters fit to take their place in society. They like the fact that 36 boys get a run in Rules compared with 22 in Soccer, 26 in Rugby League and 30 in Rugby Union. The influx of so many more players into the code must lift the standards of the game.

Here is a game where a boy can get the satisfaction of being a brilliant individualist and at the same time blend into his team's overall plan. One of the most gratifying aspects of the game is the great feeling you get from being a cog in a winning machine. That is why I say that no responsible parent should hesitate in putting a boy into a district club once he leaves school. The companionship, the fellowship both of his fellow clubmen and opponents will last all his life and help him tremendously in private life because of the discipline it teaches.

Nor should there by any fears that professionalism will spoil a boy's makeup. It is true that some of the topliners make a few dollars on the side from the game but in general I think the Victorian Football League and their counterparts in the other Rules States have a very sane and practical attitude toward payment of players. At least we don't have any shamateurs.

We are paid on a sliding scale fixed by the VFL for the number of matches played, so that no player can make a living entirely from football. There is no buying of players from rival clubs for astronomical sums as there is in overseas soccer and in Sydney Rugby League, where poker machine profits have created a Fairyland rate of payment and players change clubs for sums up to $60,000. Indeed the rules of VFL forbid lump sum payments for transfers. The administrators of our game are very mindful of the duty they have in not allowing one State to milk another of all its star players. Our players may be offered a good job or a house by influential club supporters as an inducement, if his club agrees to release him, but these lures are exceptional.

With the tremendous increase in publicity for the game, the 'fringe' benefits open to glamour players were bound to come. We get fees from TV appearances, newspaper articles for advertising certain products and fees for training are added to our match fees. There are good provident funds for most of Melbourne's 12 senior clubs, and some clubs reward players after a tough season with an overseas or interstate trip. But nobody can say we can get rich from the game. And we certainly envy the $200 per match which we read that players earn in Rugby League.

So great is the impact of this remarkable game that it is almost impossible for me or anyone of the other well known footballers in Melbourne to walk down the street or ride in a tram without someone in the city's two million button-holing us for a discussion about football. For 100 minutes every Saturday these fans can be kings. They can say what they like and do almost what they like at the games and as one writer said, what they see is "a tribal feud that affects their lives."

LILITH NORMAN

Pymbles

Illustrations by Joan Saint

IT WAS a day; just like any other.

Cassie hammered on the bathroom door and yelled again at Steve to hurry up. Trust Steve to get up early and hog the bathroom the one day everybody was in a hurry to go on a picnic. In fairness, though, Cassie realised that was obviously why. Only the promise of a picnic would rouse Steve Van Winkle from his nightly twenty-year sleep. Cassie could smell the bacon beginning to cook, and she raised her hand to pound again; or to break the door down if necessary.

Instead, it opened, and her fist nearly collided with Steve's head. He grinned at her, his hair standing up spikily and dripping onto his bare shoulders.

"Don't be long," he said, "breakfast's nearly ready."

Before Cassie could think of a suitable reply, Steve had scampered off to his room leaving a trail of damp footprints and a frayed pyjama cord. With an irritated shrug, Cassie closed the door behind her and turned on the shower.

They were all at the table when she finally went downstairs —Steve, Mum, Dad and Grampa. Steve swivelled round on his chair and whistled, "Wow! Who's got a brown belly-button?"

"Yours is in the stove, dear," said her mother at the same time.

Cassie felt the patch of bare skin between her hipsters and her bra top blushing. She scowled ferociously at Steve and smiled simultaneously at her mother.

"Lucky there's no wind today," said Grampa with a wink. "If there was, and it changed, you might stay like that."

Cassie tried to scowl at him, too, as she sat down with her plate of bacon and eggs; but Grampa gave her such a fierce scowl first that she burst out laughing. She could never stay cross when Grampa was about.

Breakfast over, and the dishes done, they all piled out to the car, stowing picnic baskets, rugs, folding chairs and a Portagas stove carefully into the boot. Genghis Khan, Steve's Afghan dog, lolloped and pitched about in front of them like an animated bathmat.

"Get that blasted dog away!" yelled Dad as a leap from Khan sent him ricocheting against the car. "If he scratches the duco with those great hoofs of his, I'll cut his toenails right up to the elbow."

Steve grabbed Khan by the collar and forced him down onto his haunches. "Sit!" he commanded. "Stay!" Khan gave him an anxious grin and charged off to peer into the boot.

"Steve, chain that overgrown haystack up," said Dad.

"But you said we could take him with us."

"Oh? Well, all right, but put him *in* the car, and make him stay there."

Steve opened the car door and Khan bounced in, trampling across the back seat from side to side and leaving wet nose-prints on the windows as he excitedly followed the final packing.

At last they were off. Dad, Mum and Steve in the front seat; Cassie, Grampa and an Afghan demented with anticipation in the back. Dad started the engine and backed carefully out of the drive, handling the car as though it were made of meringue.

The picnic, of course, was for the car. Dad's new car which he had picked up yesterday. Cassie studied her father as they rolled smoothly through the northern suburbs towards the hills that ringed Sydney. It was, thought Cassie, probably the most hideous car she had ever seen.

Its styling was sleeky pugnacious, while its colour . . . ! It was a glossy metallic purple, with a flashy red stripe slightly off-centre running its whole length over engine, top and boot. A mutant Martian bug, thought Cassie, and strictly poisonous. There was a sudden roar as Dad forced the sporty gear stick through with a ferocious double-shuffle. Cassie gazed at the back of her father's head.

There he was—Dad. Thin and slightly stooped, with grey hair thinning to a tonsure in the centre. A professor's meekly professional face, and a tendency towards drily pedantic jokes and tiny blusters of rage. What was inside? Did Dad have dreams of wild adventure? Was he, somewhere inside, a golden knight charging through the tapestry heroics of his specialty of mediaeval history? Was that why he wore bright shirts and that awful hairy jacket with knobbly bits that looked as though it was woven out of steel wool and bindi-eyes?

They were out of the city now, swooping over partly wooded hills and beside green paddocks, each with its small reddish-brown clay dam. Steve was stolidly and tunelessly singing his was through "We're off to see the Wizard", beginning each round with a different letter of the alphabet. He was now up to "Te're toff to tee the tizard, the tunderful Tizard of Toz". Cassie rapped him smartly on the head with her knuckles, but he only stuck his tongue out at her and continued doggedly, "Ve're voff to vee the Vizard. . . ."

Grampa suddenly leaned forward and whispered "Ssshhhh!" in a menacing way. Steve looked round, startled. Grampa never ticked him off as a rule.

"What's the matter?"

"You'll disturb them," said Grampa.

"Who? Cassie? She doesn't care——"

"No, them." Grampa pointed out the window as a sign flashed by. RESTING PADDOCKS, it read.

Steve began to laugh convulsively. 'Really,' thought Cassie, who had found it quite funny herself, 'children!'

"I know," said Steve. "I'll sing them a lullaby." He stuck his head out the window and bellowed, "Rockabye paddocks, by the road side."

A breeze shivered across the grasses as though the paddock had stirred slightly.

Spooky, thought Cassie.

Steve spent the rest of the day finding signs. It was better than that endless singing, thought Cassie, and before long she was joining in, then the whole family. Dad found CAREFUL SOFT SHOULDERS, where the asphalt road gave onto clay edges. "Very sexy," he remarked smugly. Cassie found SHEPHERDS DRIVING SCHOOL—but there were no shepherds in sight, and the school was not being driven anywhere. Steve got quite cross when they passed a DISPENSING CHEMIST and Dad wouldn't stop.

"But I've never seen a chemist being dispensed," he complained.

It was Cass who found the pymbles.

It was just on dusk as they swung through the streets towards home.

"Look," she said, "there's a place for pymbles to park."

PYMBLE PARKING read the small sign, and an arrow led up

a narrow one-way street.

"Let's have a look at them," said Grampa. "It's a long time since I've seen a pymble."

Dad gave a wry shrug, and turned into the lane. They drove along slowly, but when they came to the large asphalt parking square it was deserted. Dad drove on, turned right and headed back towards the highway.

"There's one!" shrieked Mum. "Quickly! Stop!"

Mum was pointing excitedly to a large neon sign PYMBLE EATING HOUSE. Behind it, silhouetted against the sky, was the arm and serrated metal jaws of a large mechanical grab. The family gazed at it with vast pride and satisfaction for a few moments. In the dim light the shovel seemed to sway slightly as though it were munching thoughtfully.

"I knew there was something familiar about it," said Grampa as they drove on.

"What?" asked Steve.

"Those pymbles." Grampa paused to tamp down his pipe.

"Not another one of your tall tales," said Dad with mock dismay.

"Tall tales be blowed. This is as true as I'm sitting here," said Grampa.

"What is it? Come on, tell us!" Steve bounded up and down in his seat, and Khan gave a deep woof of encouragement.

"Well——" Grampa said teasingly, "you know the suburb of Pymble? It was named after these pymbles of Cassie's. They go right back to the Dreamtime; but they were horrible monsters then."

"They still are," said Cassie, remembering the dinosaur-like skeleton of the grab.

"Yes. Well they were worse then. Great monsters sixty feet long they were, and just as much feared as the bunyip. In fact they were bunyips, only land ones instead of water ones. The Aborigines called them Bunyip-imbilli. They were even worse than the ordinary old billabong bunyip, for you never knew where they were. They could disguise themselves to look like anything—a gum tree, or a rock—and then *pounce* they had you."

Grampa did some more pipe-tamping.

"Of course, when the white man came here, the natives warned him about the Bunyip-imbilli, but he didn't take any notice. He couldn't speak their language, and he just thought the word must be the name of the place or the tribe or something. So he called it what he thought the Aborigines were saying . . ."

"Pymble!" shouted Steve.

"That's right." Grampa grinned and lit his pipe.

The others laughed. But Cassie, remembering the mouth of the grab seeming to move in the half light, felt suddenly chill.

"What happened to them in the end? The Bunyip-imbillis?"

"Don't know," replied Grampa. "Most of them must have died out or moved away. But some of them are still around, camouflaging themselves as something else—like mechanical grabs, for instance."

"Let's hope we didn't disturb it, then," said Mum with a laugh.

"There's always a danger," Dad said with a straight face. "Perhaps even mentioning their real name is enough."

"You mean Bunyip-imbilli?" said Steve.

"Oh shut up!" said Cassie crossly. She felt tired and cranky, with a nagging unease she couldn't shake off.

That night there was the first sound. Cassie heard it as she lay in bed. She got up and padded to the window. The lawn was in bright moonlight, but tall gums dappled the drive and the garage with shifting shadows. Cassie stared hard, and it seemed that the edge of the garage door eased down and gave a soft thunk. Should she wake Dad? It might be car thieves, or burglars. Cassie stood there undecided and watched. Nothing else happened. No noise, no lights, no voices; only the slight patter of leaves in the breeze. Her feet felt cold and she shuddered, then turned back to bed and huddled under the clothes.

She was crazy, she told herself. It was only one of Grampa's tales. Pymbles! Cassie laughed softly and uncontrollably into her pillow.

Dad wasn't laughing next morning. His roar of rage could be heard three streets away. They hurried outside. Dad had backed the car into the drive and was now gazing at it, stunned and furious.

The metallic purple duco was criss-crossed by streaks a foot wide. Wherever the streaks were there was no duco, no under-coat—only bare metal. It was like an insane road map.

Or, thought Cassie, as though a giant tongue had taken half-a-dozen licks to test the flavour.

Dad ranted and raved. He was sure it must be some sort of

student prank. The police came. They brushed at the metal, and dabbed at it out of jars, and tested for fingerprints. One policeman tapped experimentally where two streaks crossed, and his hand plunged through as the shell of metal gave way in corroded flakes. Finally, with deliberate authority, the police gathered up their gear and departed, saying nothing. Dad stormed inside to ring the car company, and call for a taxi.

Cassie said nothing. There was nothing to say. What was the evidence of shifting shadows and a half-heard thunk late at night by a girl who might have been half-asleep?

That night it came again. Cassie stole to the window. The garage door was wide open, and she could hear a soft, creaky rasp, like someone turning a crank very quietly; or a cat's tongue licking a plate. She crept down the hall and shook Dad awake.

"Dad! The garage door is open. I think there's someone inside."

Mum slept on, but Dad grunted, then sat bolt upright. He grabbed his slippers and a torch, and flung his hairy sports coat over his shoulders.

"You stay here," he whispered. "If there's anyone there I'll yell, and you ring the police." He went downstairs, and Cassie returned to the window to watch.

Dad sneaked across the lawn, keeping to the shadows till he came to the entrance of the garage. Suddenly his torch beam came on and swept across the darkness. There was no yell. Cassie watched for a few minutes longer. Dad had gone inside now and she could see flashes as the torch moved about. Then the garage door came down and the torch went out. Cassie didn't wait for Dad to come out the small side door and back into the house. He'd be cross and sarcastic at being woken up for nothing. Cassie plunged into bed and squeezed her eyes shut, feeling like a five-year-old who has had bad dreams in the night.

It was Mum who woke Cassie in the morning. Woke her before the alarm went off; white-faced and stunned.

"Cassie! Wake up Cassie! It's Dad. He's not here."

"What do you mean, not here?" Cassie tried to function through the fronds of sleep.

"He's gone. And the car—they're both gone."

The police came again, this time smugly. It was obvious,

their faces said. First yesterday and now today. Obviously some sort of elaborate hoax so the bloke could do a flit. Nothing to it. Blokes doing flits all the time. No evidence of foul play. He'd turn up again in another State, under another name. Give them time and they'd track him down. They patted Cassie's mother kindly, and advised cups of tea.

When the police had gone, and the doctor who had given Mum a sedative had gone, and Steve, white and taut-faced, had left for school, Cassie went out to the garage.

There was nothing. No marks of violence, no car, nothing. Every tool and oily rag was in its right place. Cassie gazed at the oil stain on the cement where the car had stood and tried to think. The cement was dry and slightly sandy under her bare feet. She moved back towards the side door and felt something prickly under her sole. She stooped and picked it up. For a moment she thought it was a burr; then she knew what it was. It was a bit of the bindi-eye tweed from Dad's coat. The coat he had worn down here last night.

Clutching it, she turned and walked dazedly inside. Grampa was sitting in the sun room, puffing at his cold pipe. Cassie walked up to him and slowly unclenched her hand. Grampa looked at Cassie, then at the grey bit of burr in her hand.

"Dad went down to the garage last night. I thought I heard a noise and woke him up. He was wearing this coat."

Grampa said nothing for a while. Then he gazed searchingly at Cassie.

"Don't blame yourself, Cass. He must have been worried, or very tired——" Grampa's faced looked very old and bleak. He was Dad's father.

"It's—it's not just that," said Cassie. "It's—are you really sure he's just gone away. Couldn't it be—something else?"

Grampa looked up sharply. "Something else? No. No, he's just gone away for a while. I never thought Donald would. . . ." He paused. "Never mind, Cassie, he'll be back soon." Grampa held Cassie to him, and she felt his bones hard and brittle and unreliable beneath the old, tired skin.

"Grampa," said Cassie, "where did you hear about pymbles?"

"What? Oh those! I don't know; I just made them up."

"They never existed?"

"How do I know? 'There are more things in heaven and

earth. . . .' Perhaps everything has existed somewhere. Or will exist once it's thought of. We can only think up what's possible to our own human minds, not what's impossible. Maybe there *are* things waiting to be thought of, so they can exist."

Cassie said nothing.

"Did they upset you, hey? Come on, sweetheart, you're upset about Dad. Don't let it prey on your mind. It'll turn out all right."

Cassie sighed and turned away. There was nothing to say.

The week dragged on. The garage door stayed closed now, and there were no more noises in the night. Twice more a police officer came round, full of sympathy and stolid good hope; but there was no word of Dad. Mum seemed to shrink away day by day. Cassie kept the tweedy bindi-eye always with her, knotted in the corner of a handkerchief.

At the end of the week Mum took Steve and went to stay with her married sister at Forster. Grampa stayed on in case any word should come, and Cassie asked to stay with him. She couldn't leave. Not now. Not without knowing.

Two days later a demolition team moved onto the site opposite, where a row of old houses were to be pulled down to make way for a block of home units. Soon the site was noisy and crowded with tractors, bulldozers, and pneumatic drills.

One evening, as Cassie walked home from the shops, her heart gave a lurch. There, familiar against the skyline, was the gaping jaw of a huge scoop. She had known it would come. This was what she had been waiting for.

It was a stormy night. Cassie lay in bed and listened to the trees creaking and groaning, their leaves slapping like the applause of bony skeleton hands. The house gave a slight shudder, as of a sudden gust of wind. Then another, as though a huge blind animal was bumping against it.

In the morning Grampa went out to inspect the storm damage. Part of the guttering hung down in strips, and tiles were missing in a strange pattern, as though someone had been nibbling along the edge of the roof. Grampa climbed up and fixed them back on temporarily until they could call in a builder.

"Strange," he said, pointing to a jagged edge of guttering. "There's a whole length missing here, and most of the tiles. Must have been torn off and blown away by the wind." He dragged it up and tied it securely, then scrambled down the ladder.

The last night was calm and moonless. Cassie lay in bed, waiting.

The first slight juddering bump came. Then another. Then a soft grinding whir, like a juice-extractor; and the sound of a brick falling to the ground.

Cassie leapt out of bed and dragged on some clothes; then she ran down to Grampa's room, shouting as she went.

"Get up, Grampa! Get up! We've got to go!"

Khan was whimpering outside Grampa's door, but he slunk away as Cassie came near.

Grampa was still sleeping deeply as Cassie burst into his room.

"Grampa!" she screamed. "They're here!"

Grampa opened his eyes and gazed at her dully.

"You said they were only made up, but they're true."

Grampa tried to speak, and Cassie saw with horror that one side of his face was dead and twisted downwards.

"Grampa! What'll we do?"

He jerked his head slightly, beckoning her to bend down and listen to him. Cassie stooped over.

She could hear his rattling breathing, and his voice was slurred and tired.

"Nothing," he said with an effort.

"But we must. We'll run away. I'll get the doctor. Help me, Grampa."

The tired old voice whispered on again. "Nowhere to run. Can't—escape. They know those—who know them." His eyes closed, and the papery hand which had been clutching her wrist fell to the blanket. Cassie shook him, but he didn't move.

She turned and ran wildly, down the stairs and out the front door, leaving it swinging open behind her. She ran up the dark street and paused at the corner to look back. Faintly, by the street light, she thought she could see grinning, jagged jaws looming above the house.

What was it Grampa had said? They could look like a gum tree, or a rock, or—a mechanical grab? That car? That grocery shop? These telegraph poles?

There was no escape. *They know those that know them*, Grampa had whispered.

Cassie turned and began to run.

J. R. KINGHORN

The Cicada Mystery

CICADAS are not locusts, though they are often called locusts. Cicadas belong to a large group of insects which have a tubular, or sucking, mouth and not the biting jaws of a locust. In fact they are related to shield bugs, and are themselves a kind of tree bug.

They have a very broad, short head, with the eyes placed at the side. In most species there is a small triangular shield, or ocellus—a light-reflector, rather gem-like, and generally called a brooch. Cicadas are heavy-bodied insects with transparent wings like cellophane.

Cicadas belong to a most ancient order of insects, and fossil forms are found in many countries. One genus, *Tettigarcta*, is a very hairy type. One of its species is found in Tasmania and the other, not nearly so hairy, in Gippsland, Victoria—and these two are the sole living representatives of the fossil species *Clatrotitan*, of which specimens came from Brookvale brick pits.

The largest present-day cicadas are not so large as the fossil forms, and specimens between two and three inches may be called large. There are a number of small species, the Tom Thumbs, living mainly in the grass, which measure between one-half and one-third of an inch.

In Australia today we have round about 150 species. All except a few conform to the well known cicada shape. The extreme is the Bladder Cicada, in which the abdomen is swollen to a huge, rather sausage-shaped bladder.

To the naturalist, common names mean very little. Yet to children, especially those who collect cicadas, common names mean a great deal The name that we spell as Yellow Monday is derived from the name of an Aboriginal, Yellowmundee, whom Captain Tench met at Parramatta in 1791. The name Yellowmundee was given to a creek in the Parramatta district. Probably that means that the original yellow or green cicada was collected by, or at, Yellowmundee. So you can now, without fear of correction, spell and pronounce the name Mundy or Mundee.

Our largest cicada is undoubtedly the Double Drummer, a dark brown, almost black, cicada known here and there as Union Jack and Washerwoman. 'Union Jack' comes from the crossed bands of yellow, or near-red; while 'Washerwoman' refers to a rasping voice something like clothes being rubbed on an old-fashioned corrugated washing-board. The Double Drummer is not as common as other species, except perhaps in some inland areas. It is distributed from south-east Queensland to South Australia.

Perhaps the best known of all, and certainly the most widely distributed, is the Green Mundy, known also as the Green-grocer. The Yellow Mundy and the Black Prince are regarded as mere colour varieties of the green one. Yellow is perhaps not the best description, because generally this cicada is a light tan. A more modern name for the Yellow Mundy is Brown Bomber, perpetuating the common name for parking police in New South Wales.

There is a black cicada with a red nose generally called the Cherry Nose (but sometimes the Union Jack, though it is not like that cicada at all); and a very appropriate name, Fiddler, because of its high and penetrating song. It is also known in some localities as the Whisky Drinker, because of its red nose or proboscis.

A half-sized species, black all over except for red eyes, is known by the obvious name Red Eye.

A dark brown, half-sized, species with a very large area of white on each side and rather powdery under the wings is called Floury Miller or Floury Baker. A closely related one restricted to Western Australia, greyish white on sides and back, is called by the uninspiring name Mottled Grey in most areas over in the west; but I have heard it referred to as Flour Bag, which suits it very well. Perhaps the most striking one from Western Australia is blackish in colour, with banded wings and a broad white band across the centre of the back of the abdomen. It has no common name yet recorded, though no doubt children from the west could supply one.

The Silversmith or Razor Grinder is so named because of a silvery patch on each side of the body, while the sound produced by the wings in flight was said by early settlers to

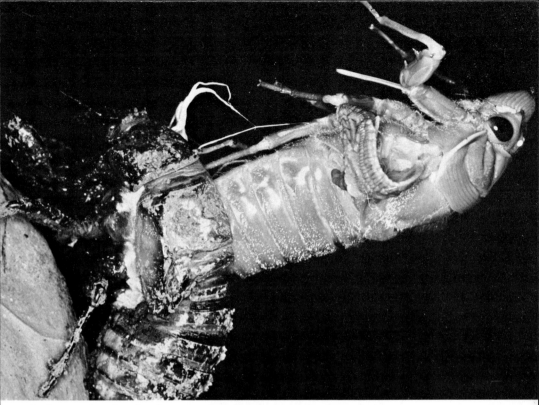

As it emerges the cicada comes out leaning over backwards . . .

THE GREEN MUNDY (*Cyclochila australasiae*)

. . . it then leans forwards grasping the head of the shell to release the lower part of its body.

The wings are then fully opened to dry before the cicada can fly.

The empty shell remains on the branch.

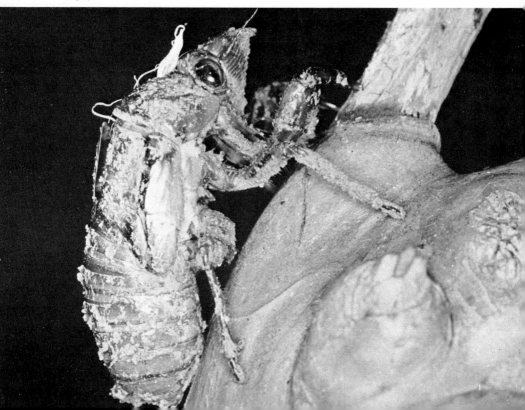

resemble the grinding of a razor. It has been found in several coastal areas north of Sydney, where it used to be much more common than it is today.

Throughout the world there are many other species of cicada that do not come into this story, but no doubt children have given them all interesting names. In England there are some exceedingly small cicadas; some so minute that they need to be examined with a powerful hand-lens.

The colour of cicadas varies from tan to dark brown, and from yellowish green to bright green. There is a rare blue variety of the Green Mundy which is found from time to time. The earliest recorded blue cicada was brought to me by one of my Television Naturalists, Stephen Way, a ten-year-old boy.

Stephen found the blue cicada at Bexley, New South Wales, on 26th November 1957. It was a female, and he was asked to keep a lookout for a male. He found a second one within two days, and it too was a female. In November 1958, a year later almost to the day, a blue male was collected at Bexley.

In nature, blue is a somewhat unstable, changeable colour, associated more with refraction than with pigment, and not so brilliant in a dead specimen as in a living one. Because of this it was decided to keep watch on the blue specimen from day to day. Within three months of being set out in a proper collection box, the original blue was changed to blue-green.

The Mystery

The life history of the cicada remains a mystery. We know only of its life above ground as an adult, and very little at that; there is a lot to be learned in this direction too. We can only guess at the time spent underground; it is all a matter of circumstantial evidence, after noting the years in which cicadas are in great numbers and those in which they are scarce. This has worked out at three years, though some entomologists say it could be four.

In New South Wales there were enormous numbers of cicadas in the coastal belt, central tablelands and some inland areas in 1954, and not again until 1957. In that summer the song of cicadas was deafening in the country between Hartley, Cox River and Jenolan; and at a general estimate the Double Drummers were by far the most numerous. Following that summer, a most devastating bushfire burnt out the country through the entire central Blue Mountains. Many millions of adults, eggs and perhaps young must have been destroyed. Some proof of this was noted in 1960, the end of the normal three-year cycle: there should have been great numbers about again, but cicadas of all kinds were few and far between. The area has been visited for about six years since then, in September, December and April, and the cicada population has never picked up since the disastrous fire. Double Drummers have been decimated beyond belief. Yet careful observation shows that there still appears to be a life cycle of three years.

On the other hand, late snow and frost may play a big part. Mr A. Musgrave, who kept regular and detailed notes, recorded that a temperature of 50-60 degrees is low enough to kill most nymphs, as the young cicadas are called, except the few that happen to emerge just before a sudden rise in temperature. I was with Mr Musgrave one spring when we noted that, while fence-posts and tree-trunks and rock-faces carried thousands of empty pupal shells, the ground below was littered with the bodies of cicadas killed by a sudden cold snap. Many had died before they could dry their wings and fly away.

It is almost impossible to be definite about a three-year life cycle. It is quite probable that some species have a longer or shorter life cycle than others. This uncertainty, this unsolved puzzle, should make the study an interesting one to any young naturalist who has time to follow it up.

As Much As We Know

The female cicada has an egg-placer not visible when at rest, because it is retractile. It is hard, like the shell of a beetle, and perfectly adapted for cutting or jabbing into the soft bark of green branches or twigs. Into these slits, or egg-pockets, she lays one or two eggs, which are long oval, hard or rather tough-shelled, and brownish in colour.

According to several experts on insects, the eggs may take from six days to six weeks to hatch. This variation would call for some definite explanation, and probably depends on the weather, the heat, the dry or humid atmosphere. Most observers say the hatching period is between six and twelve days, and that is more likely to be correct. The tiny cicadas such as Tom Thumbs or Squeakers, which live mainly in the grass, apparently make their egg-slits in some likely shrub or large weed.

The young when hatched are like fleas, and are known as nymphs. It is not long before they find their way to the ground, but whether they jump down or crawl is still unknown. Here once more is guesswork that calls for expert observers. Having reached the ground they begin, almost at once, to burrow down, to get away from their enemies and find succulent roots for food.

It is not known how far a cicada travels underground before it emerges to become an adult. It is generally thought that they go down to a depth of two or three feet, which saves them from being killed in a freeze above ground. One entomologist, who found an escape-tunnel under a house and three feet inside the foundations, suggested that the nymph had tunnelled that distance horizontally. It was then discovered that the house was built only two years earlier, and on a site where a tree had been demolished. So the nymph had tunnelled straight down, as is generally thought. I met with the same problem in the Sydney suburb of Wahroonga in 1959, where quite a number of the holes were under a house and were declared to be those of funnel-web spiders. It was found that the house had been built less than three years, and that two large gum-trees had been removed to make way for it. The owner was very pleased to hear that the holes were made by cicadas, and said he had found the empty shells of nymphs on the outside walls.

It is not known how long the adult lives above ground; some entomologists have suggested a week, others anything up to three months. There should come a time when the marking of newly emerged adult cicadas will be tried by some interested observer. Until then the time above ground will remain another mystery, when it should be so easy to determine.

Cicada Towers

At times, following very wet weather, lumps of hard-set mud or clay appear on lawns and gardens; lumps about two inches high, and two or three inches across. There may be an occasional tube or tower, about four inches high and with a hole at the side near the top; or the top may be turned over like a tiny ship's ventilator. Both the lumps and the towers have been built by cicadas. They were built because the nymph at the bottom of its burrow was being flooded out. The nymph, probably ready to emerge into the world above, digs its way to the surface and finds the weather unsuitable. It begins to build a lump or tower, partly to keep the rain out and partly to get rid of watery mud from the bottom of the burrow.

With its powerful forelimbs it carries the mud to the surface and packs it down hard. The size of the lump or tower depends entirely on the amount of mud to be removed; the nymph does not build to any pattern, like the mud-wasp and other builders. It may be regarded as merely closing the door.

A few years ago a number of towers were found in some of the western and northern suburbs of Sydney. The soil in those areas is mainly red clay and one very wet one showed signs of movement. It was opened to show a muddy nymph at work, building from the inside, and pushing the whole tower up as it added more mud to the base.

Though not yet recorded, it is most probable that the fully grown nymph can delay its change to adult form, or metamorphosis by remaining below in the cold, damp or wet tunnel until a better time presents itself.

The time arrives and the nymph emerges, sometimes very wet and covered in mud. It climbs a nearby trunk, or post, or rock, and clings tightly. After a while the skin splits lengthwise along the back and the head protrudes, followed by the body. But during this process, which may take half an hour or more, the emerging adult turns over backwards in its efforts to free itself; and when the forelegs are free they move about, pushing at this and that, helping the head and body from the pupal case. The legs are pulled out very carefully, or, in their soft condition, they would certainly be torn or broken. The whole process is smooth, apparently effortless, even though there must really be a struggle going on.

Once free, the adult cicada moves a few paces and begins to spread and dry its wings. Eventually it flies to the higher branches of a tree and begins to sing, as a call to the female.

If the newly emerged cicada is a female (who is incapable of making any sound) she awaits the call of some nearby male. Some time later, hours or days, she lays eggs and perhaps dies very soon afterwards. Then the whole process of life begins over again: several years underground, and maybe only a few hours above as an adult. On the other hand, the female may live longer than the male and spend the whole season above ground, laying successive batches of eggs.

The Song And The Singers

The female cicada is voiceless, having no apparatus for producing a song, drumming, or whatever other sound may be made by the male. The sound-producing organ is complicated, and will be described only briefly. It consists of a large air-chamber or bladder, situated under the body. In this is a thin membrane, rather glass-like, with bundles of special muscles attached to two flat knobs, called drums. The muscles push and pull, expanding and contracting the drums, causing them to vibrate rapidly. The vibration makes a crackling sound. Such a sound would not travel far but for the specially constructed sound-box, which greatly magnifies it. The magnification is so great in some species, especially the Double Drummer with the big bass voice, that it can be heard for almost half a mile. This sound is regarded as a mating call, like the calls of many animals and birds.

Dr Segel, a zoologist, says that it is possible to pick out the everyday song, the wooing song, and the challenge to the female; sounds of pairing and rivalry; cries of distress and exhaustion. Apparently all this was found under controlled experiments, though many readers must find it hard to believe. Another experimenter wrote that because the female cicada has no ears she cannot hear the song of the male, but must register sound-waves by some means not yet discovered. After all, registering sound-waves is in fact hearing, though it may not be hearing melody. Perhaps she responds to slow, fast, and intermittent tempo. In whatever way she does interpret sound-waves, she apparently cannot single out a particular male when a whole colony is in full blast.

The chorus of a large number of cicadas is probably controlled by a leader, as with frogs in a swamp. One observer noted that when hands are clapped under a tree the cicadas stop singing, and some will actually land on the hands of the clapper. He did not say whether they were females, but that is probably so.

Another scientist discovered that in tropical rain forests cicadas cheep during storms that make the day seem like night, but stop as soon as the sun comes out again. Normally, cicadas start singing as soon as the morning warms up, and will stop if a cold snap comes along. During a very warm night, and especially if it is moonlight, they are often heard as late as ten o'clock.

Dr George Bennett, a well-known naturalist late last century, tried to put words to the cicada song as is often done with bird-calls. 'The incessant drumming is the *ziz* . . . *ziz* . . . *ziz* . . . *ziz*, interrupted by an extra loud and shrill *ohoi* . . . *ohoi* . . . *ohoi* . . : *ohoi*, or varied to *whocko* . . . *whocko* . . . *whocko* . . . *whocko*.' Probably the modern word would have been *whacko* . . : *whacko*. . . .

The ancient Greeks, and also the Chinese, used to keep cicadas in cages to enjoy their song. Perhaps these ancient people would understand *ohoi* . . . *ohoi* and *whocko* . . . *whocko*.

Work For The Observer

There is a lot to be done before we can unravel the secrets of the life of the cicada; and much of it does not require a degree in science. Today we are ignorant of these simple matters:

Whether the eggs take days or weeks to incubate.

By what manner the young get to the ground.

How fast they burrow down.

How deeply they go into the soil.

How often the nymph moults during its time underground.

How long it remains underground.

How long the adult lives above ground.

A special area of ground could be prepared and marked off, and a branch containing eggs could be arranged so that the young would fall on the marked area. Nymphs could be dug up every six months to follow growth. Adults, above ground, could easily be marked, and observed to see how long they lived. And so on, and so on.

There is much to be learned, and it could all be done within the space of three or four years.

N. L. RAY

Gumboil and the Golden Belt

Illustrations by Noela Young

MR WEBSTER had lumbago. It was such an undignified indisposition, and so very painful, that the whole family winced in sympathy with every groan. Mrs Webster did her best with hot flannel and tempting dishes, but Mr Webster only groaned louder.

Sarah-Louise could bear it no longer. She slipped out through her father's store into the street. As she breathed deeply to get the clean air into her lungs, she saw a solitary horseman coming slowly down the street. Sarah-Louise turned away, then turned back to look again.

"Gumboil!"

The apparition on the horse raised its battered hat. "Sarlouie! Where are you bound?"

"Father has lumbago."

"Poor man!"

"And I'm to go to school. Tomorrow. Alone in the coach."

"Goodness to gracious."

The two looked at each other. Sarah-Louise, with her clean print frock and her shiny ringleted hair, seemed an odd acquaintance for Gumboil.

He was a skinny boy in clothes too large for him, his neck and the lower part of his face swathed in a long, brown, knitted comforter. The mare he rode was not exactly roan and not exactly fleabitten grey, but a half-and-half, in-between colour that went with underdone damper, and toothache, and foggy mornings. She had long yellow teeth and hairy heels and the boniest backbone of any horse in the whole of the Turon valley. It didn't matter how fat the rest of her became, her backbone was still bony. She was very clever at standing still and pretending to be somewhere else, a trick she had learned in her youth when she didn't want to be caught. Gumboil (whose real name was Augustus, only everyone called him Gumboil because he usually had one) knew all her tricks. She was called Serenity, and was now a kind of heirloom. Well, she had been handed down from father to son, and that's an heirloom. If there was a hole anywhere she managed to put her foot in it, and that's how she became an heirloom. Gumboil's father had been riding along the river bank when Serenity put her foot in a hole and tossed him into the water. Although Gumboil's mum had all but put her husband through the mangle to squeeze the water out of him, he died a few weeks later. Before he died he gave Serenity to Gumboil and made him promise to keep her as long as she lived. Gumboil promised.

Not long afterwards his mother died too, and Gumboil was left with half a bag of flour, a quantity of tea, sugar and treacle, a long woollen muffler, a saddle-rug knitted from wools of different colours and lined with sugar-bag, and, of course, Serenity.

If Gumboil felt lonely he never told anyone. He kept the bark hut tidy just as his mother had done, and worked when he had to just as his father had done. He didn't want to be a miner, like most of the population, but there was plenty of work for an able-bodied lad and everyone liked Gumboil. He was quiet and never pushed himself forward, was always ready to listen and was never known to break a confidence. He knew all the country between the Macquarie and the Turon: the canvas and humpy towns of the miners, the claims from the valley up to Hawkins Hill, past Hill End to Tambaroora, Dirtholes, the Green Valley and Dun Dun. He could name the reefs from Nuggetty Gully up over the top of Hawkins Hill, and leases he liked the names of he used to recite to himself as he went along—the Never Despair, Gigantic Struggle, the Sons of Freedom, the Bang Bang, the Jolly Sailor, Hit or Miss, Pat the Rambler.

Gold! It was on the tip of every man's pick, in the glitter of every man's eye, on the end of every man's tongue. Some found it in such quantities, they declared the metal was rolled off the reef like a carpet; some found it in small nuggets; some worked till they dropped and found nothing; some gave up and went away, still carrying their swags but not their fine illusions; some stayed on, hoping that the next bucket of stone would show the golden seed of fortune.

Gumboil watched and listened and, as little as possible, worked. Serenity worked for him. Sometimes she worked as a whim horse, walking round and round, winding up the buckets of ore from the shaft far below; sometimes as a packhorse, carrying the ore up the steep side of Hawkins Hill to the Ore Paddock on the crest. Each load was two hundredweight, and Gumboil was paid at the rate of seven-and-six a ton. When Serenity turned stubborn about working, Gumboil took her back to the valley to rest, and while she grew fat on good grass and no work, he lived on wallaby, pumpkin and damper.

Mrs Webster was fond of Gumboil and liked to cook things for him because she was sure he didn't have enough to eat. One of Gumboil's favourites was Spotted Dog, a pudding boiled in a cloth, the plums poking through its white skin making it look like a dog with spots. "Sticks to yer ribs, Mrs Webster," he always said.

So now Sarah-Louise stroked Serenity's neck. "Are you coming in, Gumboil? Mother would be glad, though Father's too ill to care."

"Thank you, yes." Gumboil slid off Serenity's back, dropped the reins over her head and followed Sarah-Louise into the store. You could buy everything you needed in that store— picks, shovels, clothes, flour, horse-shoes, nails, wheelbarrows, buckets, billies, fryingpans, rope, pins and needles, cloth, tea and sugar, treacle, boot blacking; and if you wanted something that was not in stock you could order it, and it would come out on the coach from Bathurst or far-away Sydney Town.

Gumboil squatted down on the floor, his back against the counter, while Sarah-Louise went to tell her mother he was there. The assistant was at the back of the store, talking to a customer. Bits of their conversation drifted to Gumboil.

". . . daughter . . . going to school . . . morning coach . . . stands to reason he can't go . . . worth a try . . ." and then, in a louder voice, "Absolutely first quality, sir. You won't get better, not in Sydney Town itself."

Sarah-Louise came back, beckoned to Gumboil and led him through to the living quarters. Gumboil's eyes missed no detail of the gentleman who was interested in first quality. He knew the face, but where had he seen it before?

In the kitchen he forgot about it. Mrs Webster's cooking seemed to improve every time he tasted it, and he told her so rather shyly. Mrs Webster was pleased. As Mr Webster was indisposed, it was arranged that Gumboil should stable Serenity there

for the night and see Sarah-Louise on to the coach in the morning.

As they stabled Serenity and rubbed her down, Sarah-Louise said, "I wish you could come with me, Gumboil."

"You'll be all right, Sarlouie."

"Oh, I know Mr Maloney is a good whip; but it isn't much fun being rattled round in the coach like a nugget in a cocoa-tin for twelve hours. Why can't females sit outside, like the gentlemen? The only good thing is the Club House Hotel and its feather beds. You'd never believe it, Gumboil, you have to climb into your bed on steps, it's so high; and when you get into it you sink fathoms deep in feathers."

Gumboil grunted. He slept on corn-sacks slung between saplings, supported on Y-forked branches driven into the ground; or on the ground itself, or in hollow trees. Feather beds were beyond his imagination. The bark hut had a floor of beaten earth that could be scrubbed, it was so hard; a split log for a table, stumps to sit on. A blackened kettle hung from a wire S-hook over the open fireplace. Gumboil thought the furnishings quite adequate.

Next morning, long before daylight, Sarah-Louise was wakened and given her breakfast. Her mother helped her dress, and buckled round her waist, under her petticoats, a heavy belt. Sarah-Louise squirmed.

"What's that for, Mother? It's very heavy."

"Your father will tell you, my dear. Run along and say goodbye to him."

Sarah-Louise rustled her petticoats, trying to be comfortable. Then she entered her father's room.

"How are you today, Father?"

"Ah—ouch—dying, my dear. Did your mother dress you?"

"Yes, Father." She wriggled a bit. "It's so heavy. Do I *have* to wear it?"

"Yes, my girl, you must. When you reach Bathurst you will be met by Mr and Mrs Custiddy from the Bank. In the belt is the gold from the store's takings. You will give Mr Custiddy this note and the belt. You understand?"

"Yes, Father."

"I would go myself but for this affliction. Goodbye, Sarah-Louise. Be a good girl. Your poor parent is—ouch!"

Gumboil was waiting, and Mrs Webster kissed Sarah-Louise tenderly before leaving her in his care.

"Cold," said Gumboil, settling his muffler more closely round his face.

"And dark . . . I don't want to go, Gumboil."

"Never mind. School's over soon enough. You have to be learnt if you're to be a lady."

"I'm a lady now."

"Well mind the mud-hole, then. What are you jiggling round for?"

"I have to wear this heavy belt under my clothes, and it's so uncomfortable. Father says I mustn't take it off until I reach Bathurst. I've a letter, too, for Mr Custiddy at the Bank."

Gumboil hissed through his teeth and shifted Sarah-Louise's travelling box to the other shoulder. He began to put together in his head some of the puzzling conversations he had overheard.

The coach was waiting outside the Company's depot, the breath of the four horses steaming in the cold air. People, waiting, stamped their feet to keep the circulation going. Gumboil saw his charge into the company of a lady with two children, who was also travelling, and went to dispose of the box. Then he leaned against a verandah post and watched the people. Presently he saw a face he knew, and slipped away.

Sarah-Louise was mortified that Gumboil had not waited to see her off properly. The lady was voluble, the children were inclined to tears. There were fifty-three jolting, bumpy miles to come, with a chance to stretch her legs only when they changed horses at Monkey Hill, Sofala and Black Flat. She sat quite still, remembering she was a lady. The belt dragged at her waist, and once she put her hands to her waist to ease it. As she did, she saw a man looking in at the window. He withdrew his head quickly. The rest of the passengers climbed aboard, the lads let go the horses' heads, and Cobb & Co.'s coach was on the way again.

Not far out of the town they ran into a thick fog. The jolting and swaying grew worse, for the road was scarcely visible. The voluble lady broke off a tedious recital of her children's ailments.

"Why are we stopping?" she asked.

"We are going up a hill, ma'am. The poor horses can't be expected to gallop and pull this load."

"Oh yes, the gentlemen are walking. It must be . . ."

Sarah-Louise never heard what it must be. There was a confusion of horses' hoofs, exclamations of alarm or distress from the gentlemen, and a shout coming out of the fog: "Bail up! Bail up!"

"Bushrangers!" cried the voluble lady, going off in a dead faint. Her children set up a loud wailing.

"And what have we here?"

Sarah-Louise stared. Only the eyes of the man were showing. His hat was pulled low on his forehead, and a spotted handkerchief was tied over his nose and chin.

"Go away!" shouted Sarah-Louise above the din.

"So I will, miss, if you'll spare me a few favours. Your locket, please. And the rings from the fainted lady. And you're wearing a belt, miss. I'll shut my eyes while you take it off."

"How did you——? I will *not!*"

The man raised his hand. It held a pistol. "I think you will, miss."

Sarah-Louise hesitated. The man pointed the pistol. "Shut your eyes, then," said the girl; and then, "Here. Take it. And take yourself off."

The man took the belt and passed it back into the fog, to someone standing behind him. "Here, Toddie, take this and guard it well." To Sarah-Louise he said, "I like your pluck, miss. You can have your locket back—here." He passed the locket to the white-faced Sarah-Louise, and stepped back into the concealing fog.

For a short time the sound of hoofbeats could be heard, then nothing but the passengers bewailing their losses. Sarah-Louise sat in dumb misery, wondering what her father would say, and how she could explain to Mr Custiddy. The children went on screaming.

Back on the hill, Gumboil crept out of a hollow tree, shook himself and whistled softly. Serenity came out of the fog. Gumboil took off the saddle, turned his bright saddlecloth the other way up so that the sugarbag showed, and resaddled her. He slung the belt he was carrying over his shoulder and strapped it under one arm, then put on his coat and wound the muffler round his face. He seemed very pleased, almost laughing.

"Git!" Serenity jumped as Gumboil kicked her flanks with his heels. She decided to take no further notice. Gumboil kicked her again, so she knew he meant it and broke into a loping run, looking rather like a sore-footed spider. She could run like that for hours, and it was comfortable if you were used to it.

They went through Hill End as they always did, minding their own business, Gumboil lifting a hand in greeting if greetings were given. Then he headed Serenity down over Split Rock, over Fingerpost, and down to the Macquarie Valley, following a track along the river. The hills went up and down like a bird flying, and as steeply. The sheoaks in the river were green and friendly. The water rushed over rapids, down along reaches where wild ducks rose, past great cliffs of rock thrusting up from the soil, and round islands of flood debris. This was the Bridle Track, a shorter way to Bathurst than the coach route. Sarah-Louise had once asked Gumboil what the country was like. "Lumpy," Gumboil had said tersely. Lumpy it certainly was.

The fog lifted, the sun shone through, and the crisp winter day was suddenly glad. Gumboil gave Serenity a short spell and ate some of Mrs Webster's provisions. Quartz glittered in the sun, mushrooming up out of the grass. Parrots flashed screeching into the trees and whip-birds rounded up invisible flocks.

Soon they were off again. Hour after hour they travelled, and Serenity's coat grew rough with sweat. Gumboil encouraged her when she stumbled, and they were both glad to see the town coming into view.

In front of the Club House Hotel, Gumboil slid off Serenity's back. The mare stood with drooping head and heaving sides, and only her ears flicked as the rumble of coach wheels came down the street. People came out to see the Cobb & Co. coach from Hill End draw up. Gumboil wondered which could be Mr and Mrs Custiddy. He unbuckled the belt and pulled it off, easing his shoulder. A heavy thing. Too heavy for a girl.

Sarah-Louise was as white as a sheet as she stepped down from the coach. The time had come to break the news that the precious belt was lost. Her anxious eyes searched the crowd, and widened as they fell on an old friend—Serenity, head lowered, sides heaving. She had no time to look further before a couple stepped out of the crowd.

"Miss Webster? Your father asked that we meet you."

"Mr Custiddy! Mrs Custiddy. Yes . . . yes."

"Poor child, come along inside, you must be worn out."

"But th—eer—message your father gave you for me. Is it safe?"

"I have the letter," Sarah-Louise produced it from her bag. Mr Custiddy scanned the note, and his eyes bulged as he read.

"The belt, Miss Webster, with the—er—deposit in it. Did you . . .' Was it . . . ? Have you . . .?"

"Yes," said Sarah-Louise, holding out her hand behind her. Gumboil and Serenity! She felt something thrust into her hand from behind. "I did. It was. I have. Will you take it now?" Mr Custiddy seized the belt with relief, and she added, "Will you excuse me a moment? This friend from Hill End will take a message to my parents."

The Custiddys waited politely as Sarah-Louise and Gumboil stepped aside.

"Gumboil! Where did you get it? How did you know? Oh, I'm so thankful I could kiss you."

"Unnecessary," said Gumboil hurriedly. "Heard someone in the store tipping off someone else about you going in the coach. Knew the feller. Seen him before—in bad company. Saw him again at the coach, and he tipped off his mates. I followed—in the fog." He chuckled at the memory. "Feller passed the belt behind him without looking. His mates were busy with the other passengers. I took it. Hid in a holler tree till they went, then came by the Bridle Track. Your family's been good to me, Sarlouie. Least I could do."

Author's Note: *Details of reefs and claims at Hill End are taken from* The Hill End Story, *by Harry Hodge,* Hillendiana, *by Donald Friend, and* Ghosts of the Gold-fields, *by H. H. Neary. The country along the Bridle Track is to this day lumpy and wild and beautiful. You can go all the way by car if the river crossing is low enough and you are brave enough. The fogs are just as thick these winters as they were then.*

My own grandmother, as a girl, wore a belt of gold dust (miners paid in gold dust then) to Sydney and was taken to the vaults of the Bank of New South Wales, where she undressed and handed over her precious cargo. She went to school at Bathurst, and told us about the feather beds at the hotel.

The Bunyip

The water down the rocky wall
Lets fall its shining stair;
The bunyip in the deep green pool
Looks up it to the air.

The Kookaburra drank, he says, then shrieked at me with laughter,
I dragged him down in a hairy hand and ate his thighbones after;
My head is bruised with the falling foam, the water blinds my eye,
Yet I will climb that waterfall and walk upon the sky.

The turpentine and stringybark,
The dark red bloodwoods lean
And drop their shadows in the pool
With blue sky in between.

A beast am I, the bunyip says, my voice a drowning cow's,
Yet am I not a singing bird among those waving boughs?
I raise my black and dripping head, I cry a bubbling cry,
For I shall climb the trunks of trees to walk upon the sky.

The little frogs they call like bells,
The bunyip swims alone;
Across the pool the stars are laid
Like stone by silver stone.

What did I do before I was born, the bunyip asks the night;
I looked at myself in the water's glass and I nearly died of fright;
Condemned to haunt a pool in the bush while a thousand years go by——
Yet I walk on the stars like stepping-stones and I'll climb them into the sky.

DOUGLAS STEWART

The Snow Gum

It is the snow gum silently,
In noon's blue and the silvery
Flowering of light on snow,
Where upon drift and icicle
Perfect lies its shadow.
Leaf upon leaf's fidelity,
The creamy trunk's solidity,
The full-grown curve of the crown,

It is the tree's perfection
Now shown in clear reflection
Like flakes of soft grey stone.
Out of the granite's eternity,
Out of the winter's long enmity,
Something is done on the snow;
And the silver light like ecstasy
Flows where the green tree perfectly
Curves to its perfect shadow.

DOUGLAS STEWART

Flight to Fiji

MAN has always travelled. Before what we call history, all men and tribes wandered the countryside along with the other animals searching for food and water and shelter. As man became a little more organised in his patterns of life, he took to the seas and tried to fly. He became aware that part of the reason for travel was a restlessness of the spirit and a wish to see what else the world had to offer.

Nowadays we travel for business—which boils down to getting food and shelter. And we travel to better ourselves and find a new place with more opportunity. The Children of Israel did it when they walked to the Promised Land. Migrants today do it, wanting a new home and hoping it will be a hospitable one.

Of course we also travel for fun. We take holidays at the seashore or in the mountains or overseas. But this isn't new, either. Basically our holiday is the old urge to change, to explore, to make our lives more interesting, to help us understand what the world is all about. The desire to travel and to accomplish something in that travel may seem modern, but it probably is very like the urges that pushed our ancestors across the plains and seas and over the mountains.

One thing is certain. It's easier and quicker to travel today than it ever was before—whether we're going across town to visit our grandparents or flying around the world.

Some people say that the adventure is gone from travel. They claim that if travel is too easy, we don't have the same feeling of having done something important. If many people go to a particular place, then that place loses its magic, they say.

I disagree. And the reason I disagree is part of another argument about travelling. It involves the old saying that 'travel broadens the mind'. Recently some less generous people have suggested that travel nowadays is more likely to broaden the backside and narrow the mind.

I believe that both ideas can be right. Whether travel makes us better people or more narrow-minded people depends on us, not on the places we visit. Travel doesn't always broaden the mind, but it should. The key is the attitude we carry as part of our baggage when we travel. The best attitude to carry when we go travelling is a hunger, with our minds rumbling almost like our stomachs rumble when they are empty. When we are hungry food smells better and tastes better. And when we are hungry for new experiences, a different place has brighter colours and prettier shapes and more interesting people.

We need a kind of innocence—not the kind that means we don't know anything, but the kind that makes it possible for us to feel a sense of adventure and excitement. We need to get really involved.

There are three or four parts in any trip. One is planning and getting ready. Another—sometimes a very brief one these days—is actually getting there and back. The third is being in a new or different place. And, finally, there are the memories and new ideas we carry back home with us.

Not so very long ago I made my first real visit to Fiji. I knew for several months that we were going on a trip in November, but didn't decide for a while where we would go. It was to be mostly a holiday, but I would also plan to write some stories about the trip. I thought about many places in Australia and overseas. And of course I thought about money. After much talk, my wife and I decided that at that particular time, for a particular amount of money and for the particular things we wanted to do, Fiji was the right place.

This thinking and deciding was really part of the trip. If we look forward to it and are excited by it, getting ready is great fun.

Once we decided where to go, the journey became real. At this stage there is much to do. If the trip is overseas, as Fiji is, then the traveller must have a passport. In Sydney this means going down to the Commonwealth Centre, having pictures taken, telling the government some things about yourself. Sometimes a whole family can travel on one passport—but everybody has to have his own inoculations. That means another trip to the Commonwealth Centre, or to your family doctor, to have a shot or two as protection against disease.

Even this can be interesting, if you watch the huge number of people in the waiting room and think that all of them are travelling somewhere out of Australia. Some of the people are excited, some are curious, some wear the look of regular travellers to whom this has become an ordinary part of their lives.

Wherever one goes, the trip has to be planned. How will we travel? How long will we stay? What will we do there? What should we buy? What shall we take?

Part of planning the trip is a happy and hungry kind of study. You're not going into an examination, you're going on a trip, so this study is fun in two ways: first, learning about anything that interests you is fun. And second, what you learn beforehand will make the trip itself more fun—and more memorable.

The more you know about the place you're going to, the better. Knowing doesn't spoil the kind of innocence that allows excitement. Understanding a bit about the mystery of how Fijian men can walk on red-hot stones makes seeing it all the more fascinating.

When you take an interest in a place, information about it often seems to pop up everywhere. Suddenly we noticed newspaper articles about Fiji, and advertisements. We found books and pictures, heard music and watched television on Fiji. We got information from travel agents and airlines and the Fiji government in Sydney. And we studied it, finding more and more things to do and to look for.

All this information helped build our excitement: Half the population of Fiji is Indian. The time of independence was near. New hotels were being built. Cruises visit small Fijian islands where village life is almost the same as it was before the Europeans came to the area.

There is much sugar cane grown in Fiji, and the company which manufactures the sugar runs a free railroad for passengers. Gold is mined there. Shopping is 'duty free'. Fijians make a kind of bark cloth called 'tapa'. In Fijian villages there is little private property; everywhere belongs equally to the villagers.

Facts, hundreds of facts, helped make the place seem real before we even left. And we found out what the climate would be, and how casual or formal the place was, so we'd know what clothes to take. We learned that the Fijians, so friendly and easygoing in person, were fierce warriors and cannibals only three generations ago, and that they fought with great distinction in World War II.

It all helped. It gave us a kind of pleasant tension, so that in a way we were straining to see what we had read about, to check our impressions against the real thing.

As the day approached, we got ready. We made lists—"don't forget the tickets, the reservations, the passport and health card with its inked stamps. Check the cameras and remember the film, carry a book for the airplane, and to read while lying under a tall palm tree."

Then we packed—"bring the beach towel and an extra swimming costume. Never mind that shirt, I'll buy one in Fiji. Is the case too full? Try sitting on it."

Off to the airport. Here it really begins. Whether you arrive in an airline coach or a taxi or your own car, suddenly you are away from the place where everybody goes about their daily business. You're in a place that exists for only one reason—to move travellers from one place to another. The airport is, if you want it to be, another world. There is a babble of various languages, the constant call of aircraft coming in from foreign places and going out again to different countries. It is a place for parting and reunion, of laughing and crying.

At the airport it's business first. Find your airline counter and give them your bags. It goes quickly, a sheet torn out of your long airline ticket, a cardboard label stapled in to identify your luggage. "Gate six at 12.30," you are told.

Waiting—for you must be at the airport an hour before an international flight begins—usually includes a stroll out on the observation platform. Which plane is ours? Perhaps that one with the fuel tanker at one end and a food truck at the other.

On the huge runways, giant jets take off and land, adding one more row of black rubber marks with their tyres to the hundreds along the grey tarmac. Sometimes a big jet roars impatiently while a tiny private plane uses the runway to taxi in under the jet's nose.

Then your plane is called. "Now boarding from gate six . . ." the voice over the loudspeaker says. Another queue, another person in uniform, another mark on your ticket that says what seat you will have—and you're aboard.

Seat belt fastened. Watch the men outside finishing their work, hear the whine as pilots start up their engines and check hundreds of instruments. You're moving; the engines get louder and the ground hurries by. You don't feel the exact moment when the airplane is free of the ground, but it looks as though the airport and the city are falling as the aircraft climbs and turns toward the ocean. You're really on the way.

Going toward Fiji there isn't much to see out the window except the great blue expanse of the Pacific Ocean, and perhaps some cottonwool clouds. The trip itself is about four hours long—or four hours short, depending on your attitude toward it. You'll get a meal on the plane, read something, talk to the hostess, have a drink, look out the window. And soon there it is.

Spread out below the wing is a green curve of land. From one side of the plane you can see the dark mountains rising in back of the airport town of Nadi. From the other side you see the town and the black airstrip, the ocean and beach. As the aircraft noses down, trees and houses take shape, ribbons become roads, dots become people and cars. You touch down, the engines howl then soften, and the plane heads for the terminal.

The famous writer Robert Louis Stevenson, who spent much of his life travelling and writing about it, once said, 'To travel hopefully is a better thing than to arrive. . . .' Mr Stevenson was making another point not necessarily connected with travelling —that work is more rewarding than winning. Still, there are many people who feel that anticipation—the looking forward part of a trip—is better than actually being in a new place.

Many people are disappointed in the places they go. They are not excited, they feel cheated, they take away few new ideas. Their dream was better than their trip. On the other hand, there are travellers for whom the thrill of experiencing a new place is like an electrical shock. Most of their store of emotion is saved for the real thing, for living new sights and sounds and smells. If anticipation is good, experience can be better.

Our plane rolls up to the terminal. And the first Fijian we see is a government man who paces along the plane spraying insecticide from a pressure can. We've arrived, and for that moment, he *is* Fiji.

Most likely he will be a tall man, nearly black, wearing sandals and a white skirt called a sulu. Fijians tend to be tall, strong and cheerful. The chances of getting a smile and a wink are pretty good.

In the terminal, as in any foreign country, you must go through some formalities. One is a look at your yellow health card, to make sure you are protected against certain diseases. Another is a check of your passport. And finally there is a customs check, to see that you bring into the country only what you are supposed to.

Just walking from the airplane to the terminal building, and from there to a taxi or bus, is enough to make your heart pound and take away your breath—if you let it—with the sheer, total foreignness of the place. Fijians are striding strongly along; Indians glide more smoothly on their way. The warm air is sweet with the scents of frangipani and oil and the ocean and dust.

Almost any new place can give you the same feeling. It is like the top of another mountain, climbed because it is there. When you do get there, another new view greets you.

Only some of the particular things really change. For example, some of the flowers in Fiji also grow in Australia. Many of the beaches and boats and hotels and crops and cars and buses and shops are similar to some of those in Australia. Some of the food is the same.

But the world, to a traveller, is something like a set of building blocks. With the same blocks you can create entirely different things, just by arranging them differently. So nature and people, using largely the same raw materials and ideas, create different places and different cultures.

So it is in Fiji. Only a few things exist that we never saw before: the way Fijians fish with spears and nets—sometimes an entire village fishes with a single long net. The way they can walk on the hot rocks, and the way the women of one island can call giant sea turtles by singing to them.

Until we came to Fiji we hadn't seen sugar cane burning at dusk, with orange flame and black swirls of smoke against the green hills. We had never eaten raw fish soaked for a day in fresh lime juice and coconut milk. For that matter, we never had eaten fresh coconut meat after the husk has been slashed open by a man whose big knife just misses his toes every time he swings it.

There is a balance in travelling. Travellers usually want to do as many different things as they can. But they must be careful not to spend so little time at a place that they can feel none of its reality. A colour slide of a palm tree is not enough. The tree is more real to those who sat under its shade or climbed in its branches or ate some of its fruit.

We had decided to drive in a circle around the big island, called Viti Levu, and to take a cruise around some of the smaller islands of Fiji.

We began with the cruise. About 20 of us went on board a boat roughly twice as long as a big house. The captain was a New Zealander. His wife and the rest of the crew were Fijians, except for the cook, a young Indian boy who had never seen Western-style food when he left his village just a year before. We steamed north from the port of Lautoka, a sugar town near the airport at Nadi. The Pacific Ocean here is deep blue, and little islands, the tops of ancient mountains, pop their green and brown heads out of the water everywhere.

Travelling isn't meant to be all excitement. Much of the cruise, for example, was pure relaxation. But this is part of what Fiji is all about—accepting the sea, the sun, the islands. We learned from the crew members, who sat in the stern of the boat singing softly to themselves, and strumming guitars whenever they were off duty.

Occasionally there would be a moment of excitement when one of the fishing lines hanging from the back of the boat would snap taut like a clothes line. Amid great shouting and pulling, the boat's engines would stop and we'd try to land the fish. Everybody cheered when we pulled in the first tuna, which the cook baked for dinner that night.

There is great beauty in Fiji. We anchored for the night in a calm lagoon. As we ate our fish the orange sunset cast long shadows from the trees and Fijian canoes along the shore. We had to look hard to pick the thatched houses out from the groves of coconut palms that grew down to the edge of the hard sandy beach. In bright sunlight, everything seems to be shades of dazzling green and gold and brown. In the evening, dark shapes form against the dusk and jump in the light of the Fijians' cooking fires.

Another kind of beauty came to us the next day, when our boat edged close to a different kind of island, where a cave opened from a rocky cliff. We had to climb up the side of the cliff a little way, and then down inside the cave's slippery walls. When our eyes adjusted to the light, we could see a deep pool stretching into the darkness. At first we all hesitated, but when a Fijian jumped into the pool with a yell and a great splash, we all followed. In the cave our voices echoed everywhere, and

While driving around the north of the Island on the King's Road you can stop to watch the raft from the local village.

The colourful wharf at Suva.

little shafts of sunlight made silver mirrors in the still, cool water.

In Fiji there is bright colour everywhere—the greens spiked with red and yellow flowers, greenish bananas, turquoise water, and the cities of pink and white and blue coral around the islands with their own populations of tiny, brightly coloured fish.

But for us, most beautiful of all were the people. Very probably people everywhere are beautiful in this way, but most of us notice new people more than those we are used to.

The Fijians, first of all, seem to the visitor to be the happiest people he has ever seen. I'm sure they have troubles and problems like everybody else, but we kept meeting sunny, cheerful people who liked what they were doing.

Fijians also have great dignity. On the cruise we went ashore one evening to be greeted with the traditional Yaqona ceremony. In past days, the ritual was to greet visiting chiefs; today tourists are the honoured guests. The ceremony lasted for at least a half hour. We didn't understand a word, but it's not difficult to figure out that making the drink Yaqona from the roots of a special tree is an old and symbolic ritual.

When the drink is made, the first cup is solemnly handed to the leader of the visitors. He drinks it down in one gulp, to the accompaniment of a loud 'ahhhhhh' and a series of handclaps from the Fijians squatting in two lines. Then it is the turn of other guests. The procedure is the same as everybody takes his turn to taste the slightly bitter, muddy-looking drink. During the ceremony, women and children kept out of the way of the village men, each in his skirt of palm fronds, and with his face and body and hair brightly painted.

Afterward everybody gathered for the singing. The fierce looking warriors became cheerful young men with guitars and drums made from hollow logs and bamboo poles to be thumped rhythmically on the ground. The village group sang of love and of travel, of battles and gods from the sea, of good crops and bad storms.

That was part of the 'meke'. The other part of this miniature festival is dancing. Girls, for the most part, danced gracefully, sometimes kneeling and dancing with their bodies and hands only. The men, bodies painted and shining, dart back and forward in war dances that celebrate great victories of days past. Their excitement is so convincing that we almost believed the straw spears and shields were the real thing.

Sometimes, as on this particular night, the visitors are asked to join in, too. Even on the quiet little islands the guitars can change from the old melodies to the modern, and the young people relax with a strenuous watusi or frug on the dirt floor of their big thatched *bure*.

One of the best parts of a trip for me is to go to bed, tired, with the events of the day wandering through my mind. On this night of the meke the thud of feet and bamboo poles, the strong voices of the singers and the whisper of palm leaves were the sounds we thought of. The happy faces of people doing something which gave them pleasure—and which they knew gave pleasure to us—were our last memories before falling to sleep.

There is much to remember about Fiji. But as with all places I visit, the memories become like photographs. I seem to remember a moment in time, and what we were involved in at that moment. I have a mental picture of an elderly German woman on the cruise with us, whose stiffened legs gave her constant pain. She was a real traveller determined to take part in everything. The picture locked in my mind is of this pale old woman being carried onto an island in the dark arms of a big Fijian man. Both of them were laughing as they splashed ashore.

After the cruise, we took a car and drove down to a resort hotel called The Fijian, on its own little island just off the south coast of Viti Levu. We treasure several mind-pictures from there. One is of thin Indian boys at dawn moving silently through the shallow water with their fishing spears. The older boy was so skilful that he sometimes pulled back two or three little fish on the prongs of his spear.

Another picture: sitting by the beach in the evening as one giant Fijian man beats a great log drum as a call to dinner and another runs around the gardens and lawns with a flaming torch, lighting a series of other torches stuck on poles.

Another picture: we run out of the ocean with our dripping bodies warm and covered with salt and sand that has stuck to our suntan oil. We lie down in the shady grass and watch Fijian girls pick big red hibiscus to tuck behind their ears.

And another: walking a hundred yards or so out to sea at low tide, to the coral reef where the tropical waters have left an assortment of seashells. We were looking for the Golden Cowrie, a famous shell of the area. There was no cowrie, but we remember laughing at one another stumbling along in our canvas shoes (coral cuts your feet), eyes down on the thousands of tiny sea creatures stranded by the tide.

After a quiet week at The Fijian, which included some walking trips to nearby villages to talk with the people and see how they lived, we drove on to Suva. We drove for most of the day, taking it easy, stopping to look at the coast, to take some pictures and visit with the shy children. The road is bumpy and dusty and full of curves, so that there is no choice but to drive slowly. Everybody along the way smiles and waves and shouts the Fijian greeting, "Bula!"

Suva is the capital city, not very big as cities go, but the main centre of the 300 Fiji islands and a substantial trading port. For the visitor, Suva is mainly for shopping. One of our still pictures of memory is a very old Indian man with a beautiful, bearded face. He wandered in the Suva markets, where Fijian and Indian merchants sell everything from souvenir canoes to fresh fish, from seashells to bananas. The old man spotted us before we saw him, and came over. My wife asked if she could take a photograph and he nodded. My picture is the look on her face when he asked for two shillings payment.

Suva has beautiful parks, and a good museum in one of them. Nearby, at Government House, the police guard parades up and down, British in everything except his dress—blue shirt, red sash, white skirt and sandals.

The main streets of Suva are crowded with shops, where many things are less expensive than at home. There are big shops with familiar Australian names, but the real bargaining goes on at smaller stores where Indian merchants put on their best act for the visitor.

A Suva picture: an Indian merchant accuses us of taking the bread from his children's mouths because we said the price of a transistor radio was too high. And yet when I decided to argue no more, he was disappointed. Bargaining is half of doing business for some merchants, and the visitor who pays the first price asked is thought to be foolish.

There are always thousands of tourists in Fiji. They are most noticeable in Suva and in the resorts like The Fijian along the south coast. Very few go around the north side of the big island. In a way, that's a good reason to make the trip, for one of the best ways to see and feel how people really live is to see them when they aren't on their best behaviour for visitors. So early one morning we set out to drive around the north coast.

Our little car jolted along, going uphill for miles, past the airport and some suburbs. And suddenly we were in the highlands. This country is very different from the tropical island atmosphere of the south. There are flat grassy plains where cattle graze, and jagged mountains, some of rock, some wooded. Children played football in school playgrounds surrounded by brilliant flowers.

We have still pictures in our memory of that morning, too. One is stopping to soothe our dry throats with a fresh pineapple bought beside the road and cut open for us by a village woman with one of those big, mean-looking knives. One is stopping to marvel at a crystal waterfall spilling out of a rock and disappearing into a mass of soft reeds and lilies beside the mountain road. And another is looking down a sheer cliff at a broad lazy river where a man poled himself along on a raft. Nearby was a group of village wives doing their laundry in the river while their naked babies splashed happily in the shallow brown water.

The road wound through the highlands and the hills, finally turning down toward the sea. About halfway between Suva and the airport at the other end of the island is a tiny place called Raki Raki, where we stopped for lunch. The day was hot, so we sat outside to have a drink in the garden of the little pub, under some giant vines.

After lunch, for the only time on our trip, we hurried. We had to get back to Nadi, for the holiday was nearly over. We drove past the goldmines of Viti Levu and through a bare, tan-coloured landscape that looked like a series of moon craters. Through the towns of Tavua and Ba with their heavy Indian influence, a quick stop for final shopping at Lautoka, and back to Nadi. After some quick packing and a few hours sleep, we took a taxi to the airport and huddled together with a number of other sleepy people waiting for our jet to arrive.

I think travellers are allowed sadness as their trip ends—not so much because a holiday is over as because it means leaving a place and people that we have come to like and feel close to.

At the Fiji airport the bamboo decorations look less warm in the fluorescent light of the pre-dawn hours. Even the cheerful Fijians are quieter. Only a few soft conversations and the rattle of teacups breaks the melancholy sound of the Fijian song of farewell, 'Isa Lei' which plays over the loudspeaker.

We board the plane, have breakfast, dream of music and warm ocean water and laughter. And soon enough we see Sydney glowing red against the sunrise. We are home.

From there, the trip is in its final part. It becomes memory, and it becomes a part of our lives. If we were open to the beauty of the place and the warmth of the people, we accomplished something. If we let ourselves be taught, we are better people. Broadened, as the old saying has it.

Bushman

F OR THE good bushman, who knows what he is doing, there's fun and interest a-plenty in the Australian bush—and adventure, too. Have you ever been in the bush in the late winter or spring, and seen the wild flowers? At that time of the year, areas of rock and drab shrubs suddenly become gardens, colourful and beautiful.

It is no use trying to see them as you speed past in a car. You must get Dad to stop, and spend an hour or two wandering in the bush. Then you can see the display of boronias, eriostemons, tea tree, banksia, heath and many others. Some of them are not only beautiful but interesting too. The trigger plant, which grows in the bush in most States, has a small sensitive area (the trigger) in the centre of the flower. When this is touched, the pollen-laden stamens come down with a bang on whatever touched the trigger. It is quite spectacular. The idea, of course, is that when a bee (or other insect) visits the flower for nectar the trigger works, and the bee gets bopped on the bottom with a liberal dusting of pollen which it carries to the next flower it visits.

When you see a gum-tree bursting into flower, have a good look at the buds as the flower comes out. You will see a very interesting thing that does not happen to any other plant. Each bud is covered with a little cone-like cap which falls right off as the bud bursts open. This is how the eucalyptus trees get their name. *Eucalyptus* means 'well covered', and refers to this little cap.

In almost any part of Australia you will find Casuarina trees—the she-oak, bull-oak, or belar, with needle-like leaves. It is very easy to distinguish them from pines. A pine needle is all in one piece. A casuarine needle is made up of small segments which separate easily if pulled. If you look carefully at one of these segments you will see that it has a number of points at one end. These are really the leaves, and the rest is the stem. Casuarina flowers are interesting, too. At certain times of the year some she-oaks turn a lovely russet colour instead of the normal olive green. The colour is caused by large numbers of tiny flowers on the ends of the twigs. With the aid of a magnifying glass you will see a beautiful sight: each twig-end looks like a tiny head of gladiolus coming into flower.

Having gone into the bush to look at all these, it is good fun to light a fire, boil the billy, and maybe cook a meal. It is pretty easy to light a fire in the bush. In fact it is often dangerously easy. So if you do light a fire, make quite sure that you do so safely without any risk of causing a bushfire. You must take care at all times, but especially in the warmer months from the beginning of October to the end of March. Each State has its own laws and these must be observed. In general, fires should be lit only in properly prepared fireplaces or on clear ground well away from stumps, logs, and flammable material. A ring of stones or sand around the fireplace will prevent the fire from spreading accidentally. At no time should you leave a fire unattended; and of course, when you are finished with the fire it should be extinguished with water. These are simple, easy, and sensible precautions anyway. They should not hamper your enjoyment of a fire, nor the fun of cooking a meal on it.

As I have said, in dry weather it is very easy to light a fire; but after rain a little care must be taken to get dry wood. It is useless trying to get a fire going with damp fuel. Wood lying in contact with the ground generally stays damp a long time after rain, but dead branches and twigs on standing timber are practically always dry except when it is actually raining. Collect enough wood and some small dry twigs, dry brittle gum-leaves, or bracken, for kindling. Over a small pile of dry kindling build a pyramid of fine twigs and a few light sticks. When this is alight feed the flame carefully, gradually increasing the size of the sticks until you have a substantial fire.

Don't be in too great a hurry to put your billy on, but wait until the fire is established. A billy boils quickest if suspended over the flames. If there are rocks around, a little pile on each side of the fire will enable you to put a stick across them from which to hang the billy. A green stick is generally recommended, but there is no need to destroy living plants to hang the billy. A strong dead stick about an inch in diameter will do just as well; it will not burn unless you have a fire that is needlessly big.

If you want to cook a meal, grilling and frying are very

quick and easy. An efficient cooking fire is one with a good base of hot ashes and a few decent-sized sticks, say two to four inches in diameter, burning steadily. A roaring fire with flames leaping high is not necessary or desirable. A sausage can be cooked in a few minutes if a long, thin, pointed stick (or a bit of stout wire) is pushed into its side, so that you can hold it over the hot ash. If you have a number of sausages or chops, they are best held firmly in a wire griller. You can avoid holding it over the fire if you rig up a support for the griller. Don't be in too great a hurry, or you'll burn the outside and leave the inside raw.

Every good bushman can make a meal from flour. It is good fun to experiment, and not a bit messy if you go the right way about it. Here are a few suggestions.

Damper: A damper is as Australian as kangaroos, and quite easy to make. You are not likely to have a real cast-iron camp-oven, and if you are using a picnic fire you are not likely to accumulate enough hot ashes to bake a damper in, in the real dinky-di way; but you can still bake a golden-brown damper in a camp-oven that you can rig up yourself. All you need is a frying pan and an aluminium plate—or two aluminium sponge-tins will do just as well.

Before you start mixing your damper, get the fire going. Establish a nice hot fire of small sticks and then add a few sticks between one and three inches thick. These will burn merrily while you are mixing, leaving a fire of hot coals when you are ready for it. For your first effort, a good quantity is two or three cups of self-raising flour. Put this into a deep plate, add a little salt, scoop a hole in the centre, and pour water into the hole— say a couple of tablespoonfuls. Mix this around with a fork until you have a ball of dough in the centre of your plate. Then gradually add water and mix it in until you have a cake of dry dough. It is wise to have some flour in reserve in case you accidentally put in too much water. The dough should be quite dry to the touch when ready for cooking. Grease, or lightly flour, the frying pan (or one sponge-tin). Drop in your damper, and cover with a metal plate (or the other sponge-tin). Now scrape away all burning embers from your fire and set your oven in a smooth bed of *hot* ash. Cover the top with a half-inch layer of ash from the fire, and then replace a few burning embers or coals on top of the ash. With an average fire, a damper of this size will take 20 to 30 minutes to cook. Time it

Bushwalking can be enjoyable in all kinds of country.

If lost keep your head; maybe by climbing a hill you will see a river, road, or telephone line which is familiar.

It is fun to try and find fresh water on the beach using the Aborigines' method of digging at the foot of a cliff.

with your watch, and after twenty minutes scrape away the ashes from the top plate. Lift the lid and inspect your damper. If it is a good golden-brown colour you can be sure it is cooked, but if in doubt push a thin stick into the centre. If it comes out clean, the damper is cooked; if it comes out doughy you will need to cook it a few minutes longer. All this may sound long and complicated, but the whole thing is really very simple. Dampers can be improved or varied by adding some powdered milk to the flour, and perhaps dried fruits such as sultanas.

Johnny Cakes: These are really small dampers and are very quickly cooked. Mix the same dry dough as for a damper, and put enough of it into a well-greased frying pan to make a cake a little less than half an inch thick. Cook this over hot coals, and keep moving the cake to make sure it doesn't stick. When brown on one side, turn over and cook the other side. One cake should take less than ten minutes to cook.

Flapjacks are made from the same mixture but with more water added, so that you have a creamy mixture which will only just flow. Put fat into a frying pan, heat it until it smokes, and then pour in enough mixture to cover the pan. When brown on one side, turn and cook the other. They take about five minutes. The addition of powdered milk to the flour will improve the taste of all these items.

In mountain country, far from towns, water may be safe to drink straight from the creek or river; but with the growth of population more and more streams are polluted. If the water is muddy, green or discoloured, it is wise not to drink it at all. If the water is clear, it may be made safe by boiling it for ten minutes, or by using water purifying tablets. Of course, in many parks and reserves there is piped water and water in tanks which is quite safe to drink.

There is nothing better than a swim in a waterhole or river. A few simple precautions will guard against accidents. Don't dive into water before you have tested it for depth or hidden snags. Never dive into or swim in muddy water. If some of the party cannot swim, a special watch must be kept to see that they don't get into trouble. Beware of swift-flowing water. In short, use common sense and enjoy a swim without risking a tragedy.

In the sandstone country around Sydney there are Aboriginal rock carvings. They are all in the form of grooves in the rock in the outline of some animal or object, most of them easily identified. There are figures of men with spears and shields, figures of women, whales, sharks, fish, jellyfish, emus, kangaroos, and so on. Boomerangs, footprints and many other objects are clearly shown. Scientists do not fully understand the meaning of all these carvings, but the purpose of many is clear. Some are apparently just fish stories. A whale may have been washed ashore, and the local artist would record this rare happening on his only canvas—the rock. Other carvings are connected with *increase ceremonies*: rites meant to ensure the increase of animals needed for food supplies.

On the rocky banks of many streams you can find canoe-shaped grooves, about 9 to 12 inches long and 2 or 3 inches wide. These are the grooves cut in the rock in the process of grinding a hard river stone to make an axe-head.

Rock carvings are nearly always found on the top of ridges, particularly in saddles. More rare are hand caves. These are cave-like overhangs in which the roof and walls have been marked with human hands by a form of stencilling. There are red-hand caves and black-hand caves in many areas as well as around Sydney. In a park, the park authorities will direct you to them, but there are many carvings outside parks which you may discover for yourself. Your local museum will also give you information about Aboriginal relics in your area.

These relics of the original inhabitants of this country must never be interfered with or damaged in any way. Don't scratch them with sticks or stones. Don't walk on them.

All along the coast there are Aboriginal shell middens. They often look like sandhills, but where the wind has blown the surface the sand will be dark from the ashes of ancient fires. A little digging will disclose masses of shells that have been calcined or burnt. These middens are the result of thousands of years of shellfish-eating. The men who gathered the shellfish baked them in the shell, and left the burnt shells in great heaps, some over fifty feet high.

There are places on the coast too where you can find old spear-head factories, where the skilled stone-workers made sharp points for spears and cutting tools. Mostly, the tools and spear-points have long been collected, but there are interesting flakes and 'core' stones still to be found. If you ever find a good stone axe or spear-point, you should show it to your local museum.

By the way, water is often scarce on these beaches. It is

interesting to try to find fresh water as the Aborigines would have done. Fresh water is lighter than salt water, and when percolating through sand will actually float on top of the salt water. Try digging at the foot of cliffs where water would tend to run, or among dunes where reeds grow, and not very high above high water mark. When you find fresh water, dig with care lest you dig through to the salt water on which the fresh is floating.

There are lots of active things to do in the bush—exploring, scrambling up rocky ridges, and so on—but there are quiet things, too. Get up before dawn one morning, and go to some quiet place. As the first daylight comes, the birds come to life and greet the dawn. You will hear more bird calls in a few minutes than in the rest of the day. If there are lyre birds, they put on a tremendous performance, especially in winter, going through all their repertoire of mimicry. The magpies' flute-like notes, the kookaburras' raucous jollity, the resounding call of the whipbird, all make a mighty chorus with the background filled in by the screeching of parrots.

All these things can be enjoyed by intelligent and observant young people, but there are a few precautions to be observed. You don't want your enjoyment to be marred by accidents, or to cause anxiety by not getting home when you are expected. Most accidents need never happen.

If you go into the bush, go with a grown-up who knows the area. Even if you are capable of finding your way around and back again, never go in a party of less than three. Always let someone know where you are going and when you will be back. When planning a trip, make plenty of allowances in time. It is simply amazing how many people think they can walk twenty miles in a day. Maybe they can, along a road or a clear track— but in the bush, half that distance is often too far. In the thick scrub of south-west Tasmania, I and three others walked from 8 a.m. to 2 p.m. and covered a forward distance of two miles.

If you are in strange country, keep checking your direction by landmarks or compass. Keep a written or mental note of ridges crossed, of streams and their direction of flow, and so build up a picture in your mind of the country you have travelled. Check with your map and see if it confirms your mental picture. Keep turning round and looking back, so that if you have to retrace your route you will recognize what you see.

When you reach high points, note the ridges and valleys and check them with your map. You will not only know about a thin ribbon of country that you can see on each side as you travel, but what lies on the other side of the ranges that you may never see. Travelling in this fashion you can never truly be lost.

But if you are 'lost', keep your head. Sit down, have something to eat, and then work things out. Maybe by climbing a hill you will see a river, road, or telephone line—and become 'unlost' in the twinkling of an eye. Mostly a little discussion, tracing your route since leaving home, will show a certain direction, or a feature such as ridge or river, that you can follow to safety. If you are completely bewildered, don't rush round aimlessly but sit tight and await rescue. If possible, go to water and light a fire; smoke can be seen from a great distance from a height. Put green fuel on the fire from time to time to make smoke.

There are pests in the bush that you must learn to live with. The chance of snakebite is very remote; but if one of the party is bitten by a venomous snake, act as follows.

1. Keep the patient at rest without panic.
2. Immediately apply a lightly constricting bandage, towards the heart from the bite. This must be released for one minute every 30 minutes. Do not cut.
3. Send a written note to the nearest doctor or police station, naming the type of snake if possible.
4. Make sure your messenger can lead helpers back to where you are.

Ticks are easily dealt with: pull them out with tweezers, or shave them off with a sharp blade. If part of the head is left in, it will do no harm. Leeches are unpleasant, but comparatively harmless; a pinch of salt or a burning ember will make them let go. If there is much bleeding, put a pad of cottonwool on and bandage firmly.

Wherever you go, prepare for possible changes of weather.

Always carry matches.

Take a little emergency food, and carry water unless you are sure of your water supply.

Always carry a compass and the best map of the area you can get.

The bush is beautiful. Leave it that way. Don't destroy living plants. Don't spoil it for others by leaving litter anywhere.

E. BELL

To Make Life Richer

Illustrations by Astra Lacis

Boys of Rosehill Primary School, near Sydney, tell how they make the most of the time that is just their own.

MODEL PLANES

RAYMOND JEFFERS, who is eleven, writes: I was fascinated by planes that were so small but could fly. There were some on wire or some that were radio-controlled. At the end of the field were even smaller planes that couldn't fly but were exact in every detail from the rudder to the cockpit. There were Spitfires, Stukas, Hurricanes, Zeros, and many more.

That was one year ago. Now I go to a club called Air League. We learn about the great pioneers of flight, from the Wright brothers who first flew powered flights to today's modern jets. Man has always envied the birds, and many men have died trying to fly.

My own collection is only small but I have a wide variety, mostly representing the period of the two wars. My favourite is the famous Spitfire, which performed well in the Second World War. I found out that the models were hard to build at first but got easier after practice. I can't paint them very well but I try to make them as exact as I can. I am trying to buy a control-line aircraft but they cost quite a lot with the motor. I like seeing the radio-control planes and one day I hope to have one. I like flying model gliders although I can't fly them very well at all, but it's fun. After Air League we have contests for the best model. I haven't won anything as yet.

SOCCER

MALCOLM TASKER plays for the Granville Waratahs Under 12: I played in England for my school as fullback. I have been playing for two years and have been awarded three pennants. This year we tried for fourth in the Division, winning the Round Robin 2-nil.

My position is centre-half or No. 5. This is a very hard positon to play in because if a man gets past you, then gets past the goalie, he has scored. When you play centre-half you mark the centre forward.

Every Tuesday and Thursday from 4.30 p.m. to 6 p.m. are our training lessons. We usually start by running around the field four times which is over a mile. After that we do exercise like heading the ball, trapping it, racing each other, etc. Then we pick sides and have a game.

A soccer field is 130 yards in length and 100 yards in breadth.

FOSSIL COLLECTING

CHRISTOPHER DICKSON finds this a fascinating hobby for young and old: You need to have sharp eyes because you need to be able to see the bones and fossils which are often hidden under rocks and piles of rubble.

It's very inexpensive to start. All you need are: pick, shovel, glue, knives of various sizes, paper, and last of all a bag.

You never know what you are going to strike when you go digging for fossils, and that's why you need a great deal of patience. You must be careful because some collectors go past places which should certainly contain fossils.

Fossils when unearthed have to be cleaned with vinegar to remove all dirt. The fossil than has to be washed with soap and water, dried, and put into your collection. Unburying the bones takes about ten minutes depending on the depth they are buried. When you are digging them up you must be careful because you might smash the fossil.

After this stage you must apply glue to the fossil and wrap

paper around it. This prevents the fossil from breaking when it is handled.

Petrified wood, which is wood turned into stone, is one of the most colourful of all rocks. Bluish green is the most beautiful but the rarest.

The best place to look for fossils is near the beach. Millions of years ago fish died and were buried with sand and mud which has dried hard. The flesh of the fish must have perished by now, leaving the bones. Now that the sea has gone down the fossil would remain in its original place where it died.

HORSES

MICHAEL IBBETT has been riding for about six months: I started when it was my sister's birthday. She had asked if we could go to a horse-riding club for one of the sessions. The head lady and man chose a horse named 'Saint' for me on that session. The next time I went I had 'Star'.

I had learnt to ride by watching other people. I couldn't ride well then but I can now. I read all kinds of books about horses: working horses, racing horses, all kinds.

Equipment for horses: Egg butt snaffle, short cheek double bridle, plain snaffle, long cheek bridle, a half-moon Pelham. Parts of saddle: Pommel, tree, stirrup leather, stirrup iron, girth, seat, skirt, flat, cantle. Tools in a stable: Hoof pick, dandy brush, body brush, scraper for removing water or rain, curry comb used to clean the body, water brush for cleaning hoofs and soaking coats, hay wisp for polishing the horse's coat, tooth rasp for filing teeth that have become as sharp as the blade of a knife, hand clippers for hogging manes, stable rubber for the finishing touches. There are two switches, and one is against the law to use.

STEPHEN HOOD's father is a trainer, 'the best in Rosehill': I have a horse, which I look after now, called 'All Cab'. He has won six races. I get up at 7.30 a.m. on school days and clean out his stable. In the afternoon I walk him for forty-five minutes around my dad's exercise ring.

I have won a ribbon in show riding. We call our pony 'Rubber Duckie'. He can jump 3′ 6″ high with me on him. In the Parramatta River he swims, and is an excellent show pony.

The main thing about looking after a show pony is to keep his coat nice and glossy. I use a soft brush, then a hard dandy to brush his mane and tail. I have his feet done by the blacksmith at least every two months, and also keep his teeth checked. I keep his feet clean at all times. If I do these things and am kind to him he will be an excellent pony.

JONATHAN VIDLER also rides at a riding school, and hopes to have a horse when he is older. He gives a colourful account of his first ride: The horse looked so big and muscular, I could have fallen over backwards. With slow movements I urged myself towards the horse. Its side was white with foam. I slowly but surely mounted myself on the horse. This was it. Then with a bit of courage I kicked the horse's flanks, and a slow, easy trot was developed. Soon this was fun.

TRAINING GREYHOUNDS

GEORGE CHRARA writes: The responsibility of training a greyhound is a great experience. This aggressive, unique dog has the qualities of a long neck, a lean figure, and of course its fabulous thighs packed with muscles.

These dogs must be walked long distances so they are fit before racing. The food is Weetbix for breakfast and mince-meat for tea. A dog must go through breaking-in before going in any races. The person who is doing this must teach the dog to have a killer instinct on the track. He shows the greyhound a couple of live rabbits so when the electrical bunny comes it will chase it with great enthusiasm. One of the main things in racing is making them jump fast out of the box.

A stayer goes to the distance of 880 or 760 yards. Sprinters' distance is 440, 580, and 330 yards. Bitches are smaller than the dogs, so they work out that the bitches like a tight track and the dogs a loose track. The greyhound must qualify before running in a race, but you get no money for a qualifying run. Races are the only occasions when you get paid for wins and places.

During the week you must take your dog to a track to give it its practice.

GARDENING

JEFFREY GALLAGHER has taken up gardening as a hobby that is interesting and useful too: Now if you have a garden, or if you wish to start a garden of your own, if you want to add new plants to it, to start with you dig a hole big enough for the plant. Then you put some water in the hole, so the plant has enough water to last him to the next day. If you see a weed pull it out, or it will take the water that the plant needs.

You will find vegetables you grow in your garden will taste a lot better than the vegetables you buy in the corner shop which have been sitting there for days. You can use the flowers to decorate the home, and the fragrance is beautiful and refreshing. When they are in full bloom they are so beautiful and colourful. Let's face it, flowers and vegetables cost a fair bit of money these days, so look at all the money you will be saving.

So the water won't run away from the plant you dig a rim round the plant, then you won't waste any water when you are watering. Make sure you give the plant enough water, or it will die under the extreme heat of summer.

Each week you will have to air the garden. You do this by getting a fork and turning the top part of the soil up. This stops the soil from going sour.

SURFING

MARK FAULDER says: In the summer when all of my family and I go on holidays, I find that surfing takes up most of my time, but I always enjoy it.

Before I go in the water I wax my board. This wax is put on the board to stop you from falling off and hurting yourself. After that you are ready to go in.

You paddle out about 100 yards, out to where all the big waves are, and you wait until a good wave comes, and then you paddle as hard as you can with your hands and feet. As soon as you are sure that you are on the wave, stand up and stay up.

If the nose of the board starts to go under, you move to the back of the board to keep the board on the waves. It takes a great deal of skill. Sometimes you have a wipe-out. This happens when a wave is too big and you can't handle it and your board goes flying up in the air and you have to be careful that the fin doesn't hit you.

I have a twin-finner board, and with this kind of board I can spin around once when on a wave.

CHESS

GLEN COLLINS: I became interested in chess at the age of about eight. Dad had tried to teach me previously but I had not been interested. Now I began to wonder just what it was like, and what all those funny pieces did.

I finally persuaded Dad to teach me, and after that, by playing Dad and the occasional challengers at school, I became better at the game. My great moment came when I was ten. I received a chess set for Christmas, and in the first game with this set I was for the first time victorious.

Next year I met Mark Sheen over a chess board, and suffered the defeat of my life. We played two more games that year, in both of which Mark was victorious.

However, the next year, while repeating sixth grade, Mark and I had more chances to play. After a good equal game I finally won the first game of the year. In two more games I was successful, equalling the score and, I'm sure, giving Mark something to think about. My glory didn't last very long, for Mark soon made a comeback and was successful again. I caught up again, though, finally, and ever since Mark and I have been equal and determined to beat each other. We both promise each other that next time we're going to win.

This game has a mathematical precision about it, and one cannot lose concentration for long without suffering the consequences. The cry of "checkmate" brings the game to a glorious or an inglorious end.

ATHLETICS

MARK XENITA chooses a hobby to keep fit: I train every Tuesday and Thursday. When I first arrive I do four warm-up laps and then I do exercises. Then I do ten sprints and another two laps. When I finish, I go over to the long-jump pit till the trainer comes.

He makes us do two laps. When I finish the two laps I do a hundred 10-metre sprints. After them I do shot-put training till my mother picks me up. I train at Merrylands Oval. I run for Merrylands Youth Club under 12.

On Saturday I run at Makepeace Oval in Fairfield. The meeting starts at twelve o'clock and finishes about five o'clock.

Every Saturday you would have shot-put, the baton relay and the circular relay, but other events are held on different Saturdays. One Saturday you might have the 100 metres and high jump. Next Saturday you would have 200 metres and long jump.

At the end of the year you have the State Competition and an Inter-club Competition. In the State Competition you run against competitors from all clubs in New South Wales. If you come first you receive a silver medal, second a bronze medal, and third a certificate. In the Inter-club Competition if you come first, second or third you receive a certificate.

It is better to run in spikes than bare feet or sandshoes, because it gives you more drive, and gives you an advantage over the competitors that don't wear them. It is better to use starting blocks than a standing start. It takes a while to get used to them.

The season starts in October and finishes in March.

STAMP COLLECTING

MARK SHEEN: Many times I have sat on a chair fixing or preparing, adding or even sometimes subtracting, stamps from my stamp album. Sometimes I look through the album and find some stamps that are valuable. Some, of course, are more valuable than others; but it's a great feeling if I do find one that worth something, and it's a very enjoyable way to spend any leisure time you might have on your hands.

It was my third birthday, or maybe my fourth, that I received this present. The older I grew, the more interested I became in stamps, and by the time I was seven or eight I was looking for price, age and watermarks. At that age I had about 500 stamps and about 50 countries.

Now I have not many more countries, but I have accumulated about double the amount of stamps. I have become really interested, and have found out many other stamps that are valuable. I have accumulated a few with watermarks from Italy, Rhodesia and Germany. If I can afford it, I will buy one or two stamp catalogues, so I can look up approximate prices.

My oldest stamp is from Eire, which I found to be approximately ninety years old. I don't know its price, but I saw in a stamp book that it was pretty rare.

I have quite a varied range of stamps, and I think they are one of the most enjoyable hobbies anyone could possibly have. Most of the pupils in 6A have stamp collections. One of my friends has a good one.

But it's amazing what they can make out of a simple piece of paper, isn't it?

Outback Tales

READERS' STORIES FROM *The Bulletin* NEWSPAPER

Illustrations by Will Mahoney

No rain had fallen for three years, and all the stock were watered at bores on various parts of the run. One evening a terrific thunderstorm broke, followed by steady rain.

Just at daybreak, one of the boys came stamping along the homestead verandah and woke me. "Come out and look in the creek, Boss. Cattle coming down."

I jumped out of bed and ran to the front of the house. The creek was running a banker, and amongst rubbish of all descriptions floated a long iron cattle-trough. Swimming along beside it were about fifty yearlings and two-year-olds, trying to drink from the trough.

'Tamornie'
8 January 1930

When I was a youngster, the vineyard country around Rutherglen (Victoria) provided scenes of flagrant drunkery amongst cattle, pigs and fowls. It would have broken the heart of any temperance lecturer. The degraded creatures would eat the fermented must when it was cleared out of the presses, and the results were shocking.

Cows would be seen sitting in the road, waggling drunken horns at passing vehicles and mooing defiantly. Roosters would stagger at each other, too tight to lift a spur; while processions of glassy-eyed hens meandered in zig-zags like ladies leaving a gin-parlour at closing-time. Pigs were the most shocking. They hiccupped continuously, and kept on falling down and staggering up. Even the bush birds got full.

Some of us kids tried it once on the way to school—but the teacher's reaction kept us teetotal after that.

'Notaden'
9 January 1935

Charlie was a hard-working Swede who seldom had time to look up. He was felling timber in Western Australia, and one day he got to work on a trunk three feet thick. Charlie was feeling even fitter than usual: chips the size of a portable gramophone littered the surrounding country to a depth of three feet.

At last it came down—the top two-foot-six of a stump five feet high. Charlie knew two languages, and strained both of them.

'Dan Bay'
8 January 1930

At Swan Creek (New South Wales) a party was building a bridge. Close to the line of the bridge was a sturdy English oak growing in midstream. It reached up about ten feet or so above the water hyacinth which blocked the creek. As some of the toilers were admiring it, the tree suddenly sank from sight like the *Fata Morgana*.

The dumbfounded men learnt later that it was not unusual for acorns from the trees bordering the stream to take root in the dense mass of hyacinth. These developed into trees which sometimes grew for years, until their weight was too much for their floating support and they sank through it.

'Seeing Em'
23 January 1935

Where's Charlie?

Illustrations by Joyce Abbott

"WHERE'S CHARLIE?"

At the teacher's question, every head in the classroom turned, and every pair of eyes looked at the desk where Charlie always sat. The eyes registered astonishment as they turned back to the teacher. Charlie wasn't there!

"He came to breakfast," volunteered one, his dark face very serious.

"Yes, yes," agreed all the others. "He came to breakfast."

"Did anybody see him *after* breakfast?" the teacher asked.

The class thought deeply about this. Nobody could be sure. There were some whispers, but no, no one really remembered seeing Charlie after breakfast.

"Tommie Wulpa, please go and find Charlie and bring him to the class."

"Yes, Miss." Tommie leaped up, pleased with his assignment.

"Don't dawdle on the way," the teacher reminded him, but Tommie had already slid out the door, across the verandah and down the steps into the yard. The sun was warm and the red sand between his toes was warm, too. Tommie slowed down. Now where should he look for Charlie first? Perhaps he had better look in the dining room and see if he was still there. He had been there at breakfast. But when Tommie reached the long building which housed the kitchen and dining room for the Settlement, there was no sign of Charlie. Only the rows of tables and benches, set ready for lunch, and the cooks, laughing and chattering and producing the most delicious odours of meat pie and custard.

"Go 'way," they shouted at Tommie.

"Have you seen Charlie? I'm looking for Charlie. Teacher wants Charlie. He was here at breakfast time."

"He's not here now. Go on, it isn't lunch time yet."

Tommie turned away. Perhaps Charlie had not been feeling

well and had gone across to the hospital. He would go and look there.

The hospital was set apart in the shade of trees, with green lawns of kikuyu grass growing round it. Tommie felt the difference through the soles of his feet when he stepped from the hot sand on to the cool grass. He peered through the fly-screening of the hospital verandah. He could hear voices: Sister's voice, her lecturing voice, and the softer hesitant voices of Aboriginal women. It must be the Mothercraft Lectures. Tommie stood on tiptoe and, sure enough, there were eight or nine mothers sitting very still on hospital chairs which were drilled in straight lines in front of a blackboard. Just like school! They had their babies on their laps, and were looking at Sister with dark, earnest eyes. Some of them were wearing bright scarves on their heads. One of the mothers saw Tommie, and Sister saw her smile. Quick as a flash she turned round and caught Tommie peering through the screen, and quicker still she was out the door and had grabbed his arm before he could run off.

"What do you want?"

Tommie looked up into the blue eyes, and wriggled his toes. Sister's veil was snowy white, and her uniform was starched stiff. Tommie had never been so close to her before and quite lost his voice.

"Ch-Charlie . . . looking for Char-lie," he stuttered at last.

"Charlie's not here. Go and look somewhere else and don't interrupt my class. Go on. Run off."

Tommie did.

Perhaps Charlie had gone into the workshop and had forgotten all about school. Tommie went to look, stopping to play with one of the dogs on the way. Looking for Charlie was fun. But when he looked round the door of the workshop there was no sign of Charlie. Big Harry was there, covered with grease, doing mysterious things to the inside of the utility's engine. Tommie went to look and Big Harry let him hold a greasy spanner while he wangled a difficult bolt into place.

"Why aren't you in school?" Big Harry asked at last.

"I'm looking for Charlie. Have you seen Charlie? Teacher sent me," Tommie said.

"No, Charlie hasn't been here. You'd better go and look somewhere else."

"Perhaps he's gone to the woodwork class," Tommie suggested.

"It wouldn't hurt to look," Big Harry grinned at him. Tommie grinned back. Big Harry was a qualified engineer, but he was always friendly.

In the woodwork room, the white teacher was showing a class of senior boys how to use a plane, and the floor was covered with lovely curly shavings. Tommie sniffed the clean smell of freshly cut wood and picked up a big shaving between his toes. The big boys pointed towards the door, but Tommie took no notice. Then the teacher saw him.

"What do you want, Tommie Wulpa? Why aren't you in school?"

"Please Mr Clarke, teacher sent me. I'm looking for Charlie."

The teacher looked carefully round the room. "Charlie isn't here, and you'd better not be here either. O.K.?"

"O.K. Mr Clarke," Tommie replied cheerfully, and left the room.

He wandered towards the vegetable gardens behind the administrative buildings. How was he to know where he might find Charlie unless he looked everywhere? He could see Mr Ballantyne busy in his office, and heard the Galah Session coming from the Flying Doctor wireless. No, it wasn't likely that Charlie would be there.

On the way to the gardens he had to pass the brick-yard. Two or three men were mixing the red sand with cement and water, then putting the wet mass into wooden forms to dry and set. A heap of dried bricks was stacked up waiting to be used for building.

"School out?" asked one of the men at last, looking at Tommie leaning against the fence.

Tommie shook his head. "Looking for Charlie," he said. "Teacher sent me," he added virtuously, to show that he was on a real errand.

When he came to the vegetable gardens, he stopped to admire the rows of green in the bright red soil, the onions, spinach, lettuce, beetroot, cabbages. Behind the meandering rows were orange trees laden with fruit, and the hen-house where fowls were busy laying eggs. Tommie felt sorry for the fowls. They were not free to scratch about in the dust, to roll

over in the sand cleaning their feathers, and to lay eggs where they had a mind to. They were secured in wire cages with food and water in front of them, and all they could do was eat and lay.

Beyond the hen-house was the fence and then outside the fence was Australia.

Tommie stood on one leg, remembering the time before he and his family had come to the Settlement to live. He remembered the wonderful taste of wild potatoes, the days of feasting when the game was plentiful, the horrible days when there was nothing much to eat. He thought of the fascinating tracks on the sandhills, the learning to know what each track meant. He remembered the shivering nights when the cold got through right into his bones, and the long sleepy days when a patch of shade was reason enough to lie down and have a nap. The white people always expected you to be busy, busy, busy, and only to sleep at night. It was warm sleeping in a house on cold nights. There was never any worry about whether they would eat or starve. Tommie looked at the garden, then at the unwatered desert outside the fence, and couldn't make up his mind. He knew he would have to go to school to learn how to earn his living in the white man's world. His father and mother knew that by coming into the Settlement they were giving their children a chance to learn about these things. There was no rule to keep them in the Settlement and they could go walkabout at any time and still come back. But they did not go very often, because they wanted the children to go to school.

"Hi, Tommie!"

Tommie started. "Hi! Have you seen Charlie?"

Rosie leant on her hoe and considered the question. "Not since breakfast. Why aren't you at school?"

"Teacher sent me to find Charlie, he's not at school."

"No, he's not here. You'd better be off and look somewhere else."

"O.K., Rosie." Tommie grinned at her. "Vegetables looking good-oh."

Rosie beamed. "Yes. But not for you. Go on."

Tommie laughed and went. He looked under the big water tanks and along the dusty roads where the cottages faced each other across hedges of oleander. But no one had seen Charlie. He helped Old John take cuttings from the trees and stack them in drums of water in the shade. When the cuttings grew roots they would be handed out to anyone who wanted a tree or shrub to plant in his yard. Old John worked slowly and silently, and Tommie didn't like to break in on his silence. At last Old John stopped and looked at Tommie, holding a great bundle of cuttings in his arms.

"Why aren't you at school?"

"Looking for Charlie," he said. "Teacher sent me."

"Charlie was in the craft shop. You better go."

"In the craft shop? I haven't been there. Thank you, Old John."

Tommie dropped his load of cuttings and trotted across the road towards the entrance to the Settlement. Old John shook his head and stooped down to pick up the scattered sticks.

In the craft shop half a dozen men were busy, sitting on the floor and making weapons, music sticks and seed necklaces. Tommie squatted down to watch them. There was a small fire in the middle of the floor, where pieces of wire were heating. Ernie was burning holes through the hard beans with a piece of red hot wire. He had a heap of the orange-brown beans beside him, a patch of colour that pleased Tommie. He would have liked to pick them up and dribble them through his fingers. Bobo had smoothed a piece of mulga wood into the shape of a snake, and was busy burning circles on it with hot wire. It would take a long time to burn enough circles to cover the snake. It had red seeds stuck in its head for eyes. Tommie loved that snake with his eyes. Tib was making boomerangs, and Oscar was making tapping sticks. The finished articles would be sold to tourists. There were coolamons, too, the curved baskets the women used for carrying babies or possessions, and there were spears and digging sticks and waddies. Tommie wanted to handle them, but he knew better than to touch them. The men were all looking at him now.

"Have you seen Charlie?" He asked his question again. "Teacher sent me. Charlie's not at school."

"He was here after breakfast. Gone now. You'd better go and tell Miss you can't find him."

Tommie got to his feet. "Yes. Perhaps I'd better." He turned away, frowning. Where could that Charlie have got to?

There was a sudden silence as he entered the classroom, where before there had been a buzz of voices reciting a lesson. Teacher raised her eyebrows at him.

"Well, Tommie Wulpa? What have you to say for yourself?"

"Please, Miss, I looked just *everywhere* for Charlie. I looked in the kitchen and in the workshops and in the garden and round the houses and under the tanks, and behind the trees, and near the brick-yard and in the craft shop and Miss, he's just *not there!*"

The class giggled. Tommie looked at them, frowning. He looked towards the empty desk where Charlie should have been, and his eyes widened in disbelief.

"Why, Miss, THERE's Charlie!"

Everyone laughed, Charlie most of all, doubling over with merriment at the astonished look on Tommie's face.

"Yes," said the teacher. "Sit down, Tommie. Charlie arrived just after you went to look for him."

Spike

Told in Town

FROM *The Bulletin* NEWSPAPER

Illustrations by Will Mahoney

Years ago there was a Willoughby (North Sydney) blacksmith who was rather sensitive about his very large and shiny bald pate. A customer one day left his horse to be shod while he went for a drink. During the shoeing the nag turned its head three or four times and idly licked the smith's glistening cranium.

When the owner came back the angry smith snorted: "You ought t' muzzle that blasted horse of yours. What does it take my head for, anyway?"

The owner turned in the saddle. "Rock salt," he said, truthfully and sweetly.

The blacksmith's hammer just missed him.

'Darker'
20 November 1929

I wanted to ignore the unsavoury type who was trying to put the bite on us, but my friend was unable to free himself from the grip on his sleeve. He was forced to halt and listen to a tale of woe. In vain he tried to escape by declaring, "I haven't got any change just now." The firm hold on his arm was not released, so he added: "But I'm going to a shop just along there, and when I get change I'll give you something; that is, if you'll be here when we come back."

The cadger considered for a moment. Then he announced, "Well, I reckon I'll just walk along with yer. Yer see, mister," he confided to me, "I've fell in before through givin' credit."

'Mr Cats'
13 November 1929

Jones was a keen angler; but when he extended his arms to illustrate the size of his catch, his friends scoffed. So Jones bought a pair of scales. When he returned from a fishing expedition, he weighed his fish in the presence of his next-door neighbours. Since *they* were pillars of truth, their word was accepted throughout the town. Jones soon won a fame that he would not have bartered for the honour and dignity of mayor.

One day Mr Stork paid a visit to a neighbour's house, and the doctor borrowed Jone's scales to weigh the new baby. Baby went forty-seven pounds.

'Spica'
26 June 1935

I remember an exhibition at Geelong wheat-sheds when the lads of one of the public schools were given a half holiday. On one stall was a pile of literature on agricultural and pastoral notes issued by the Immigration Department, bearing a neat card with the invitation 'Please take one'.

Close at hand was an exhibit of the goods we export to England, its chief feature a tall pyramid of luscious Jonathon apples. With unusual thoughtfulness for others, two of the schoolboys removed the card from the literature to the apples and passed on.

Delighted visitors, including the respectable citizens of Geelong, accepted the invitation and disposed of the pyramid.

'D.D.'
19 June 1935

Shane Gould, Swimmer Extraordinary

Forbes Carlile, former Dutch and Australian Olympic Swimming coach, writes about his star pupil.

IN DAYS to come better swimmers than Shane Gould may emerge, but in mid-1972 the fifteen-year-old girl from the Sydney suburb of Pymble must be reckoned the greatest female swimmer the world has seen—some say the greatest swimmer. This is saying a lot when you consider that the great Dawn Fraser won the 100 metres freestyle in three Olympic Games, and held the world record for sixteen years until Shane broke it in 58.5 seconds in 1972. With this history-making swim Shane became the second woman ever to hold *every* available world freestyle record.

The other woman who accomplished this feat (no man has ever done it) was the American Helene Madison, far back in 1932. But her records were set over a period of several years. Shane's records were set in less than a year. Helene Madison' time for the 100 m was 66.6 seconds—which would have put Shane some *12 metres* in front of her at the finish. In the 1500 m Shane would have been approximately *5 laps* of the 50 m pool in front! Shane is a very much faster swimmer than Helene Madison forty years ago. Why? Even the fact that Shane is outstanding human material could not account for the huge margin between the champions of different eras.

I think there are two main reasons why Shane Gould, 5′7½″ and 9 stone 3, is so much the better. The reasons may be summed up in two words: *training* and *technique*.

Swimmers are very much fitter today because they start younger and because they train much harder for practically every month of the year. In the 1930's the champions were swimming at the most two or three miles in a day's training, and this for three or four months of the year. They would be lucky to cover more than 300 or 400 miles in the year. Compare this with the 1500 or even 2000 miles today's champions would cover.

Nowadays an average of thirty miles in the week is reckoned only moderately hard training. Many cover forty and even fifty miles, especially in their hardest weeks of preparation. Some swimmers take one complete day off every week. Shane does not.

Training is seldom at an easy pace. Boys and girls do not always swim 'flat out', of course, but most swimming would be quite fast 'interval' training. The interval is the short rest taken between each effort, at distances of 50, 100, 200, 400, or 800 metres. Distance swimmers often swim straight 3000 metres, which is 60 laps of the Olympic pool.

At each of the styles—butterfly, backstroke and breaststroke —Shane with her squad does some kicking-board practice to strengthen her leg actions. Some swimmers do a lot of 'pulling' with the legs tied, but we don't seem to find enough time in training for much of this. The theory is that it strengthens the arms. Instead of 'pulling', Shane and our other pupils do a lot of special exercises with a resistance machine they can carry around with them. This is called the Dynastic. We coaches ask for 15–20 minutes a day. *Some* days they do find time for this much. We reckon even five minutes a day is worth while.

In her hardest training (in November, December and part of January, when preparing for the championships in Australia) Shane covers about nine miles a day, split into two sessions, each of two hours: from about 5 a.m. and from 4 p.m. This is fairly standard around the world these days. Each day Shane writes up her training log book and makes notes and remarks about her swimming. We coaches collect the books at the end of the week and check them. In our swimming organization I am chief coach at Pymble and Ryde, but we have a number of other coaches who often take our senior squad including Shane.

So much for training. To appreciate Shane's technique at the crawl we must look back into the past. Man has swum long into antiquity, and techniques have evolved through the years. The first racing stroke appears to have been the breaststroke, then the sidestroke with *single* arm over, and later with both arms over. In those days ladies did not swim with the men but had segregated sessions. There was not much chance of developing a Shane Gould. Girls did not race.

The sidestroke was the popular racing style when 12-year-old Alick Wickham introduced the *crawl* to Australia and the world. It was in 1896, in the Bronte rock pool near Sydney. The dark-skinned boy surprised swimmers and coaches when he brought *both* arms over the water (though there were other swimmers who could do this in what they called the double overarm) and, more important, *kicked his legs vigorously up and down* in the vertical plane. The knees were not drawn up to make the trudgen-like rounded kick which nearly everybody did in those days. The Wickham stroke was much faster than anything his rivals could do, and soon the new 'crawl' became the sprint stroke everybody aimed to copy.

Dick Cavill soon took up the crawl technique that Wickham demonstrated so well, and became the fastest swimmer in the world. He proved it in England in 1902, when he broke the world record. There they called him Splash Cavill—he swam with head down, legs thrashing, and a big splash.

About this time, in Sydney, Cecil Healey developed a style of crawl which became famous as the Australian Crawl. Cecil Healey was not only a teacher and writer of note, but fast enough in the water to set a world record of 65 seconds for the 100 metres. This was in 1905. The stroke he used was a very definitely defined *two-beat* crawl: there were two beats to each revolution of the arms. As the left arm entered the water the right leg, bent at the knee, would lift up high and thrash down. With the entry of the right arm the left leg would kick down— with such a thud that it was said you could hear a good Australian Crawler a hundred yards away from the pool.

From 1905 to 1912 is called the Golden Age of Australian swimming. Australia led the way, as it was to do again for a short time after the 1956 Olympic Games in Melbourne. The majority of Australia's great swimmers of that period swam the Australian Crawl. In 1912 Fanny Durack of Sydney was an easy winner in world record time of the first Olympic swimming race for women. She used the Australian Crawl with the heavily accented two beats of the legs.

That year marked the end of the Australian Crawl as the leading style. American swimmers and coaches experimenting with the kick developed the six-beat crawl known as the American Crawl. The six-beat (one, two, three kicks to each pull of the arms) took over as the fastest stroke, and the legs came to be accepted as very important in adding speed to the crawl.

The interesting thing is that Shane Gould today (and some other good swimmers like Karen Moras as well) use the two-beat kick. They do not get much propulsion from their legs but they still go very fast, in fact they can make world records with this method. It was *almost* a return to the Australian Crawl, but there was really a great deal of difference. Whereas the early Australians *bent their knees* considerably and lifted their feet far from the water before thrashing them down, Shane Gould keeps the legs nearly straight and the heels barely break the surface. The timing is the same as Fanny Durack and Cecil Healey but this is where the resemblance ends. Many say that in the modern two-beat the legs act mainly as a balance. We are inclined to think that they do more than this, that in the high-rating arm action the kick is fast enough to contribute to the propulsion of the body. We think they do contribute some speed, although we by no means stress the importance of using the legs hard.

Shane was thirteen when she moved down from Queensland with her parents and started training with us. She had had a number of good coaches and had shown promise in the age-group ranks. Before she and her parents (and parents have to be involved in competitive swimming nowadays) decided in 1970 to commit themselves to hard training, Shane was in fact only a light trainer. We doubled her mileage to over thirty per week.

Her crawl technique was altered within a short time. Shane had been using a fairly straight-armed wide swinging technique which she was able to transform into the high elbow recovery used by others in our squad including Karen Moras who was with us at that time.

Both Shane and her parents were predisposed towards the sprint distances—probably, we suspect, because they thought that this would mean less arduous training and shorter sessions. The desire to train as a sprinter did not concern us too much because Shane did what the rest of the squad was doing—everybody trained for endurance, at long distances, whether they thought they were sprinters or not. Our pupils all do much the same programme of training.

Shane's leg action could be described as a broken tempo (that is, there was a pause during the action) and a flutter kick. It was not a regular six-beat but it was not a two-beat either.

Her kick posed a problem for us. It was quite suitable for distance swimming but it was wide—'slow and lazy'. We pondered whether it should not be speeded up for sprinting. However, the whole thing was settled for us when Shane developed the kick of those around her and got into the regular two-beat. When she continued to make good times for the 100 metres freestyle we reckoned we could leave things be.

Even at this stage, in August 1970, we were quite sure we had a potential record holder. Shane made good even earlier than we had thought possible. Within eighteen months she was to hold *all* the world freestyle records. Her first world record came on April 30th 1971 when she equalled Dawn Fraser's 58.9 seconds for the 100 metres. The next day she did the 200 metres in 2–06.5, knocking two-tenths off Debbie Meyer's world record. She was well grooved by now into a regular two-beat at all distances, including 'the hundred'.

Shane kicks with a pure two-beat with no balancing cross-over of the feet as seen in the successful four-beaters (countrymen Grahame Windeatt, Brad Cooper, and Debbie Meyer). Shane's technique in the 100 metres had broken new ground in modern swimming, though it had its echoes from the past with Fanny Durack nearly sixty years before.

Shane's elbows are high in the arm recover, her hands enter almost straight in front of the shoulders. She does not stretch out far in front, in fact she looks 'short'. She makes up for this with a long pull back. The high elbows are kept this way in the arm pull, high and forward. This is accepted as very efficient, because the hand then tends to be pushing the water backwards and not down towards the bottom of the pool.

The rate of stroking is high, fifty or more strokes to the 50-metre lap. There is very little gliding action with the arms stretched out in front. We always say that 'while you are gliding somebody else will be swimming'. The glide of such great swimmers as Lorraine Crapp, Ilsa Konrads and Dawn Fraser has given way to the high tempo perpetual motion technique.

Shane keeps the right muscles strong by doing special swimming exercises with the much-used Dynastic exerciser. She tries hard to do her fifteen minutes daily. We do *no* weight training, only the special resistance exercises copying the arm action in the water.

Shane's mental and physical attributes are those of the

Shane Gould relaxes after setting a record of 58.5 seconds for the 100 metres during the 1972 New South Wales Championship Meet.

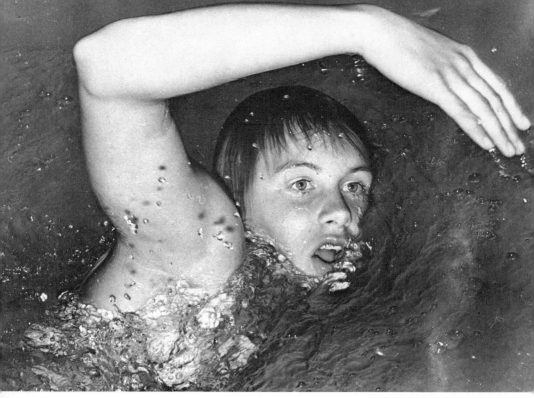

Shane, who now holds every available world freestyle record, starts another practice swim. During her hardest training period she swims about nine miles a day.

The start of another record breaking swim for Shane — the 800 metres.

champion. She is very good at her studies and concentrates hard on her schoolwork. Even though she misses more school than she would like owing to swimming tours, Shane manages to keep up enough to put her in the top bracket at her examinations. In 1972, at the Turramurra High School, despite time out for the Munich Olympic Games, she did extremely well in her fourth form examinations, gaining the maximum pass of six A's in her six subjects.

From the end of 1971 honours have been heaped on Shane and she has won scores of international and Australian awards. Her greatest achievement of all was at Munich in 1972 when she won the most medals ever for a girl at the Olympics. Shane won three gold medals (the 200 metres, 400 metres and 200 metres individual medley) all in world record time and in addition a silver medal (for 800 metres freestyle) and a bronze in the 100 metres sprint.

In January 1973 Shane received a wonderful compliment from her fellow Australians when she was named 1972 Australian of the Year, a tribute not only to her prowess in swimming but also to her fine sportsmanship.

There has been tremendous pressure on Shane. Every move she has made has been watched and reported on by press, radio and television. When she was resting during the afternoon between heats and final (she made a world record for the 100 metres with 58.5 seconds) at the New South Wales Championships in 1972, no fewer than six newspapers phoned for permission to send out photographers and reporters to 'get the story about her relaxing' that day. Shane has learnt to smile and say no when the demands of press and television intrude too much into her private life. Thanks to her mature approach to life and to her parents' guidance she has enjoyed a very good press and an excellent public image. It has been well deserved, because Shane is a happy, shy and gentle girl. Her success has not gone to her head.

Australia may find more great swimmers in the future; but I cannot imagine that I personally will ever have the opportunity to coach and guide a greater champion than Shane Gould who has achieved the position of being the greatest female swimmer of all time.

DENNIS HALL

Naturalization At Kiley's Cowshed

Illustrations by David Rae

THE ONE thing the Higginses couldn't take was the pair of emu eggs on the mantelpiece. Since coming to Australia they had learned to put up with rheumatic railways loud with howling transistors, roads smoking with Holdens, and weekends full of the snarlings of motor-mowers. They had even learned to smile at these things, when they hadn't been too worn out.

But when Sam Higgins left the city to work at Ross's place, and took his family to live in the farm cottage near the township of Kiley's Cowshed, they had to face those emu eggs. A fine pair they were, all dark-green and shining, with a sort of mossy knobbliness under the polish. And they were too much for the Higginses.

"Ain't they whoppers, though!" little Timmy Higgins used to shout. But he was only eight.

"Just fancy havin' birds that'd lay eggs that big," marvelled Muriel Higgins, who should have known better at eleven.

"Don't reckon we'd eggs like that back 'ome," said Stan Higgins, who was a traitor of twelve.

"Na that'll be enough from you," Sam Higgins would say over his paper. "Just remember where you come from, young Stanley."

"And I'm sure there's bigger eggs back in Lunnon, in the Queen's drawing room at Buckin'am Palace, or at some of them toffy hotels," declared Mrs Higgins. "Bound to be. Stands to reason."

But the green eggs had done their evil work. The Higgins family was divided, with the junior members sticking up for the Australian eggs while their elders championed the better British product.

At last Sam Higgins lost his patience and his temper, and found a memory.

"Na then!" he shouted. "How about your great-auntie Florrie's egg?"

"Where is it?"

"What about it?"

"We've never seen it," chorused the young Higginses.

Sam Higgins dropped his pipe on the farm cat, which smelled like scorched ironing for a week after.

"It'd make them little things look like tom-tits' eggs," he triumphed. "Mother, you write a letter askin' can we borrow it off her. We'll even pay the postage," he added recklessly.

Three months and two postal strikes later Auntie Florrie's egg arrived. All the Higginses fidgeted round while Sam opened the box and pulled out the hundreds of crumpled sheets of *The Daily Mirror* and *News of the World* which had cushioned it against the best efforts of peevish postal clerks and snarling stevedores and demented delivery men. It was worth waiting for, and it was quite unsmashed.

"Though you'd think a three-months' egg'd be pretty hard," as Muriel was heard to murmur.

They all looked. The egg was golden, softly golden and somehow fragile-looking, as though its shell was made of gold dust so thinly powdered that an inner light shone through.

"That wouldn't be a British egg," young Stan said suspiciously.

"It come from Britain, didn't it?" his father demanded. "Don't that make it British?"

"But where did it come from in the first place?" Muriel wanted to know.

"Your great-uncle Murky brought it from foreign parts," said Mrs Higgins firmly. "Out past China and South America or such. And that'll be enough from you," she added.

Timmy Higgins tapped the egg. It didn't sound hollow, and he said so. But no one was listening to him.

Well, they found a pink plastic bucket, into which the geat golden egg fitted as if in a giant egg-cup, and they placed it in the centre of the mantelpiece fair under the picture of Queen Elizabeth in her royal purple robes.

The emu eggs seemed suddenly small and dull, and Sam Higgins was satisfied. The British egg was clearly better, and bigger, and a whole lot brighter. Even the cheeky young 'uns could see that.

The egg hatched next morning. The night had been one of those Australian nights, breathlessly hot and fiercely uncom-

fortable. The sort of night when you have to choose between suffocating under a damp sheet or being feasted upon by ferocious mosquitoes. A night like the inside of an incubator, only not so smelly.

They were all having a good British breakfast of porridge and eggs and chips when the golden egg broke. It didn't crack. It broke with a musical chiming like a chorus of temple bells.

The thing in the egg fell to the hearth with a leathery thud, but it quickly recovered. All the Higgins, silent for once, looked at. it.

It was patterned all over in golds and purples and strange sea-greens. It had a musky smell, rather like a crocodile which didn't believe in washing too often. Even before it opened its bright green mouth, from which wisps of smoke were even then beginning to curl, they could see that it was a dragon.

And before they had swept up the bits of the tea-pot Mrs Higgins had dropped, or comforted the cat which had copped the tea, they were worried.

"It must've come from China," Muriel said. "Wouldn't that make it a communist dragon?"

"Belt up!" Stan snapped at her. "They were breeding silkworms and dragons and things in China ages before communism was invented. Teacher said so last week."

"Don't you go telling them at school, now," Mrs Higgins warned.

"You'll get a right proper tannin' if you do," Sam Higgins backed her up.

"We're in Australia, don't you forget," Mrs Higgins reminded them.

"And they're mortal strict about no fires in the open all their bloomin' summer," Sam worried.

They were sure, though, that kindness to animals had to include dragons. So they put the little creature in a sort of play-pen Sam made from asbestos sheets; but by the end of the week there was nothing little about it. It must have been three or four yards long by then. It was growing like a politician's expense account and, as Mrs Higgins said, it was fair eating them out of house and home.

They did have arguments about whether it was British, because the egg came from England, whether it was Chinese because China seemed to be the last country to have domesticated dragons, or whether it was Australian because, being born there, it baffled the immigration authorities. But they all agreed that it was good tempered, apparently intelligent, nicely house-broken, and that they were worried.

The worry was, after all, a pretty good thing, because at least it cancelled out some of their other troubles. Mrs Higgins stopped fretting about whether Australian ladies were better or worse than British ones and joined the CWA, where she had a high old social time.

Sam Higgins stopped worrying that the men thought he was a blinkin' Pommy and joined the local cricket club, which soon found that he was a tricky slow bowler.

Muriel and Stan and Timmy played longer after school with the township children so that they wouldn't get home in time to feed the dragon. Not that they minded throwing mutton chops into its gently smoking jaws, and seeing them instantly grilled; but they were pretty sick of Mum's moaning about what they were going to do with the brute.

They did all right out of their new cobbers, too. Because as soon as they were accepted by the local kids they were presented with all sorts of fascinating Australian information, about Ned Kelly and Phar Lap, Kingsford Smith and bunyips and gold-diggers. They even learned the names of all the Australian Olympic champions for ten years back, and the winners of the Kiley's Cowshed butterfat contests for at least twenty.

Anyway, everyone around Kiley's Cowshed began to say what a nice family the Higginses were, or how Pommies could be fair dinkum sorts, The trouble was, the Higginses got to hear of this, and they felt terribly guilty. After all, if you live in a district full of dry grass, on which sheep live, by which people live, and if you have a fathom or two of waddling blowlamp at your place—well, you must feel a little uneasy.

But they kept the dragon a family secret, and their popularity went up faster than doctors' fees, which at that time were Australia's contribution to the rocket race. So they were naturally offered a lift to the Duncan's Dip picnic races.

They went. They had a proper good time. And when they got home that evening the dragon was out.

Well, all the Higginses were fair flummoxed. To come home full of tea and hospitality and fruitcake and Australian good wishes, and to find their fiery dragon in the forty-acre was the most shaming thing that had happened to the family since Auntie Lil's elastic broke outside Fortnum & Masons.

But shamefully worried as they were, the Higginses couldn't help noticing the dejection of their dragon. It stood with its head drooping towards the dry grass in the middle of the paddock. The sad light of evening fell like a mourning robe over its dusty scales and failed to light a gleam in its dull, despairing eyes.

It had been a splendid dragon. Now, marooned in a dusty paddock with twenty rather moth-eaten sheep and the last grey kangaroo left in fifty miles, it was simply hopeless, alien and forlorn.

Timmy Higgins was quick to notice the important thing. "Look, Mum!" he piped. "The dragon's give up smoking."

It had. Quenched by the Australian desolation, its inner fires had smouldered and died. Here was another worry for the Higginses.

"Quick, you nippers!" snapped Sam. "Run and get that ten pounds o' lamb chops from the larder. We got to revive the poor beast somehow."

But his kindness was in vain. While Stan stood by with the garden hose, chop after chop fell rejected to the dusty grass. The dragon wouldn't look at raw mutton.

It might have died there, creating a fine old pollution problem, if it hadn't been for Mrs Higgins. In a shop at Duncan's Dip she had found the one delicacy her family had yearned for in the wide open spaces of Australia. She had bought it triumphantly, and promised them fish and chips for their tea.

"Quick!" she cried. "The fish! Try it with the fish."

It says a lot for the Higginses that they never thought of their promised treat. They tore away the wet paper until they came to the gleam of scales and the ripe aroma of well-travelled fish.

Sam Higgins threw a fine mullet. The dragon snapped. He threw another. In two minutes their tea was gone, but the dragon was saved. But his fires were quenched for good.

All next day the Higginses worried about the problem of fish supplies in a land addicted to mutton. They were still worrying on Monday when Charlies Ross sent a message asking them to attend an emergency meeting of the Kiley's Cowshed Progress Association that evening.

Well, Sam and Mrs Higgins went, and in the local hall with its dance-floor smell they soon forgot their little worries in the wider ones of the whole district.

Clancy Kleemann was the speaker. "Ladies and gents," he said. "Unaccustomed as I am to speaking in public I have to draw your attention to the forthcoming festivities convened for Back to Kiley's Cowshed Day.

"It is fitting and proper that we should honour this truly historic occasion—er, for all we're worth. But there's a snag, ladies and gents. The committee has discovered that our beloved district has never been honoured by an eminent public figure. What I mean, we've never had a bushranger nor a jockey nor a boxer from these parts. Not even a champ ping-ponger or a notable chook-thief."

This was tragedy. Everyone knows you can't have a district celebration without a district celebrity. The meeting worried itself hoarse until 9 o'clock that night.

Meanwhile the young Higginses had come home from school, tucked into the cold tea their Mum had left for them, and fed the cat. Then, naturally, their thoughts turned to their poor, neglected dragon.

"I think we ought to take him for a walk," Muriel dictated.

"What? And make him even sorrier for himself, seeing a lot more old sheep and galahs and goannas?" said Stan scornfully.

"Take him for a walk to the river," said Timmy, hopefully. He was never allowed there on his own.

"Why?" asked the others, thinking of a three-mile walk under the afternoon sun.

"Fish!" said Timmy promptly. "Rivers has fish."

So they trailed off across the dusty paddocks with their dragon drooping behind. They had to stop pretty often to help him through barbed-wire fences, and at one stage they scared three percent of butterfat out of Donovan's cows, but at last they saw ahead of them the lonely line of red-gums that marked the river.

It was evening by then, getting late, and the grey light fell cold and cheerless on the still waters of the deep reach known locally as Barney's Billabong. They were all tired and feeling pretty hopeless as they lined up along the edge of the steep bank.

"Proper mugs, we are," said Stan. "Coming all this way for nothing. Young Timmy. . . ."

"Look!" cried Muriel, almost swallowing her pink plastic hair-slide.

The dragon's fanged and craggy head was lifted. Its sooty nostrils sniffed the evening breeze. For the first time in days its eyes gleamed as though they reflected long-dead internal fires. Its three yards of saw-toothed tail quivered with excitement.

Then it was off, bounding at a waddling run recklessly down the slope, stopping at the brink in an avalanche of rattling clods. It paused for a moment, its scaly neck stretched out like a gun-dog making a point. Then it plunged into the grey steel mirror of the billabong.

The young Higginses sat on the bank till mopoke time, fascinated and forgetful of distance. Below them, the dragon swam like an eel, it dived like a seal, it hunted with the easy greed of an otter.

"Yabbies!" Stan breathed once.

"Oh yes!" Muriel agreed, remembering that Barney's Billabong was famous for its thousands of fat crayfish.

Timmy was silent. He thought they were unfair in not

praising him. After all, it had been his idea.

They toiled back across the paddocks, dragonless under the stars, to meet the scoldings of their parents who had come home bowed under the district's worries as well as their own.

And the young Higginses had added to those worries, as their parents were quick to remind them. Kiley's Cowshed was a pretty gun-happy place, and what duck-shooter could resist adding a few fathoms of dragon to his bag? For the umpteenth night in succession they all dragged off unhappily to bed.

It was Muriel who saved the situation, next day, after thinking furiously all through an afternoon English lesson. By that time her teacher was quite ready to believe that she was sick—with one of those sicknesses that attack the brain.

So Muriel took her leave from school, all her pocket money, and the bus to Duncan's Dip. At the Dip she made straight for the office of *The Duncan's Dip Declaimer*, and found Rob Holly asleep in the editor's chair. Rob was the only reporter, as well as the editor and chief compositor. He needed all the rest he could get.

I don't know what Muriel said to Rob, but whatever it was it got him out of that chair. After all, if you had spent your life writing about weddings and cows with twin calves and foot-rot and damp hay you'd be rather pleased to hear about a real, live, aquatic dragon in your district.

Anyway, in ten minutes flat, after stopping just long enough to buy some fish for her Mum, Muriel was in Rob's old car, belting the gravel towards Kiley's Cowshed. It is to her undying credit that, choked with dust and hanging on for dear life, she remembered Timmy and Stan.

Rob was a gentleman, even though he worked for a newspaper. He stopped and picked them up outside the school, jammed the accelerator back into its groove in the floorboards, and reached the river without killing more than a couple of roosters. Their hearts caught up with them about five minutes later.

Well, *The Duncan's Dip Declaimer* had headlines that week:

THE CREATURE OF KILEY'S COWSHED
MONSTER SEEN IN BARNEY'S BILLABONG
IS IT A BUNYIP?

Naturally, the Back to Kiley's Cowshed doings were the greatest ever. The Higginses were heroes, of course. Sam was made President of the Barney's Billabong Fauna Reserve. And if ever the Cowshed has another back-to you can bet who'll be the celebrities. Along with the dragon, who has grown to be a sort of freshwater leviathan because of all the tinned herrings people feed him on cool Sundays.

Anyway, the Higginses were happy. They celebrated the doings in their own way, and even at their own expense. For Sam hired an artistic bloke to engrave 'Advance' on one of the emu eggs, and 'Australia' on the other.

Jurraveel

Illustrations by Joyce Abbott

THE SONG OF DARMUNJURA

BILLY NICKEL, he reared me up. We got so fond of one another. We used to sing these songs together under a gum-tree. He was a great singer, was Billy Nickel. This is the song of the gold-*jurraveel*.

You see, out near Baryulgil there's two mountains, Yillin and Darmunjura. Billy Nickel knew that on Darmunjura there was a gold-*juraveel*. One day he thought, I'll go out and get this gold. He was a *maragun*, that's an initiated man.

Anyway, Billy Nickel went up on to the mountain. I was grubbing out stumps at the time. Billy Nickel was on a cliff, and there was a creek flowing there. He was looking for the gold. He was just starting to part the long weeds flowing in the water, when the mountain started to crack, the mountain started to growl.

The mountain was up against Billy Nickel for interfering with those weeds. The mountain spoke to him. It said, "You have interfered with this *jurraveel*. You don't belong here. You belong to the Bunjalung tribe."

Billy Nickel went back to his blady-grass camp. He was lying on the blady-grass outside his *bungin*, his humpy made of branches and grass. Blady-grass was given to us by God. He got a dream. When he woke he says to his wife, Susan, "I see those two women, the *gaungun*." Those two spirit-women, the *gaungun*, were haunting him, they were tormenting him.

His wife Susan said, "You had no right going up on to that mountain and interfering with that *jurraveel*."

Next night these two women showed themselves again in a dream to Billy Nickel. He saw them coming to haunt him. His wife, Susan, was wondering what would happen to her husband. She kept rousing on him.

Anyhow, these two *gaungun* kept on haunting Billy Nickel

till he went blind. When he was blind, he sat down under that gum-tree. He had his two *djalgai*, his song-sticks. All is quiet. He sings.

He came to me. He said, "I've made up a song. Listen to me." He was a nice man. I missed him when he died. This is the song of Darmunjura that I caught from Billy Nickel:

"What shall I do? What shall I do?
  The mountain Darmunjura has wrestled with me.
  Back there on the mountain, I thought the gold
  was in the water. Soon as I pulled those weeds,
  the mountain started to crack, the mountain started to rumble.
  I pulled only those weeds, but the mountain was offended.
  Hold me now. The mountain has wrestled with me.
  What am I going to do? You've got to hold me.
  You've got to keep me. You've got to guide me now."

> *Told and sung to Roland Robinson by Dick Donelly*
> *of the Bunjalung Tribe.*

Jurraveel: A totem place or spirit.

THE FROG WHO WAS A KING

THIS happened at Grassy Heads. This happened when the world was made, years and years ago. There was an old man, an old King, he was. He used to look after Australia, we'll say. Then one day another old feller came from the other side of the world. Where would he come from? Africa, would he? That's where the lions and tigers are.

He came across to Grassy Heads and asked the old King did he have any lions and tigers in Australia. "Yes!" said the old King. "We've got all those things here." He was telling a lie, he didn't want them animals here.

Well, the old feller goes back to wherever he came from. He came back to the old King again. "Have you got anything like this here?"

The old King says, "Yoo ngunce kunee walkung." That means, "Yes, we've got all those things here."

I suppose if he hadn't spoken like that we'd have all them dangerous things here—lions, tigers, monkeys—all them bad things. Anyway, that old feller was bringing those things over, one after another.

And anyway, this old feller from the other side got sick of bringing these animals over to the old King. So he cursed him.

"Tishure nginga ngong yatanga!"

That means he turned the old King into a frog, them big brown fellers. That big brown frog says, "Wark, wark, wark! Ngure kunee walkung. Gitjeeng boseeya." This means, "Oh, we don't want anything like that. We've got 'em all here in this place."

The old feller from the other side picked up this old King and threw him down into a crevice in the rocks, and that's where he is to this day. Because he told a lie. But he saved Australia from all those deadly animals.

So now we've got all the quiet animals—kangaroos, emus, wallabies, possums and all that. Except the crocodile. That old feller must have sneaked him in.

Told to Roland Robinson by Tom Whaddy of the Gumbangirr Tribe, near Grafton.

THE BUNYIP

OLD Billy Poddam was a real *bugeen*, a clever old-man. He used to have a half-crown. He would go and play cards. He would go through all his other silver and then play his half a crown. He'd lose it. But next day he'd have it back in his hands again. No one could get that half a crown from him.

This old feller had a bunyip. It was his power, his *moojingarl*. This bunyip was high in the front and low in the back like a hyena, like a lion. It had a terrible big bull-head, and it was milk-white. This bunyip could go down into the ground and take the old-man with him. They could travel under the ground. They could come out anywhere. They could come out under that tree over there.

Old Billy Poddam never did no harm to no one all the time he was at Wallaga. He went out to Brungle, the home of his tribe, the Red Hill tribe. Out there he did something wrong that hurt his sister's feelings. His sister caught him with the *guneena* stones. She was as clever as he was. So, when he knew that his own sister had caught him, he caught her with the *guneena* stones.

"Well," he said, "you'll die. I'll die too."

That bunyip, he went away, he went back to the swamp, back to the water. If he was coming out of the swamp you'd see the water bubbling and boiling. He'd make the water all milky.

My old dad was smoking his pipe by the chimney. Mum heard this bunyip coming, roaring. The ground started to shake. He was coming closer. He came out of the ground underneath the tankstand. He went over to the chimney and started rubbing himself against it. He started to get savage. He started to roar.

Mum told dad to go out and talk to him in the language, tell him to go away, that we were all right.

Dad went out and spoke to him in the language. He talked to him: "We are all right. No one doing any harm. You can go away."

Dad followed him across the road, talking to him.

I looked out through the window. That's when I saw the bunyip. He was milk-white. He had a terrible big bull-head, a queer-looking thing. He had terrible eyes, big as a bullock's eyes, and they were glaring and rolling about. Every time dad spoke to him, he'd roar. My old-man was talking: "Everything is all right. Don't get savage here."

The bunyip went down into the hill and down into the salt water. I have never seen that bunyip since my poor old dad died. It was the last people of the tribe who left him there. You don't often see him. He only shows himself to certain fellows. You can hear him panting: *Hah-hah-hah.*

He travels around, up and down the coast as far as Kempsey, looking for anyone who has done anything wrong. When he bites you, you die. He's even been seen in Victoria, at Lake Tyers Mission.

Told to Roland Robinson by Parcy Mumbulla, Wallaga Lake.

Autumn Wind

The wind has all the sleeping seeds
In his pocket now,
Blowing past the summer
With blossoms for the bough.

Hand in hand with rain he comes
Laughing from the hills,
With grass in his pocket,
And daffodils.

IRENE GOUGH

No Night

There is no night.
Only the world is turning
From the light.

IRENE GOUGH

Close Your Book

Close your book,
Forget your rhyming.
Birds are singing
And bells are chiming.

Stretched in the shade
With grass for a pillow,
Watch the green sun
Through the leaves of the willow.

Follow the sound
Of a lazy stream flowing,
The hum of a bumble-bee
Coming and going.

Breathe all the scents
That the warm wind is bringing——
Part of the stream-flow,
The sun and the singing.

Lie in the shadow,
Just lie and look.
Forget your rhyming
And close your book.

CLIVE SANSOM

MAX FATCHEN

No Use Crying

Illustrations by David Rae

MILK was spilt all over the place . . . and there was no use crying about it. Driver Bill Brakey was cleaning it off the front of Engine No. 27 because he kept his engine spick and span even on this little country spur line.

There hadn't been that much milk, but enough to make a splash, enough to set the guard, Ben Thompson, shaking his head. He nearly shook it off sometimes at all the things that went wrong on this line . . . hotboxes on the wheels, buckles in the rails in the heat.

It was a line with little ballast and one train a day. Usually it was No. 27, hauling one passenger carriage and a few assorted trucks and picking up milk and anything that farmers liked to send, drive or carry to the station.

Ben Thompson had enough troubles.

And now this one . . . spilt milk.

Twelve year old John Stokes was as red as fire. He looked at the squashed and shattered milk can, he looked at Ben Thompson, and then he looked at the ground where the ants raced around caring about no one.

John had left the can of milk too close to the edge of the little platform in his hurry to see a hawk's nest. He'd meant to be back, but the train was running early. He'd just reached the nest up the tree when the train had whistled. He looked across just in time to see a white splash go over the front of the engine. . . .

Several gallons of milk from the dozen cows that his father and mother were handfeeding from their precious haystack; for the weather was dry, the grass gone and the countryside dusty.

"What are your parents going to say?"

Ben Thompson knew about the struggling Stokes family and what the milk cheque from the small butter factory in the nearby town meant. Ben knew a good many things.

He liked John; a sturdy boy, big for his age, full of energy, but with a tendency to never quite finish a job.

"They'll be mad."

"What's the milk depot going to say? Look at that can."

They all looked at it. John in horror, Ben in disgust and Bill Brakey in sorrow. It was twisted and crumpled. The engine had given it a fine old smack.

"Do things properly lad," said Bill. He was a big man and always carried an oil can. Some people said he went to bed with it. Some said he kept castor oil in it for the very delicate parts of his engine, and even put a dash of it in the water tank of the tender to settle it down.

"What if I left me engine standing around for the express to hit?"

"There aren't expresses on this line." John felt he had to make a stand.

"What if there were, lad?"

There was silence except for the panting of the engine and a drift of conversation between a couple of curious heads sticking out of the train's solitary carriage.

"And what," said Ben Thompson eyeing the boy with a terrible sternness (and Ben could look terrible because he was slightly cross-eyed), "what if the superintendent had been aboard. You know they're talking about closing this line? Or did you?"

"No." The boy's face was troubled as well as a little scared.

"I think I'll call this place Bad Luck Siding," said Ben. "Everything goes wrong here. I suppose we'd better think of something to tell the milk depot about the can."

"But you tell your father, lad," said Bill Brakey climbing back into his engine where Ed, the fireman, was shovelling more coal.

Ben Thompson lifted an empty can from the guard's van. "Here's your empty. If you aren't careful, you mightn't have a train soon to run over your milk can lad."

John watched the train puff from the station, the small well-kept engine and the three trucks. As the wooden carriage went past he noticed miserably the disapproving face of Mrs Eldring, mother of Molly Eldring, a noisy and troublesome classmate of John's at school.

Bill Brakey was still hollering as the little train gathered speed. "You tell your father. . . ."

Bad Luck Siding . . . it was bad luck all right, John muttered to himself in bed that night, carefully lying on his stomach because it was sore where the strap had been.

"Bad luck . . . darned carelessness," his father had said. "Milk's as precious as money."

The strap had hurt, but the sight of his mother's disappointed face had hurt more.

He twisted in bed and the soreness reminded him, and he scowled at the wall. A cow bellowed outside so he scowled through the window into the darkness at where he imagined the cow might be.

"I don't care if the old train never comes again. . . ." He lay still a moment, thinking. No use crying over spilt milk or sore tails, he supposed.

Then he fell asleep and milk cans came marching in shining legions, a giant superintendent in an enormous stationmaster's cap shouting, "Left, right! Left, right!" The milk cans were pushing him and herding him onto a railway track. And in the distance an engine was coming and the cans kept shoving him onto the line. . . .

He woke early and was out and bringing in the cows before his parents had stirred.

They seemed a little surprised, and after the milking was over his mother said, "Turning over a new leaf, John."

"I was sorry about the milk, Mum."

"The milk's important, John."

"Yes, Mum."

Then they carried the buckets down to the cool underground dairy which Mr Stokes had built.

But the day was as hot as it promised to be. He drove old Dynamite, the horse, in the spring cart to school, picking up the two Lucas children who sat beside him clutching their schoolbags.

They looked at him with big eyes, as they roosted on the seat like a couple of small plump birds—two girls, a year between them. He always had to pick them up. His mother made him.

"Our mum was talking to Mrs Eldring on the 'phone. Mrs Eldring said you left a can of milk on the line."

"I did not," he said. "It was on the platform."

"Mrs Eldring told our mum. . . ."

"You kids want to walk to school?" he said, savagely.

That quietened them. They shifted over to the other side of the single wooden seat. They felt nervous, alone with this milk-can wrecker.

Worse awaited him at school.

The Lucas children climbed down and raced off to a growing group at the gate. They all turned to watch him after he'd tied the horse up under a shady tree.

Molly Eldring planted herself in his way, pert nose tilted and wearing the general air of a stickybeak.

"You tried to wreck the train. My mum said. Milk everywhere, my mum said."

"Your mum is a windbag."

He glared at her. "And you'd better keep away from the railway line, or I'll tie you to the rails like they do in the movies."

There was a general backing away from the monster.

The whistle went and they marched into school at the bang of the drum, but the children around him were making train noises under their breath.

Everyone knew now.

Finally Miss Prue the teacher gave a talk about responsibility and not leaving things where they could cause trouble. She'd heard. She kept flashing him stern looks through her glasses. She had nice eyes usually.

Then something nudged John in the back and a sticky hand shoved a piece of paper into his. It was a drawing of an engine hitting a milk can and causing what looked to be a tidal wave.

He didn't have to be told who had drawn THAT!

Next time he took the milk can to the siding, the train was already in. So he backed the old dray against the platform and Ben lifted the can into the guard's van.

"Well, we made it this time without spilling any."

Driver Bill Brakey climbed down from his engine and came for a chat because the train was early.

"Old No. 27 took a couple of days to get that milk out of her system, John," he said, unnecessarily winking at Ben who winked back. "Oil's the thing for engines, they don't steam too well on milk."

"I'm sick of hearing about the milk," said John, "and I'm being careful, honest."

He quickly changed the subject.

"They still talking about closing the line?"

"Yep, they're talking."

Ben changed the subject too and looked at the sky. "She's getting hotter and dustier. We could get a nice blow-up after this."

"Let's hope there's some rain. See you later, John." Bill Brakey climbed back into the engine. As the train steamed out, Ben Thompson bawled, "Watch out with the milk, lad."

John gave old Dynamite the horse a sharp slap with the reins in disgust. Dynamite didn't look too pleased either.

Next day the heat was stifling. Everyone was listless at school, and when the boy came home the cows were gathered languidly around the water trough. The wind was getting up and the dust was racing everywhere, sometimes in small abrasive drifts that cut his knees, and sometimes in clouds that rolled along obscuring the scrub and the paddocks.

The cows were restless at milking time, refusing at first to go into the cow bales where the wooden yokes were slid against their necks to keep them quiet.

There was an afternoon train, and Stokes had to milk reasonably early.

John had to put a leg-rope on his cow. It kicked and thrashed, but finally he got it milked. The wind was still rising.

"Looks like a dust storm coming. Hope there's some rain behind it."

Mr Stokes looked at the sky. He was tired and dusty. Everyone was.

Mrs Stokes pushed away a wisp of her fair hair that the wind tore loose.

"You're going to risk sending the milk?" she said.

She had just risen from milking a cow. She talked as she milked, in a quick urgent way.

"We need the money, Mother. We'll wrap some wet bags around the can. It'll be all right."

Mr Stokes put his hand on her reassuringly and they both looked at John, who straightened up from the side of the cranky, old cow which glared around at him with rolling eyes.

"You finished, John?"

"Yep."

He released the cow. She rushed back giving her horns a hoist at him as she went. She was irritated by the slamming, banging wind and the rising, swirling grit, as everyone else was.

"You'd better get the spring cart, son."

"Yes dad."

John harnessed old Dynamite who seemed restless, flicking his tail and blowing heavily through his big soft nostrils.

"Whoa, whoa."

The wind caught a big cardboard box from somewhere and sent it banging and rolling across the yard. Dynamite snorted and shifted.

A hen, lifted by the wind in her wild rush for the fowl house, was blown over in a feathery cartwheel.

"Serve you right," said John unkindly. Milk and wind and dust were making him irritable too.

His mother and father had taken the milk buckets to the cool little underground dairy and were straining the milk carefully into the can.

Gritty milk wasn't welcomed at the butter factory.

At last they'd put the lid on securely, wrapped it in damp bags, and John's father lifted it into the cart.

"What about these wooden boxes in the cart, Dad?"

"Leave them there."

There were a couple of big old boxes. Johns father put another wet bag over the top of the can and tied it with binder string.

Mrs Stokes came out of the dairy and looked at the sky again. Her face was sweaty and dirt-streaked and a little anxious.

A sudden gust of wind blew her milking apron right over her head. She was laughing as she pulled it down, but not laughing too much. John could see she was concerned for him.

"I'll be all right, Mum. It's only a bit of a dust storm."

"I've got the fencing," said his father. "If we get rain, I want that bottom paddock fence fixed. The boy can look after himself. Away you go, John."

But the storm was worse than they thought. The old spring cart wobbled along the track, and the wind slashed the boy's face as they topped the rises. He tied his handkerchief around his mouth to protect himself.

"We're for it, Dynamite," he said in a muffled kind of way.

Dynamite plodded on head down, his tail switching disap- provingly. The boy felt irritated like the horse. The milk splashed around in its can. Milk and cans. Ben Thompson bawling about them from the guard's van and that Molly Eldring drawing pictures. He was starting to hate milk.

The boy had brought some water in an old bucket and he turned and tipped a bit more on the bagging around the milk can. A branch suddenly cracked off a tree nearby and snapped with a slither and thresh of leaves into the scrub. The dust was choking now, getting into his throat. The sky was darkening. A cockatoo exploded out of a tree and pitched away, like a white feather ball, its harsh cry torn apart by the wind.

John wondered whether he ought to turn about and go home. But if the milk missed the train, it could go sour by morning. Spilt milk and then sour milk. No thanks, he told himself. Old Dynamite still battled on, but the boy had to haul him back on the track every few minutes.

Sometimes John could see only a few yards ahead, then a trick of the wind would clear the dust for a few seconds and then another great cloud would envelop him.

The spring cart topped the last rise before the siding. Here the tracks separated; one fork ran down a steep creek bed and up the other side, where it went along beside the railway line for a mile or so in a small flat valley.

The train line came around in a bend and over a small high bridge to the siding.

For a moment the dust lifted in its freakish way. And then the boy saw it. He pulled the horse up with a jerk, the sand stinging his face, the hot wind searing his forehead. Where the train line came on to the bridge it had buckled and lifted in the heat. . . .

He was thrashing old Dynamite and the cart down into the creek bed and up the other side. He had to do something. He'd seen buckled lines before, and so (usually in time) had the engine drivers. But trains were often coming off the line when a rail buckled.

Here the engine would jump the line and fall straight into the creek, he reckoned. They wouldn't see the bad rail in the dust. They wouldn't. He pictured old No. 27 lying on her side, pistons smashed and everything else smashed including Bill Brakey and his oil can.

"Giddup Dynamite. Giddup."

He had to do something. The sky was black and sometimes he could hardly see past the horse's head. The cart wheels bumped against the stone ballast of the track. He steered it off again. Here it was flat going and he could drive along the line. He *had* to stop them. He had an idea. It was crazy and it mightn't work, but he'd try.

And then he heard briefly a terrifying sound. It was the distant slamming of old No. 27's exhaust. He had the horse stopped and was off the cart in an instant. For he hadn't long. . . .

"Never seen a dust storm like it." Bill Brakey was hanging out the side of his cab, cursing and swearing and hardly being able to see ten feet in front of his engine. He was going cautiously, but they were running late and he went as fast as he dared. He knew the line like he knew the back of his old rough hand. He knew he had the line to himself. But Ben Thompson would be back in the guard's van, worrying about the schedule.

Ed Barton the fireman was alternately stoking and watching, and the dust hung in the cabin, heavy and choking.

Bill slowed her a little. They weren't far off the siding and the downgrade to the creek.

He leaned out further, his face a dirty brown, his big nose sticking out like a small sandhill. Dust swirled and eddied, thickened and lightened. Suddenly, through a momentary break, he thought he saw a short, squat outline standing on what seemed to be a little platform, plumb in the middle of the line. There was a noise in front—a bang—a clang—and a piece of wood flew past. Something splashed over his face and dribbled into his mouth.

MILK!

He slammed on the brakes, the wheels locked and the whole train shuddered to a banging, noisy halt. In the guard's van Ben Thompson was rolled on to the floor. Up in front and out of the swirling dust, an urgent figure was clambering up the side of the engine, a dirty, alarmed face was thrust over the footplate, cracked lips moving and a voice yelling in Bill's ear.

"The line's buckled on the bridge . . . the line's buckled on the bridge."

The wind tore and tugged the voice about—". . . had to stop . . . put the milk can on the boxes . . . had to stop you . . . had to stop you. . . ."

A week later a special train came into the siding. Old No. 27 was pulling it, her brass funnel band shining and Bill Brakey blowing his whistle as he came around the bend.

This was unusual for him, thought John; Bill was mean with his steam.

John stood silently, his hair parted and shining with oil, his hands hanging alongside the seams of his best pants.

His father and mother and all the neighbours were there. Miss Prue was there, and even Molly Eldring was there. There was a table with food covered over, and a big tea urn was bubbling on a carefully tended fire. There was a smell of rain and fresh earth, and a glint of water in the creek. There was also some kind of notice covered with a cloth. The train stopped with a squeak and a clang of couplings.

Ben Thompson the guard came hurrying along to help people from the solitary carriage.

John recognised the manager of the milk depot, the chairman of the district council; but there was a big impressive man too, with a great silver watch slung across his waistcoat, a watch as big as a railway buffer.

A moment later he found himself shaking hands with the railway superintendent.

And within five minutes they were all gathered around the mysterious notice.

"Ladies and gentlemen," said the superintendent, "before you start crying over spilt milk. . . .

Everyone laughed uproariously except John.

"Well, we're not closing the line."

There were cheers and clapping.

"Secondly, we're giving this siding a real name," said the superintendent. "We're grateful to this quick-witted boy." John felt uneasy and looked at the engine panting quietly. Bill was leaning out of the cabin listening and waved his oil can. "So ladies and gentlemen, I have much pleasure in calling it. . . ."

Off came the cover and there gleamed the white bold letters on a background of shining black paint:

MILK CAN CREEK.

They were still cheering when the superintendent walked up and presented John with the inscribed watch, while Bill waved his oil can wildly and Ben Thompson gave a slow, proud wink at the local hero.

ELIZABETH LANE

Mad As Rabbits

Illustrations by Walter Cunningham

HOW WE BEGAN

MOTHER often said we were all as mad as rabbits; and, after rearing a dozen of us and having hundreds of acres of rabbits to compare us with, she should have known. But then, our having eaten rabbit—baked, stewed or curried—for the greater part of our lives may have had something to do with the likeness.

Mother had a whole tribe of babies before I came along; in fact, by the time I was born a number of them were already going to school. I marvel now how any but the eldest few survived. Mother was a busy woman, so she didn't have much time to spend feeding babies; therefore one of us older children was usually given the job.

The baby usually got very little. After every one of us within coo-ee had each had a good taste, the baby had what was left.

Another hazard was that we were always sent to take the still-hungry little thing for a walk in the pram to put it to sleep. This walk would usually end in a gallop, for we had proved that babies drop off to sleep quicker that way. Once out of sight of the house we would clap on the pace, race madly up and down the bank of the dam, over gutters and around sheds on two wheels, until our passenger, from sheer exhaustion, fell asleep.

Sometimes we'd wheel the pram to the top of the hill about half a mile from the house and hold races, going flat-out downhill. One or two of us would fairly fly, pushing and guiding the pram; another one or two would race alongside in the billy-cart. More than once we had to pick up a sandy baby at the bottom of the hill and dust it down. Then we would replace it in the pram and slowly, carefully, wheel it home.

We were always afraid the baby might not wake up again, and all the way home we would ask God to 'please let the baby be all right', and promise Him that we'd never again use the pram as a racing-car. But somehow we always forgot our promises by the next time.

As we had been, we gathered, treated in much the same way by our elder brothers and sisters when we were babies, it was nothing short of miraculous that we all reached adulthood.

And nothing short of a wonder that our parents found enough for us to eat, or ever made a go of the farm at all, for that matter.

My paternal grandfather had selected this scrubby block of land, paid one payment on it, and died. He had only two children, both boys. Father, being the elder, inherited the land. So when Father, who had spent the greater part of his working life as a drover, married Mother, the poor lass not only found herself with a husband who knew nothing about how to run his poor-quality farm, but, into the bargain, with a quick-tempered, impossible brother-in-law.

Uncle Charlie was periodically away making money to entertain Uncle Charlie, coming home only when he was broke. He'd then set to work, and for weeks would slave from daylight until dark, felling timber and clearing the block. This happy state would last until he fell out with someone; then he'd roll his possum-skin swag and be off again.

During the following years Father and Uncle felled timber, fenced the farm, cleared the greater part of it, and then set to work to wipe out the rabbits. But though the family lived almost entirely on rabbits, and the dogs did live on them, the rabbits still seemed to regard the farm as theirs.

They were busy years for Father; busy ones, too, for Mother, for her time was more than taken up in the house, helping Father in the paddock, acting as family keeper of the peace, and having new babies. But Mother accepted these things philosophically; what really tried her patience were Uncle Charlie's attempts to kill Father.

They were not premeditated attempts, of course; they were mere flare-ups of different temperaments. Father was a dawdler, a dreamer, completely useless at planning things and running a farm, Uncle Charlie was a quick mover, a quick thinker, and was owned by a fiery temper. Father would never tell a lie, no matter how embarrassing the circumstances; Uncle, on principle, never told the truth unless it was of no importance.

One day the two men got into an argument over the depth of the post-holes for a shed they were building. Mother looked up and saw Uncle, while Father's back was turned, ready to bang his shovel down on Father's head. She yelled and ran towards them. By the time she reached them, Father was looking over his shoulder at Uncle Charlie.

"Good lord, Charlie," he was saying calmly, "you wouldn't have hit me with that, would you?"

By the time I was old enough to take in my surroundings Mother had bought a sewing machine, so I suppose you could say we were now prosperous. Anyhow, I don't remember our thinking we were poor, even though we girls had a bedroom where on windy nights the wind used to whistle through the cracks in the wall, and often blew the candle out. On wet nights

Mother had to cover some of the beds with waterproof coats, and we had to be careful not to step in the dishes and basins spread through the house to catch the drops.

Despite it all we were a happy mob, delightfully happy, in a contented, grateful kind of way.

I was, I was sure, going to be a singer, have a large bosom, wear flashing false teeth, long evening frocks, and loads of diamonds; spend my evenings thrilling people with my wonderful voice, and spend my days being driven around in a motor-car.

My idea of wanting to be a singer might have been inspired by Madame Melba and my Uncle Charlie. When Melba was in her heyday as a singer, and he was in his heyday as a shearer, he found himself not far from the city in which the great lady was then drawing the crowds. It cost him, he said, 'half-a-shearing-cheque' to make the trip to hear her sing.

He told us all about it as soon as he'd got back and unpacked his swag. He balanced back on two legs of the kitchen chair and looked up at the mantelpiece.

"Sing!" he said. "Holy hell, she's got a voice like a bullocky."

We sat silent and spellbound, for this, from Uncle Charlie, was the highest possible praise.

"But what did she sing!" he said. "She didn't sing any decent songs. None of them had words, she just went like this. . . ." He threw his head back and started off warbling like a magpie, and ended up screeching like a cockatoo. "Yes, she can sing all right, but it's a shame she didn't sing one decent song all night."

But Melba's repertoire wasn't the only thing that Uncle Charlie brought back from that shearing trip. Far more important was his elegant boxer hat. We'd been used to seeing him in the faded almost-yellow felt hat, turned up in front, that he wore when he went away. And now here he was, standing on the family hearth, wearing a handsome arrangement the like of which we'd only seen in catalogues.

Father looked up as the kitchen door suddenly swung open. "Holy cow!"

"Yes, it's me," Uncle told him, taking stock of the family taking stock of him. "And what are you all grinning about?"

Because he was short, slight and sinewy, and sprouted twin hearthbrooms of ginger eyebrows, and a loose ginger kiss-curl hanging halfway down his forehead; because of the dusty tan boots and the cheap grey suit, and the shearing swag resting at his feet; he was not in keeping with the dignity of that sleek, glossy, wonderful hat.

"Where the devil did you get it?" Father asked him.

"I bought her for thirty bob in the city—she's the best," Uncle said as he lifted it off. Then he pulled his sleeve tight as a clothes-brush to give his hat a good rub before hanging it on a nail in the porch. (Porch, we called it, though it was nothing but a lean-to put up to stop the rain beating in the back door.)

When anyone in the years to come saw the hat resting on the nail at night, they knew Uncle Charlie was in bed; when they saw it there in the daytime they knew he was sitting at the meal table, for those were the only times that he and his hat were ever parted. He even put it on in the morning when he went to have his wash. And whereas most men would have taken off their hats to, say, run down a rooster, Uncle Charlie left his on. His hat became one of his most valued possessions—along with his pack of dogs and his double-headed penny—the penny he had made himself and spent weeks in bringing to perfection.

When there were so many of us children that we occupied most of the sleeping space from the front door to the back, Uncle moved out to a covered van parked beside the blacksmith shop. Mother was glad when he went; she was tired of telling him he mustn't spit up the wall at night. He chewed plug tobacco, and there weren't many mornings when she didn't have something to say about it. He still ate his meals with us; that is, apart from the times when he had fallen out with Mother.

All in all, Uncle found it convenient to live in the van. He kept three or four dogs tied underneath it, and as soon as he let them off the chain for a run they'd fight our dogs. When this happened at night, and they chose to fight on the front verandah right under Mother's bedroom window, things would be a bit hectic next day.

Mother would say with an air of cold authority, "Charlie, you will just have to get rid of those dogs, fighting three parts of the night under my window. I just won't have it; it's not good enough. You will just have to get rid of them."

"Get rid of my dogs! Holy hell, where my dogs are not wanted neither am I!"

"Well, your dogs are not wanted here."

That was always enough to send him stalking off to his van

to pack. Sometimes he'd be gone only days, sometimes weeks, occasionally for months. The dogs, the usual cause of the trouble, would be left in the family care. Strange to say, this was something my brothers liked. Feeling a personal responsibility, they fed them better than they did their own, and took a delight in sooling them on to the family dogs.

Setting more traps to keep Uncle's as well as our own dogs fed meant nothing to the boys. Once, because of the extra traps they had set, Jack invited me to go round the traps the following morning. I was very excited because I'd never been asked before. Jack told me I would have to be up very early on Saturday. I hardly slept, in case I disappointed him by sleeping in.

INITIATION

IT WAS scarcely daylight, the fowls were still noisily declaring the dawn, when I tiptoed out to the kitchen. Jack had lit the fire and sat warming his feet in the oven. I pulled up a chair and slid my feet in beside his. As soon as our toes were warm we put our boots on, took our coats and crept out of the house. I felt excited and happy, sneaking off and leaving everyone else in bed.

Just in front of our house the railway embankment had been built up to a height of about twenty feet. From there it levelled out until, about half a mile away, it entered a cutting that bit into a steep hill.

Our breath steamed in clouds as we struggled up the embankment. The six wires in the fence at the top had just been strained and were hard to squeeze between. Jack put his boot on a lower one and strained the one above, but just as I went to get through he lost his grip. At the same moment his boot slipped off the lower wire. With a ringing twang the wires snapped together on my half frozen leg.

"Did it hurt much?" he asked as he freed my leg.

"No," I lied. The sudden red weal halfway round my leg spoke for itself.

"Would you like to go home?"

Biting my lip and fighting back my tears I wriggled through the fence. "Oh no!" I told him. "Of course not."

The embankment was like ice, so slippery that my boots wouldn't grip; and each tuft of grass or small bush that I grabbed came away in my hand with a frosty crackle.

"Look back," said Jack. "It doesn't even look like our place."

I turned back. Stretched below was a view like a scene on a Christmas card: everything was clean, covered in an overcoat of thick white frost. The iced cake of the haystack carried a topping of pink-breasted galahs. The thin blue smoke that curled up from the kitchen chimney reminded us we were hungry, so we hurried on.

A terrified little bunny was crouched in the first trap set in a clump of stunted wattles. Jack grinned. "One," he said.

"But it's only such a little one!" I protested.

"It doesn't matter, it'll help feed the dogs," Jack said.

By far the kindest of my brothers, Jack was forever fixing a splint on a fowl's broken leg or treating a drooping wing; yet here he was, hitting a baby rabbit on the head with a mallee stick and thinking nothing of it. Of course I knew that for years he'd been catching rabbits and killing them, but I had never seen him do it before. I was nearly sick when he passed the little thing over to me to carry. I was so upset that I nearly dropped it.

The next couple of traps had been sprung by foxes, but as we went along the line we picked up another eight rabbits. Then we turned for home.

Suddenly the sharp, clear whistle of a train split the air, almost as if it were hidden in the nearest patch of scrub.

"Sound travels a long way on a frosty morning," Jack explained. "If we hurry we can be in the cutting in time to see it go through."

"In the cutting! Isn't that dangerous?"

"Oh, Ernie and I often hide there as the trains go through; but, mind you, you have to be brave. Come on." I fell into step behind him as he started to run.

We pounded along, but Jack kept looking at the ground beside the track. Suddenly he swooped on a nail, and further along on a metal washer. When we were well into the cutting we stopped. "Watch this!" He placed them on the cold rails.

The wall of the cutting was yellow sandstone in which little caves had been worn. Jack dragged me into one of these, and there we crouched, together with the nine dead rabbits. "Keep your eye on that washer and nail," Jack said. "I'm going to show you something later."

My hands and feet were numb with cold, and my leg was so sore I could scarcely touch it. Jack saw me looking at it.

"It hurt a lot, didn't it?" he said.

"Oh, no, not much. Anyway, it's all right now."

He examined my leg tenderly. I didn't flinch. I'd never before felt so important or precious to anyone. We might easily have been the only two people in the world.

"You know, doctors use leeches to suck out bruised blood like that," Jack said.

"Could it have broken my leg?"

"Quite easy; snapped it like a carrot," he said. And for that moment, anyway, I almost wished it had.

The train was whistling at the level crossing about half a mile the other side of our house. I began to feel scared.

"Don't be frightened of the smoke and steam as she goes past," Jack warned me. "It's really nothing, but don't move."

There was a series of quick-fire, explosive stutterings from the train—chug-chug—chug-chug. "Hear that!" Jack said. "It's so cold the engine can't grip the rails."

The chugging died away. The frosty air was silent. "It's running back to get a longer run at the hill."

The chug-chug—chug-chug began again, then died away as before. Next time it came faster and made even more noise. Then it suddenly plunged ahead. "They've sprinkled sand on the rails," Jack explained. "They have to, you know; it makes the wheels grip."

With a shattering roar the train came rushing into the cutting, setting the sandstone shaking and bringing little trickles of sand down on our heads. I blinked my eyes, and then a huge monster—spitting smoke and hissing steam and firing sparks— seemed to be roaring straight at us. It passed so near that I only had to put my hand out to touch it—except that my hands were tightly clenched around the baby rabbit.

As the guard's van passed, Jack crawled out. "Stand up," he said, "and take a big breath." The clean, fresh tang of the burning coal was exhilarating. It filled our nostrils and heads, and stayed in the air.

Then we went along the rails to see what had happened to

the washer and nail. Although we searched and searched we couldn't find the washer, but the nail was squashed as flat as a piece of tin and was about three times as long and wide as it had been before.

"There, what did I tell you!" cried Jack.

We were as proud of that nail as if it were made of solid gold. He let me carry it home. When we reached home again the sun was coming up, flooding the frosty world in a blaze of colour.

OLD HOUSE, NEW HOUSE

THE BRYCE family was almost as numerous as ours. When we walked to the tiny school together we must have looked like a swarm of grasshoppers. And when both families went down with measles at the same time it was hardly worth keeping the school open.

We provided Mrs Bryce with a daily supply of milk. On weekdays we gave her a billy of it on the way to school; but on Saturdays and Sundays a couple of her children came to our place for it. Sometimes Mother would send them home with a billy of eggs as well.

The Bryces were much worse off than we were, for our father didn't drink. Our home and farm was our own, apart from the mortgage. The Bryces, on the other hand, lived in their place only because it had been empty for years and the owner felt sorry for Mrs Bryce and the children.

Ann and I shared with the children any luxuries we managed to lay our hands on. We made our biggest haul of the week the day the grocer's van arrived. The driver used to stop on a clean patch of grass and chuck a double handful of boiled lollies into the air, just for the fun of seeing our whole family of kids scramble for them. Ann and I used to dash into the fray like mad; every lolly we got hold of we used to save, to share with Renie and May Bryce when they came at the weekend.

Several of our boys had now left school and were taking a great interest in running the farm. They faced up to even the dreadful ordeal of cutting chaff almost as though they enjoyed it. Before, Father had spent the greater part of each chaff-cutting day lining the boys up and calling the escapees back from over the railway line. Now the boys were really bucking in, working with gusto and enthusiasm. From the time they left school they not only ran the farm, but in slack times they worked for the neighbours. Every pound they earned went towards machinery, horses and harness.

The boys gained most of their knowledge by trial and error; like the time brother Charlie, determined to teach a jibbing horse in the team a lesson, gathered an armful of loose hay, placed it under the horse, and set fire to it. It worked—the horses pranced on just far enough for the wagon-load of hay to be right over the blaze. Only George's quickness in emptying the waterbag over the flames saved the wagon.

The girls who had left school played their part as earnestly as the boys. We were able to keep more cows, and it was the girls' task to milk them. Thus Father was happy to be left to ride round his sheep, and Mother to be left to her kitchen. We were so prosperous that there was talk of building a new house.

Our old home, made of daub and saplings, had settled down very close to the earth. The roof, rusty with age, blended in with the surroundings so well that it might have been a monstrous mushroom with the earth still clinging to it. There was only one discordant note—the chimney Uncle Charlie had built to replace one that had blown down in a storm. He had built it of cement and flour (he thought it was lime). The result was a chimney as staunch as marble, that did everything that could be expected of a good chimney. But it refused the earthy mellowness of the rest of the house, standing out like a new false tooth in an old lady's mouth.

Within a year or so of the start of discussions our new house was built. The great day came when we formally moved in. But before the great day, came the great night when our neighbours and friends gave us a 'house-warming'. Mrs Bryce and her children were the first to arrive. We didn't suspect anything; they often walked across on moonlit Saturday nights.

Father, Mother and Mrs Bryce were sitting on the underground tank at the front of the old house. We youngsters were playing 'chasey' in the moonlight. The older girls were going through some old catalogues in the kitchen. The Bryce boys and our boys were in the stable robbing sparrow-nests.

Suddenly the dogs barked and rushed to the front gate. We heard the crunchy rumble of buggy-wheels, and the clatter of

horses' hooves on a stretch of hard road near our gate. The dogs nearly went mad as buggy after buggy, and men and boys on horseback, came stringing through our gate in a never-ending line of neighbours, all laughing and calling out to us at once. They had met at the railway crossing, and then descended upon us *en masse*.

All these people coming to see us and our new house; it was almost unbelievable! And the Bryces hadn't spoilt it by letting on, not even the youngsters.

The buggies emptied quickly. Excited youngsters tumbled out, sleepy babies were handed down, and then, while the women began carrying awkward suitcases of food into the house, groups of men stood around self-consciously, mumbling about the weather.

Everyone brightened up when old Billy Addison squatted on a box in a corner of the new dining-room and began to 'try out' his new accordion. Soon everyone was milling about, and there were so many people in so many rooms that we hadn't enough lamps to go round and even ran out of candles.

Everyone, school kids included, joined in. Barney Cameron played the mouth-organ; Jim Heinrich played the fiddle. And food, it was everywhere! The women of the district must have been preparing for days. There were sandwiches, sausage-rolls, Cornish pasties, lamingtons, huge chocolate cakes, cream puffs, and enormous cream sponges six inches high.

When we couldn't eat any more, dance any more, or keep our eyes open any longer, we children crept back to the old house and fell into bed with everything but our boots on. Any child within walking distance stayed the night; beds and shakedowns were all over the place.

Next day Ann and I were fiercely jealous of the older boys, who had managed to see the party out and had beaten us to sleeping in the new house for the first time.

Moving in was a great thrill; yet with all this, the old place took on a renewed interest for us. The front room with the stark chimney became Uncle Charlie's sleeping quarters. The rest of the building was our play-house, even though the men used the rooms to store bags and seed-wheat. In fact, romping on the bags increased the fun. It was a fine place to play.

CHRISTMAS AND PHONE CALLS

MY EARLY reading was generally confined to *The Weekly Times* and *The Australian Worker*, though I read everything I could lay my eyes on, from *Chaff-Cutting Made Easy* to *The Family Doctor's Book*, which Mother bought at the door from a persuasive salesman. I loved the glossy, illustrated catalogues the firms used to send out, and I spent hours poring over the brightly coloured pages.

Once when we were all small Mother selected an inexpensive Christmas toy for each of us from one of these catalogues, and gave the letter containing the money to the man on the grocery van. When Christmas Eve came and not a toy had turned up, Mother and Father sat up half the night making toys. Father made kites; Mother made and dressed dolls, baked gingerbread men and made up batch after batch of toffee.

The man on the grocery van had left the district hurriedly, and Mother's money, along with many other people's, had gone with him.

Years later, through another of these catalogues, Mother bought a Daisy airgun for the older boys. They were happy and excited as they took turns with it on Christmas morning. When they were called to dinner they stood the gun inside the kitchen door. As dinner was being served a sparrow flew down and sat by the tank outside the kitchen window. The opportunity was too good to miss. Tom grabbed the gun, rushed out and took aim. *Ping, ping, ping!* Tom hit three rust-weakened patches in the tank. Our one tank of water, and the summer as dry and hot as it could be.

Father and Mother rushed out, we all rushed out, and so did the precious water. Father tried to block the holes with bits of soap, then with putty, but neither would hold. And while he tried to block one hole he kept getting wet from the others.

Every bucket, cask and billy round the place was filled, but it wasn't until the water was below the level of the holes that it stopped flowing. By then the tank was half empty and the Christmas dinner was ruined. Tom disappeared for the afternoon into the scrub. The other boys spoke up in his defence and said it was an accident that could have happened to any of them, and surely Father wasn't going to hold that against Tom for life.

"No, not for life," said Father, "but at least until it rains." Then he snatched up the gun and slugs, and put them on top of his wardrobe, where they stayed for a long time. An hour's lecture on the use and misuse of firearms preceded Father's handing the airgun back, but before Christmas came round again Frank nearly lost an eye to the airgun.

Charlie, sitting on the front step of the old house, was firing at a small tin. Suddenly Frank walked into the line of fire and fell to the ground. Charlie helped him up, rushed him to the stable, and laid him on a couple of sheaves of hay. Then, with a pocket-knife, he probed until he removed the piece of lead embedded in Frank's eyebrow. To prevent the airgun being confiscated again, Charlie drove a nail into a very dangerous corner-post at the height of Frank's eyebrow, and rehearsed Frank over and over again as to how the accident was supposed to have happened.

The phone was installed the year after a Christmas when

George was ill. It was a party line, shared with about eight of our neighbours.

Because the cable for our phone had to be tunnelled under the railway line, our party-line members blames us for any faults. We couldn't resist listening in to their calls; and when we heard them abusing our phone we almost had to bite our tongues to stop from chipping in and telling them that *we* could hear them very well.

Mr Pollitt was one who realized we used to listen. In fact he often asked up to hang up, adding that he'd ring us later and tell us who he'd been ringing and why. But we knew the jerkiness of his ring and hated to miss any of his calls.

"This is 2G speaking," he'd shout; then, "G for Jesus."

We'd fall over each other to get to the phone first. "Chase the speckled rooster away," someone would whisper with a hand over the mouthpiece; for his peculiar crow would let everyone know we were listening.

Everyone had some 'give-away'. Mrs Pollitt's chair squeaked; and Mrs Brown had a habit of sniffing every few minutes; and we always knew when the Kents were on the line by the loud ticking of their clock. But no one seemed to mind. Nearly everyone expected it, and would often draw those listening in into the conversation.

Getting the phone on seemed to alter us in some way. For a long time we found it hard to lend our rubbers or rulers to those who didn't have a phone; we seemed to have so little in common with them. We felt sorry for the Bryces because we knew they'd never be able to afford such a thing as a phone. It seemed a shame.

A 'GO-IN' WITH UNCLE

ONE OF the worst rows any of us had with Uncle was the time he and Marj had the 'go-in' over his greyhound dog Skeeta. Marj was separating and, needing another cream-basin, she let the separator run while she hurried to the kitchen. When she returned she found the greyhound lapping at the milk-bucket.

"Get out, you mongrel!" she shouted, and swung him a kick as he went out the door. Uncle came round the corner just in time to see it all.

"Call him a mongrel?" he roared. "Why, he's better bred than you are." He glared at Marj, wishing she were a man so that he could defend his dog.

Marj, used to these skirmishes, ducked under his arm and went on with her job. Uncle stood in the doorway and went on talking furiously. Marj turned her back on him and began to sing. Uncle walked off in disgust. Marj didn't know he was gone until she went to the kitchen for hot water to flush the separator; then she saw that he'd taken his axe and was chopping hell out of a log, which he usually did when he was fighting mad and had no one to fight with.

When she came back to the separator she met Skeeta slinking out of the door, this time licking cream off his chops. She let fly with the saucepan of hot water. Uncle dropped the axe, ran at Marj, and let fly with a piece of wood. Marj fled to the kitchen pursued by Uncle, his eyes blazing and the veins on his scrawny neck standing out like twine.

They ran round the kitchen table twice. Then Marj shot out the back door with Uncle, clutching a loaf of bread from the table, close behind. "I'll brain you, I will!" he roared as he raced out the side gate. But she doubled back through the fence, leaving long strands of hair on the barbed wire. Back they came through the kitchen, making for the front door this time, and the dry patch of ground we called the garden—Marj zig-zagging this way and that, Uncle still clutching the loaf of bread.

Suddenly he cornered her and let fly. She ducked, and the bread went over her head into a post; but he'd thrown it with such force that it hit her as it bounced back. Marj screamed, and when Mother arrived on the scene she was in tears. Uncle was just standing there, stupefied.

"And what do you think you're doing?" Mother asked.

"She threw hot water over Skeeta and no one's going to do that to my dog and get away with it!"

"He was at the cream when I went in with the hot water, so I threw it over him," sobbed Marj.

"And what right," Mother demanded of Uncle, "have you to go throwing good bread about?"

The sound of a crash saved Uncle from having to reply, and they all raced to the separator room. When they got there, Skeeta was again slinking out the door. While the chase was on he had gone back and finished off the cream and, trying to lick

out the last drops, had knocked the basin from the stand and smashed it.

"That's finished it, Charlie," Mother said quietly. "Either you keep that dog on the chain, or you know what you can do."

Uncle took Skeeta to the shed and tied him up. Then he went back and chopped an armful of wood. That didn't relieve his state of mind, so he put his axe away and stalked off up the paddock.

"I'll bet he's going to earmark Baldy," Mother said. We watched him march into the cow-paddock, settle his precious boxer hat firmly on his head, and start chasing the half-grown calf. Any other time he'd have asked one of the boys to give him a hand, but not today.

After much running, swearing and panting, he managed to

lasso Baldy. Then the tussle began. One minute he'd be dragging the calf, the next minute the calf would be dragging him. And through it all the hat stayed firmly on Uncle's head.

Finally Uncle proved the more determined, and turned the earmarked calf loose in the house-paddock. He had closed the gate and was taking a short cut through the small, stoutly fenced paddock when Bingo the Jersey bull came galloping up. The activity had roused Bingo's fighting spirit; he pawed the ground and threw up dirt for yards around.

"Get back, you!" shouted Uncle as he made a running swipe at Bingo with a cow-yoke. But Bingo was in no mood to be bluffed. He threw up another shower of dirt and advanced menacingly. Yard by yard, step by step, he closed in on Uncle. Uncle stood his ground till Bingo was about six feet away, then bolted for the nearest tree with Bingo after him.

It was a huge old gum-tree with no low-hanging branches, and since Bingo didn't stop Uncle had to keep circling the tree. Just as we hurried down to help him, he made a sharp dash for the fence. He reached it with a few feet to spare, and as he threw himself through his braces caught on the barbed wire. There was a rending of cloth, and the buttons on the back of his pants flew into the air as he fell on his face in the dirt.

He was dirt from head to toe; his bushy eyebrows sprouted bits of leaves, and dry grass and twigs stuck to the dust on his face. His trousers were ripped in several places, oddly white skin shone through. And the junction of his braces had slipped up his back until it was tight behind his neck so that he was forced to stoop.

He brushed himself down a bit, then bent to pick up his hat. It wasn't there. He began frantically searching for it.

He needn't have bothered. On the other side of the fence, the calf was watching Bingo horning the hat: the hat that had been part of Uncle all these years. Each time the hat landed, Bingo would make another ferocious run at it, catch it on his horns and flip it into the air.

Uncle just couldn't face us. He turned his back and stumbled off to the stable; a tough, wiry little man slinking off with the back of his trousers almost down to the tail-end of his shirt, and the torn strips flapping in the breeee. But we didn't feel like laughing.

When he disappeared into the stable we looked at the hat

and then at each other. It was now completely ruined. Not one of us could find anything to say.

SNAKES WE MET

"Don't play in the chaff-shed," was one of Father's constant warnings. "There may be snakes there. And keep away from the haystack, there may be snakes there too." And Mother was always telling us to keep out of the wheat-crop, and off the thatched roof of the stable, for fear of snakes.

Strange to say, we had more snakes in the house and around it than I ever remember round the sheds. But I suppose the ones away from the house didn't create much excitement and were soon forgotten, whereas the snakes round the house certainly livened things up.

When we lived in the old house there was a huge, black, shiny one that Mother, without knowing it, shared a nightly mug of water with for weeks. Each night she put a mug of water on the dressing-table near her, in case any of us should wake and want a drink. In the morning it would be almost empty, though she'd only taken a sip or two from it and none of us had been in her room.

One night she woke to hear a slither and a plop beside her bed. Almost stiff with fright, she managed to strike a match in time to see the tail of her drinking companion disappear through a hole in the paper-covered, hessian-lined wall.

She woke Father, and got him to light a lamp in each of our bedrooms. They examined the hole, and found a darkish, greasy ring round the edge of it. Since they also found several such holes in our rooms—all as greasy—they spent a worried night.

At first light Uncle Charlie was called in, and Mother couldn't get us all shepherded into the washhouse quickly enough to please him. He was like one of those tough snake-killing dogs, prancing around with a 'let-me-at-him' expression. He had no fear whatever of snakes, and no sense of property either. It was the same when there was a blowfly or moth buzzing round the lamp—he'd get it, even if he broke a lamp-glass or two. And now here he was with a butcher's knife, slashing Mother's prized paper off the walls; while Father stood at the door with the snake-killing stick and the older boys stood guard outside, each with a stick or a bent piece of wire.

Even the ceiling did not escape, for everywhere the paper-covered hessian had sagged Uncle slashed, and, standing on a ladder, popped his head through; though how he would have killed a snake with just his head I don't know.

When he failed to find his quarry in the walls or the ceiling he turned to the earthen floor. After a great deal of digging, he found the hole between the hessian and the mud wall. He then dug the snake out and killed it, but by that time we didn't have very much house left.

One day Ann and I were home on our own when we saw a snake disappear under the new house. We wondered how we could coax it out and kill it ourselves, surprising the family.

"You watch; see it doesn't come out," Ann said. She then went inside and came out carrying an old mouth-organ of George's. "Snakes love music, so I'll play to it while you stand quietly on the top of the steps. When I've coaxed it out, you kill it."

Being neither musical or clever, I had to agree. Then Ann decided she'd better not let the snake see her; so she climbed a tree about twenty yards from the house and played for two hours straight the only tune she knew: 'Jesus bids us shine'.

This is how the family found us when they arrived home. We thought that as we'd risked our lives for them they'd make a great fuss of us, but they weren't impressed. We hadn't done our homework, and Father and Mother seemed to think this more important.

Then there was the time that Uncle Charlie was topping off a stack when he was bitten on the leg by a snake thrown up to him in a sheaf of hay. He killed it with his pitchfork, slid off the stack, bustled up to the house, cut and bled the bite, washed it in Condy's crystals, tied a rag dipped in kerosene round his leg, and, when Father wanted to drive him to the doctor, stared at him in disgust. "Can't you see that storm coming, man? If you want that stack finished, let's get back and finish it." In the morning we were very surprised to find Uncle still with us, none the worse.

We saw lots of snakes on the railway line on our way to and from school. The embankment was a breeding-ground for rabbits, and young rabbits make ideal prey for snakes. My brother Charlie tallied twenty-two in one year on the railway line alone, rushing his dinner down each day to go looking for them.

I was always terrified of snakes; but I must say that the two I met behaved in a gentlemanly way.

One day I was down on my knees, squeezing into a low chicken-coop to gather eggs, when I came face to face with a splendid snake. It bowed past me, almost apologising for beating me to the eggs, slid through the wire netting, and was gone.

Then another day, at the lonely little building up the yard, a snake pulled back as I went to enter. If it had been wearing a hat it would have raised it; its expression and manner so clearly said, "No, you go first. Ladies before gents."

UNCLE CHARLIE'S TRIP TO SYDNEY

I HAD an abscess on my right knee and was home from school. Mother had made up a bed for me on the kitchen sofa, close to the stove, where a never-ending change of hot linseed-oil poultices simmered, each one seeming to burn me more than the last.

Father was stamping round cursing the south wind—the "perishin' southerly". Every time anyone opened the back door, the wind swept in and swirled charcoal and ashes from the wood-stove, scattering them over the floor. The south wind always put Mother in a bad mood because over the years the stove had slowly shifted out from the back of the chimney; not only would it belch smoke into the kitchen each time the back door was opened, but it wouldn't draw properly. Bread would come out doughy, sodden and white, even if Mother used the good bull-oak wood she saved for special occasions.

Things were just anyhow at our place the day of my abscess, for the 'perishin' southerly' had chilled Father to the bone and made him decide to stay indoors straightening up his after-harvest accounts.

Uncle too found an indoor job. "Bring out anything you want soldered," he told Mother. This suggestion was so rare around our place that in a matter of minutes Mother was able to produce a kettle-lid, several saucepans, a bucket, the sifter-handle, the egg-beater, and the tap to the big black fountain.

Father sat there with his glasses on the end of his nose and multiplied, divided, added up and took away, all in a loud half-chant. Every now and then he'd stop working and rave about what it cost to keep a roof over our heads. Several times he appealed to Mother. She produced her little ready-reckoner and flung it on the table in front of him.

The boys, who were mending and greasing harness, had a bucket of unsalted mutton-fat, blacklead, and neatsfoot-oil melting down on top of the stove. The smell was vile.

Uncle was heating his soldering iron on the stove, too. As he was doing his soldering in the washhouse, the wind cooled the iron so that he had to keep galloping back and forth between the washhouse and the stove. Every time, Father would shout "Shut that blasted door!" and the cockatoo in his cage outside would give a follow-up screech—"Shut that blasted door!" They were having quite a busy time, for every time Uncle opened the door great rolls of black smoke filled the kitchen; and Father, with smarting eyes, had to gather up his papers that were flying about the room and start again. The scalloped paper on the shelves would flap, all the calendars on the wall would dance, the curtains would fling out their shirt-tails, and dried herbs tied in paper bags would spin and twirl from the ceiling.

After Father had gathered up his papers about ten times, his patience gave out. "Must you keep opening and closing that door, Charlie? Why do you have to pick today to do your soldering?"

"If that's all the thanks a feller gets," Uncle snapped, "you can do your own soldering." He turned to stalk out the back door.

"Oh no, you don't," Father said. "You can go out the front door."

Mother glared at Father. She was mad because so little soldering had been done. Dinner was a wordless affair. As soon as the dishes were done, Mother went up to the front part of the house to tidy out some drawers.

The boys took their bucket of vile-smelling grease to the stable; Uncle took his dogs and went off to shoot a few rabbits; I quietly sewed some dolls' clothes; and Father was able to work until the children came home from school.

From then on, he and the cockatoo had a very busy time.

The kitchen was like a madhouse. At last he ordered everyone out of the room, jammed a chair under the door-knob, and proceeded to work in peace. Then Uncle Charlie, not knowing about the chair under the door-knob, tried to barge in with an armful of wood. Finding his way obstructed, he tried force.

"I'll fix you!" Father yelled, whipping the chair out from the door and grabbing for the nearest weapon. It was a school-bag full of books. As the door cracked open he swung it high and brought it down, whop, on Uncle's astonished head.

The veins in Uncle's neck swelled till he looked like a frill-necked lizard. For a second he was stunned, then, freeing his arms for battle, he threw the wood on Father's feet. Father was so nonplussed at having walloped his brother instead of one of those 'confounded boys' that even the wood dropping on his feet failed to rouse him.

But Uncle wasn't stupefied. With a lightning blow to the nose he shattered Father's glasses. Mother, hearing the crash, rushed in, but the room was so full of smoke that she had trouble in understanding what had happened.

As soon as she realized, however, she led Father out to the tank, dabbing at his wounds with a wet cloth. I hurried out to join the throng of children watching. Uncle strode in lonely state to the stable, and the cockatoo kept screeching "Shut the blasted door!" Father leaned back against the tank, still dumbfounded, and kept repeating, over and over, "How was I to know it was him? How was I to know?"

Shortly afterwards, Uncle drove up in his gig and tied the horse to the fence. We knew then that he was going away. He was in the old house so long that Mother, curious, sent one of the youngsters over to ask if he'd be home to tea.

No, he would certainly not be home to tea. When he'd gathered all his stuff together he'd be setting out for Sydney.

Father, hearing this, seemed to wake up. "What, going to Sydney?" He shook his head, sadly. "I must go over and tell him I'm sorry. After all, I hit him first, and he is my only relative——"

He hurried over to the old house, met Uncle struggling under the weight of his tin trunk, and turned and followed him. We could tell by the way he was shaking his head and throwing his hands up that he was pleading with Uncle; but Uncle wouldn't speak to him. Father continued to plead until at last Uncle said, very coldly and firmly, that since it was probable he would never see any of us again, he would not go away refusing to eat a last meal with us.

So he stayed to tea, but he had no appetite. Father kept passing him things, and he kept coldly refusing them. Both left the table before we were halfway through our pudding, and went back to the old house. It seemed to be only Mother and us Uncle was put-out with now, for we watched him shake hands with Father, then get up in the gig. We watched Father open the gate for Uncle, and close it after him. Then, with a quick wave of his hand, Uncle was gone.

When Father came back he no longer seemed to be on our side; the way he acted you would have thought it was Mother who had punched his nose. Mother appeared unconcerned. She was mixing a batch of bread which she knew was sure to be spoiled in the baking, for there was no bull-oak and the southerly was still blowing.

Two days later, Uncle drove in the gate. Old Bess was in the shafts of the gig—but one of its wheels was gone, and in itsplace was a high buggy-wheel. So the gig had a terrific tilt that kept Uncle tipped down to one end of the seat. We flocked around, and it took several seconds for Mother to control her sniggering and say, "I thought you were going to Sydney!"

Uncle looked quite amazed. "What? Me, going to Sydney? You must be mad! I haven't been to Sydney since the Prince of Wales was here."

He explained that he would have been home three days ago (he'd only been gone two) if it hadn't been for breaking his gig-wheel, which caused him to wait in town for another wheel. We heard the true story later: Uncle had not got past the first pub. Some of the lads at the hotel had removed the gig-wheel, replaced it with the buggy-wheel, tied the reins to the dash-board, laid Uncle unconscious in the bottom of the gig, and, with a slap on the old mare's rump, sent her home.

He looked far from bright. Nobody was surprised when he went straight to bed.

Next morning, however, he was bustling round the house. As soon as breakfast was over he and Father set to and pulled out the stove, bricked it in afresh, and added extra bricks to the chimney-top. Then they carted in a whole wagon-load of wood, and most of it good, dry bull-oak. And then they cut up the whole lot of it, without waiting for Mother to sing out that the wood-box was empty.

The wind had swung to the west.

PEOPLE AT SCHOOL

FOR the first week I was back at school we were all driven there and back, as I still couldn't walk very well. This was great fun when one of the boys drove; but when Father was the driver I used to feel that even with my hoppy leg I would have raced the buggy to school. The lucky ones sitting at the back had several ways of brightening the journey. We would slip over the back of the buggy, place our feet on the back axle, and hang on by main strength. Or we would lean backwards until another inch would have had us falling on our necks, and hang head down; the strange view of buggy wheels going round, ground sliding by, and clumps of grass bobbing up was entrancing. We would drop over the back, hanging on with our hands, and let ourselves be dragged along; this act was very hard on our boots and caused lots of work for Mother, who was the family boot-mender.

We weren't driven to school very often. It had to be very wet, the buggy in good order, the horse easy to catch, and one of the men not too busy to drive. Otherwise we walked or stayed at home. If it came on to rain hard while we were at school, we girls were sometimes asked to stay at the Pollitts'. This was fun, but not as much fun as it would have been to stay at the Bryces'. Ann and I never went to the trouble of praying that it would be wet so that we would have to stay at the Pollitts'.

The Pollitts lived within shouting distance of the school; and Mrs Pollitt, who was an invalid, often wanted one of her children to come home. But she never shouted for them. Instead she used a bottle, which she kept beside her. When she banged this once against the corrugated-iron wall of the house, it meant that she wanted one of the boys. Two bangs close together caused the girls to look at each other and decide which one would go, then, getting a nod from the teacher, hurry off.

Mr Pollitt did the washing at week-ends, and the children did the household jobs, so all Mrs Pollitt had to do was to sit down and direct things. She spent the day sitting in a big old deck-chair on the front verandah. Mrs Pollitt's stoop and the chair fitted each other very well; and there Mrs Pollitt sat all day and watched the school.

I can't remember the Pollitts having a bath all through their school days. We had a bath every Saturday night; and if we were going to a picnic, or the Show or anything, we always had a bath the night before. Bath night was always wash-head night with us, and Ann and I would beg Mother to put our hair up in rags which, though uncomfortable for sleeping, would leave us with long, beautiful ringlets the next day.

It was never like that with the Pollitt girls. They had long, heavy plaits, and their hair was washed once a year—in February, just before school started.

I never found out what was wrong with Percy Pollitt's hair.

When he took off his hat there was always as much hair matted inside the hat as on his head. Poor Percy! He had sandy-coloured hair, weak-looking, red-rimmed eyes, and teeth like a fox. Big as he was, he never seemed to mind coming to school with his throat wrapped up for half the year.

In late autumn, strips of new grey flannel, well soaked in camphor, were sewn around the necks of the Pollitt family, and these remained in place until well into spring. They were then replaced with plain strips of sheeting for a week or so before the spring breezes were allowed to tickle their naked necks. The Pollitts hadn't any faith in doctors since the time Mr Pollitt took his wife along. The doctor asked if they had a woodheap, and then if there were a fence near it. He then told Mrs Pollitt that he wanted her to go home and throw all the wood over the fence, then throw it all back again next day; he'd like her to do that every day for a fortnight, then come back and see him again.

That ended doctors for the Pollitts.

Ann and I stayed with this family many a wet night. Although at school we didn't like the Pollitt children nearly as much as we liked the Bryces, we liked them well enough in their own home, where we didn't have Renie and May Bryce to compare with them.

At about this time Renie and May Bryce and Ann and I discovered that the water in our little dam came just to our middles, making it an excellent swimming-pool. We'd been warned away from dams from the time we could walk, so we'd never had a chance to try swimming until now.

We had several old curtains that we used for towels, and we dried them out on a bush. And the care we had to take of our hair! And how careful we were to make sure we'd left no mud on ourselves or our clothes, for Mother would have come down on us like a haystack.

One day when the dam had dried up until there was more mud than water in it, Renie was flopping around pretending she was swimming, shouting to us to watch her. In her excitement she opened her large, frog-shaped mouth under the water and scooped up a slimy, silver tadpole.

Before she could spit it out she swallowed it. We left the water, all feeling a little sick—all but Renie. She said it didn't hurt, it didn't taste, and she didn't feel any different.

Sitting on the edge of the dam with just our skins on, we

began discussing what would happen to the tadpole. Then a terrible thought struck us—what would happen to Renie? We didn't know much about sex, and at last we decided that if the tadpole Renie had swallowed was a female everything would probably be all right; but if it were a male, we hated to think what might happen to Renie.

For weeks after that the rest of us kept looking at her and asking her did she feel any different. And even though she said she didn't feel any different, every time we saw seven magpies together we crossed our fingers and wished hard for Renie. Our wishes may have come true, for Renie's life went on as before. . . .

What with tennis, football, and going to dances, Marj and the older boys began to 'knock up quite a good time'. Getting the boys off to sport on Saturday was Mother's big headache. Even though the copper would always be boiling, their clothes laid out in neat piles on their beds, and their dinner ready for them, every one of the boys was always late every Saturday. Mother was always in such a state of nervous exhaustion by the time the last of them had got away that she would not feel like eating dinner at all.

Father would nobly announce, "The kiddies and I will do the dishes for you, Jane," but before he and Mother had finished we'd be over the railway line, or down at the fowlhouse playing 'ladies'.

One day Ann and I came across a bottle of wine when we had sneaked into Uncle's room and were going through his trunk. The next day was Saturday, and we thought it would be a pleasant change if, instead of serving the teapot drainings for our 'ladies' afternoon tea, we served wine. So we emptied some of Uncle's wine into another bottle. Then we took the cold tea from breakfast and carefully strained it into Uncle's bottle to bring it up to the previous level.

We waited excitedly for the morning to pass, and began serving our afternoon 'tea' the moment we could slip away from the dinner-table. Sipping our wine in the fowlhouse, our little fingers sticking well out, we saw Mr Gregory call to take Uncle Charlie to football. He and Uncle Charlie headed for the old house, and came out about five minutes later wiping their mouths with satisfaction. We tittered at the thought of the wine warming our blood while the cold tea warmed theirs.

When the family were safely out of the way, Ann and I

moved into the sun and sat leaning against the fowlhouse wall. The sun was gloriously warm after a long cold winter. It was a hen-cackling day. White butterflies danced on new grass; the wheat paddock seemed to change to a fresh green while we looked at it; the scrub seemed taller and closer. As we sat and sipped, the wine rested comfortably in our tummies, sending exciting messages to our heads, arms and legs.

Then things began to grow a bit hazy, and the longer we sat in the sun and sipped the hazier they became. Sun and wine started our chilblains itching, and the more we rubbed the more they itched.

"It's the blood all blocked up in there," I explained to Ann.

"Well," she asked, "why don't you let the blood out?"

By that time I felt brave enough for anything, so, with Uncle's razor, I cut a cross on my toe. The way the blood gushed out, you'd have thought I'd cut off a chook's head. Then Ann cut a cross through the centre of one of her heels, and this too bled freely. After that we were sure they felt better. We were feeling so whoozy and light-headed that the blood clotting on the ground under our feet didn't seem to be connected with us.

"Does the ground keep jumping up at you?" I asked.

"No," she said, "but the haystack's going round and round."

I began to feel very strange; my eyes refused to stay open. When I woke up again, Ann was propped against my shoulder snoring in a loud, chortling snore, her mouth agape like a hole in a sock. Our cuts hadn't bled much, but we were covered with hen-lice.

I woke Ann up, and we agreed that we felt terrible. We staggered away as though we had to drag heavy chains as we walked; our heads were too heavy; our tummies squelched like half-churned butter, and nothing we looked at was on an even keel.

After we'd been violently sick we felt better. We chewed mouthfuls of eucalyptus leaves, but we were still very uncomfortable. When we had to go in for tea we felt so awful that we waited through the whole meal for someone to say something; but no one even looked at us. We itched everywhere, from head to toe, with hen-lice, but we didn't dare scratch for fear of drawing attention. When at last we got into a bath it was one of the loveliest moments of our lives.

That was the finish of us and wine—never again!

THE MURPHYS

OUR district didn't really come to life until the Murphys moved in. Ever since it had been known that they were coming, the local people had been arguing about them. Some said they were wealthy and owned a piano, a striking-clock and crystal chandeliers; but old Mrs Sullivan said she'd known Shane Murphy all his life and she'd be surprised if Ben Martin ever received more than the deposit on his mallee-block, which the Murphys were buying.

Mother, maybe spurred on by curiosity, offered to go and help the Murphys settle in. When she got back she had lots to tell us.

They did have a piano and a striking-clock, but the chandeliers turned out to be a candlestick with long crystal droppers hanging from it—and even that looked out of place in the old mud-and-daub house with its earthen floors. We were invited to visit them two Sundays later, and it seemed an eternity to have to wait. When the day did arrive we even helped round the house, so anxious were we to be on our way.

No sooner had we arrived than the Murphy boys and girls and ours were up in the scrub, hunting. Father and Mr Murphy spent the afternoon in an earnest inspection of the farm. Mother sat in the kitchen and talked while Mrs Murphy ran up a batch of scones and cakes.

"Wretched varmints," said Mrs Murphy. "Ate the batch I ran up yesterday."

Every time Mrs Murphy turned her back the young Murphys—those about my age and younger—took turns to sneak into the kitchen and pinch things. They not only pinched luxuries such as currants and coconut, but they took everyday things—sugar, sago, salt, things they couldn't have wanted— just for the fun of stealing them.

The marauding Murphys had two lines of approach. The older ones went in pairs, and while one was raiding, say, the salt, the other drew attention to herself by pretending to raid the sugar. When the first had been successful she would bustle outside with her spoil, leaving the other to chat to her mother for a moment before coming out for her share. The younger fry mainly relied on darting methods. They would dart into the kitchen, dart out again, in again, out again, until their mother hardly knew whether they were there or not. Then they made their unholy swoops, raiding what was handiest. And this would be shared equally as soon as they were out the back door.

Should Mrs Murphy catch one of her offspring in a pinching act she'd make a half-hearted swipe with the oven-cloth. "Wretched varmints!" she'd say, but by then the child would be out the back door.

And all the time the speckled hen and her chicks wandered in and out of the kitchen, much as if they were Murphys. Any crumb or scrap dropped by Mrs Murphy hardly hit the floor before it was gobbled up. Mrs Murphy walked with a foot-swinging action to shoo the chicks from under her feet.

A wire-netted box stood near the piano where it had been put the day they moved in, only now it was lying on its side and one corner of the netting had been rolled back. That, we discovered, was where the hen and chicks slept each night. And the box was very handy, for two of the 'varmints' sat on it to have their tea.

On our way home we discussed the Murphys and voted them by far the most exciting of any of our neighbours.

"Yes," said Father, "they're like ourselves—mightn't have much, but they're happy."

Mrs Murphy's calm acceptance of the unusual behaviour of her offspring shocked Mother; but after what happened with Harry Henderson, Mother was no longer surprised at anything the Murphys got up to. Our family happened to go over there again that Saturday, and Mother and Mrs Murphy were having a cup of tea when we rushed in to tell them that a man with a gig was turning in at their gate.

"Oh, good heavens!" Mother said. "It's Harry Henderson. He's the sewing-machine man. You'll have him here all the afternoon if you're not careful. Then he'll stay the night, and you'll end up giving him tea and breakfast, and his horse too feeds as well."

"Ask him in for a cup of tea, Shane," Mrs Murphy called out to Mr Murphy.

"You'll be sorry," Mother told her. "I'm warning you, you just can't get rid of him." Mrs Murphy chuckled, and whispered something to her son Shammie.

Harry Henderson came in, introduced himself, and stated his business. He said hello to Mother, but he knew he had no hope of selling Mother another sewing machine, so he gushed over Mrs Murphy's scones and tea. "The best scones I've ever tasted. It takes a country woman to make tea, doesn't it, Shane?"

Harry made a sale only by wearing his customer down, so he was soon chattering like a chaff-cutter, and the sewing machine was brought in for a demonstration. Frank had his hanging cuff sewn on while he was still wearing the shirt; Mrs Murphy worked a fancy design on a teatowel; Mr Murphy mended a saddle-cloth. Harry, seeing they were enjoying themselves, relaxed and allowed the machine to sell itself. He strolled over to the fire and spread his hands to the warmth.

He looked less happy when his eyes roved over the furniture: the kerosene-box shelves; the slab table supported by saplings driven into the earthen floor; the piano-case serving as a kitchen dresser. But his face brightened as he took in the piano, the clock, and the crystal candlestick. He relaxed, expanded, and smiled. The pendulum of the clock swung backwards and forwards. Mr Henderson was in no hurry.

Shammie, who had been heating a soldering-iron in the fire, looked as though he too were well satisfied with things. With a sly, quick lunge, he popped the soldering iron into Harry's outstretched hand.

Harry let out a piercing scream. He flew at Shammie, letting out with his fist and a well-polished shoe. When Mr Murphy rushed to Shammie's aid Harry took to his heels, scattering us round the kitchen as he bolted for the door.

There he was met by Mike with a gun in his hand.

Mike had a wild, mad look. His nostrils were dilated, his hair stood straight up on end, he showed the whites of his eyes, and his head rolled from side to side. Slowly he lifted the gun. . . .

Mrs Murphy screamed. "Shane! Oh, Shane, Mike's out, and he's got a gun! Oh, Shane, do something, quick! Mike's going to shoot the poor man!" To Harry, blocked in the doorway, she explained, "Oh, our poor Mike's mad . . . mad as a hatter, ever since he had sunstroke last summer, and we have to keep him locked up but he must have got out. I'll attract his attention while you get away, and please, never ever come back. You seem to upset him."

Mike, still rolling his head and swivelling his eyes, began to creep nearer the door, but Mrs Murphy bravely placed herself

between the lunatic and Harry. Harry, finding his pathway clear, took off for his gig as if devils were after him.

Mrs Murphy bent double with laughter. When she recovered she congratulated the boys on their fine acting and timing. Turning to Mother she said timing was important in matters like this, and didn't our mother agree?

Mother looked at Mrs Murphy, looked at us, looked at Mike, looked at Mrs Murphy again, and for once in her life remained silent.

Mr Murphy suggested that Mike had better wash the soap out of his hair and knock it down a bit because it fair gave him the creeps. That was all he said, but he had a funny proud look on his face.

After this Mother always had an excuse why we couldn't go to the Murphys'. The Murphy boys' acting and timing became so perfect in matters like this that it provided them with many sample tins of grease and kerosene. In the end, no salesman would go within coo-ee of their place.

MISS FLOWERS AND I

FOR the two years Miss Flowers was at our school she never smiled. Her favourite quotation was "The world is full of sin", and she brought out the worst in all of us.

She was a little brown mouse of a woman who darted everywhere, but there was nothing mouselike about the way she would suddenly roar if things didn't suit her.

Each morning she came to school wearing the same little brown hat with a bird's wing perched on the side, and with a brown leather handbag under her arm. She always placed the bag on a certain shelf in the cupboard, with her hat on top; then she'd padlock the cupboard and hang the key round her neck with a brown shoelace.

During school hours, whenever she unlocked the cupboard, popped the little brown hat on her head, and clutched her bag under her arm, it was a sign that she was about to pay a darting visit to the little building in the corner of the yard.

Many were the schemes we hatched to bring about her destruction. The Murphy boys rigged up a fine wire across her track, hoping to trip her up; and our boys walked out of their way each night for weeks to torment a nesting magpie in the hope that it would attack Miss Flowers. And though I did no more than the others to antagonize her I was always in trouble at school. When Mother had a talk with her about me, Miss Flowers said she realized we didn't get along well together, and added that this was because our natures were so much alike. When I heard this I was so indignant that Mother had a hard job to make me go to school the next day.

Mother promised me that if I worked well and got a Merit Certificate I could leave school at the end of the year and not wait till I was fourteen. Spurred on by this promise, I didn't have to sit for my Merit Certificate; the inspector recommended me on my year's work. On the Friday of that week I packed my books and left school for good: for my good and Miss Flowers', at any rate.

I was happy doing things I'd been thought too young to be

trusted with while I was at school. Mother encouraged me to make puddings, bake cakes, and iron the men's shirts. Because I always helped with the milking and separating, she gave me a few shillings every month from the milk cheque. As soon as I became a 'shareholder', my milking and separating methods went through a sudden change. No longer did I let the milk run over on the ground when I'd filled one bucket and didn't feel like making another trip to empty it. I improved my separating, too; instead of varying the pace at which I turned, I now turned evenly at the ideal speed.

Marj and I got on very well together when Ann was away at school. Nothing else around the place altered at all. Everyone still sang, still laughed, and still squabbled. Father and the cockatoo still shouted to us to "Shut that blasted door!" Mother still told us we were all as mad as rabbits. Uncle's dogs and ours still found something to fight about. Ann still seemed a child.

Only I had altered. I had suddenly grown up.

A Song of Rain

Mile on mile from Mallacoota
Runs the news, and far Baroota
Speeds it over hill and plain,
Till the slogan of the rain
Rolls afar to Yankalilla;
Wallaroo and Wirrawilla
Shout it o'er the leagues between,
Telling of the dawning green.
Frogs at Cocoroc are croaking,
Booboorowie soil is soaking,
Oodla Wirra, Orroroo
Breathe relief and hope anew.
Wycheproof and Wollongong
Catch the burden of the song
That is rolling, rolling ever
O'er the plains of Never Never
Sounding in each mountain rill,
Echoing from hill to hill . . .
In the lonely, silent places
Men lift up their glad, wet faces,
And their thanks ask no explaining—
It is raining—raining—raining!

C. J. DENNIS

EVE POWNALL

A Younger Land

IF TIME were a whirligig we could spin the years around to
look back at the families who lived in Australia more than a
hundred years ago. We could twirl away the Australia we know
with its towns and cities spread along the roads like beads on a
string, and the millions of people who live around the coast and
through the inland. Instead, we could see Australia as the early
settlers saw it when they came ashore from the sailing ships to
raise their families and live in a quiet, empty, unknown land.

Life was hard for those who came on the convict ships. There
were not enough clothes, bedding or other goods to go round.
What was worse: food was very scarce. Everyone, including the
children, received a ration of food each week from the Government Store. Even babies under eighteen months old were
allowed one pound of salt meat a week.

The food was mostly flour or rice, and corned beef or pork,
known as salt junk. Sometimes there was fish for the family meal
if the boats made a catch in the harbour, but no one could be
sure that any would be caught. Men went hunting in the bush
with muskets but they weren't very successful either because the
bush animals soon learnt to stay away from the area around
the camp.

Anything that could be caught was eaten. Rats, crows,
snakes and lizards made a good meal for many early arrivals.
One man wrote home to England that he had dined on 'a fine
dog'. He said it was very good and he hoped to have another
meal like it.

It was fresher than the meat served out by the Government
Store which was over three years old before the next supplies
were received. And it was certainly better than the meat at the
settlement in Hobart. This was bad when it was put into the
casks in England, so it was terrible when handed out to the
convicts and their families.

But there were plenty of kangaroos in the bush near Hobart

Town and their meat was a welcome change from the ever-lasting salt junk. Better still was a sumptuous meal of black swans, caught on the Derwent River and served to the prisoners for Christmas 1806.

That was a one-time-only treat, however. In the early years at Hobart scarcely anyone had enough to eat in spite of the kangaroos. The prisoners became weak and ill and the livestock died.

At Norfolk Island, prisoners and their families fared a little better in the mutton bird season. When the birds arrived to make their nests, the convicts ate the eggs and cooked the birds for dinner.

Vegetables were scarce also, and the settlers made do with native plants which they found were suitable to eat. The children must have helped to pick wild celery, spinach and parsley to take back to the little huts. Even when other settlements were made in other parts of the country years later those native plants helped in the family meal. One family found the wild celery very tasty in making pea soup.

Later still when settlers moved so far out that bullock drays took many months to bring supplies from town, the wild plants were served for dinner. Rosa Campbell Praed who was a child on a Queensland station in the 1850s said the family ate mutton, pumpkin (which grew easily), and a plant called fathen, day after day for weeks when the drays were held up by floods along the track.

But not everyone had to eat weeds in place of vegetables, or have only mutton, mutton, mutton served up every day. Annabella Boswell in the 1830s and 1840s never had that experience at all. She remembered that splendid melons grew on the river bank near her home, and pumpkins so large that she was certain they were the kind the Fairy Godmother turned into Cinderella's coach.

At her home near Bathurst the family grew its own wheat. Annabella saw it growing in the fields, then harvested with reaping hooks, and eventually ground into flour in steel hand-mills. She said wheat ground that way made the best dampers. But they had plenty of other food as well:·

We often rose early to go . . . to the milking yard for mugs of new milk, warm and frothy, from our favourite cows. Butter and cheese were made for home use, and occasionally for the Sydney market.

We had a variety of jams and jellies, dried apples and peaches, and preserved grapes for use until late in the season by covering them with paper bags while still on the vines, which bags we had, of course, to make.

'We had a great variety of poultry, and more eggs than we could possibly use. Delicious cakes were of everyday use, sugar being the only thing we had to buy. Our Highland maid was a famous baker of bread, and made also delicious rolls and scones. Sometimes we children made a cake and had it baked in primitive fashion on the hot·hearth under an inverted pot with hot coals piled on the top.

Annabella Boswell was born in 1826, in the days before coaches and trains, and when roads were few and not well made. Yet Annabella's family, like other people of the day, never stayed at home if there was a good reason for travelling. When she was twelve years old she went with her family from Bathurst to Port Macquarie north of Sydney. The whole journey was more than 500 miles.

A bullock dray loaded with tents and food was sent ahead to prepare the first camp. The family followed the next day. Annabella wrote:

It was a lovely morning in the first week of March when we set off in a large and comfortable carriage and five, in other words a large dray well piled with mattresses and pillows, and drawn by 5 strong bullocks. A steady old driver walked at one side, carrying a long-handled whip which he waved over them, or cracked cheerfully from time to time. Miss Smith (governess), Margaret (sister) and I were seated in the dray. Papa and Mama followed in the gig.

Annabella said it was a pleasant ride, not in the least uncomfortable because

. . . the great wheels (of the dray) move so slowly and seem so little affected by going over a stone, or sinking into a wide rut, that we never thought of being afraid.

They arrived at the camping spot to find the fires alight and the tent up, with a carpet spread inside it. They ate a hearty meal set out on a travelling chest. They slept snug and warm, and awoke next morning when the men began to light the fires and bring in the horses and bullocks.

We soon started up, and, seizing clothes and towels, flew to bathe in the clear, cool stream. We soon found a sheltered palm, and there arrayed ourselves,

wrote Annabella.

The second day's journey was much more strenuous. They left the valley and began to climb the hills, up the slope and down the other side of each rise as the track went steadily upward. Many times they had to come down from their 'comfortable carriage and five' and walk up the steep stretches to ease the load for the bullocks. Whenever the beasts stopped, someone had to place a large stone behind the wheels to prevent the dray slipping backward.

The girls walked on, gathering flowers and berries as they went. These they had to throw away as the track grew steeper, and they needed hands and feet to scramble up. Sometimes they were given a horse to hold or to lead, and that, said Annabella, took some managing. Best of all, they were occasionally allowed to drive in the gig for a short stretch, and this felt like flying after their slow progress on foot.

When they reached the top of a rise, the dray had to be prepared for the steep descent. This meant fastening a heavy chain from the dray to the wheel to hold it fast, otherwise it would have kept turning and would overrun the bullocks. It made a grating sound all the way down, and the dray and its load swayed alarmingly.

On a very long descent, the chain was often not enough. Then a small tree was cut down and fastened behind, to act as a further brake.

Everyone was anxious to reach the next camping spot where there was water for the stock, but suddenly part of the harness gave way and the stone jar full of water which they were carrying for their own use was broken.

They managed to bring the party to an old camp site a little way ahead, and there they had to spend the night. There was no water for the stock, none to make tea, and everyone was thirsty. Even the grapes they ate made them feel worse as they were so sweet. They ate their supper without interest, and crept rather miserably into bed.

In the night some of the men brought them water they had found, and the girls drank thankfully. But, to their horror, in the morning they found it so polluted it was nothing but green slime! Poor Annabella! She had hoped for a cup of tea with breakfast, but instead could not bring herself either to drink the water or wash in it.

The worst of the track was behind them, however, and they

set out more cheerfully. They reached some waterholes where they rested and the animals drank. By nightfall, they arrived at the place where their father had arranged for a carriage to meet them. It was at the junction of several roads and a meeting place for drays travelling to and from the stations. The family camped out another night and this time had milk and supplies from a nearby hut.

Annabella was astonished to see several drays arrive, piled high with wool, and with a woman and some children riding on top. How did they climb up there, she wondered, and once up, how did they stay there without tumbling off?

The next morning, one dray was sent home to Bathurst, the other went on to Sydney with the luggage. Miss Smith and the girls and their mother set off at a smart pace in the carriage while their father drove the gig.

That night they stayed at an inn where they spent an uncomfortable night, because, although Annabella would not say so outright, the beds were infested with bugs.

The next day they reached Penrith. They had taken four days to come a little over one hundred miles. It was no use being in a hurry when travelling in early Australia.

The girls and their governess stayed with an aunt about twenty miles from Sydney while their parents went on to make arrangements for the last part of the journey. When they were together again, Annabella said:

> We had some shopping to do for ourselves, which was a great treat, and mamma got us pretty grey silk pelisses, and neat poke bonnets of fine straw, trimmed with straw-coloured ribbon.

The visit to her uncle's handsome house at Lake Innes, near Port Macquarie lasted seven months. No one thought that too long. It was no use travelling so far and only staying a couple of weeks. The girls went on with their lessons, drew wildflowers, sewed pincushions and did embroidery, went to the beach and called on friends. They had no work to do.

But when families were struggling to make a living on their properties, everyone had things to do. Mothers and children set up hurdles to make yards where the sheep stayed at night. Children acted as shepherds. One little girl was only five years old when she began taking out the sheep on her father's property in South Australia. She spent the long hours while the sheep grazed playing with a handful of smooth pebbles, her only playthings.

Alexander, the eldest son of a family on the Murray River flats, was only eleven when he helped clear the land, plant crops and build the family cottage. His sister Minnie was only nine, yet she also helped by mixing the mortar to bind stones together to make the walls.

And it wasn't only country children who began working young. Australia's first newspaper, the *Sydney Gazette*, printed an advertisement for Boys Wanted between the ages of ten and fourteen. The elder lads were to be taught shipbuilding. The younger ones were to go to sea.

There were all kinds of jobs children could do. Water had to be hauled up from the family well or brought by cart from the nearest creek. Wood was always needed for cooking, and twice a day the cows had to be rounded up and milked. These were tasks for the boys. Girls helped make candles, hanging a length of cotton in each mould to act as the wick, and pouring melted fat around it. When it had set hard, the candle was loosened by standing the container in boiling water for a few seconds, just as a jelly is freed from its mould.

Girls also worked in the dairy, setting the milk, skimming off the cream, churning the butter and helping to make cheeses which had to be turned over every day to make sure that they cured properly.

Children who worked very hard, like Alexander for instance, didn't have time to spend learning lessons. Anyway, there were schools only in the towns and larger settlements. Boys and girls who lived any distance out had little chance of learning unless their parents taught them. Many parents did, and one girl said she used to follow her mother about the house as she did the housework. Her mother held a book in one hand, a duster in the other while her daughter recited a lesson, or spelt a list of words.

Families who could afford it sent their children to school in England. Others had a tutor for their sons, a governess for their daughters. But other children had little or no schooling, and it is not so many years since there were people in Australia who could neither read nor write.

Not so Annabella Boswell. She had her first lessons on her fifth birthday when she was staying in the home of some friends whose boys had a tutor. Annabella was allowed to sit with them on her birthday and work in a copybook, the usual way of teaching children to write in those days.

In 1834 when she was eight years old, Annabella went to boarding school in Sydney. The older girls at the school would tell spooky stories to the young ones, and then send them upstairs in the dark alone. Annabella was glad when her father came to take her home to have lessons with a governess.

Annabella studied the history of England and Scotland, of Greece and Rome. She learnt grammar and had a great deal of spelling. It was a time when people wrote many letters, and part of Annabella's work each week was to write a letter about what she had been doing. Here is part of a letter she wrote to her uncle at Port Macquarie, telling him first of all about her guitar:

> I made my fingers so sore and my arms ache but now my fingers have got quite hard at the points, and I am getting on very well with it. . . . I am reading the history of England, have got the length of James the First, who began the reign of the family of Stuarts in England. I like my studies very much indeed; they are a pleasure to me. Miss Willis (the governess) explains them as I go on, which makes them easy to be understood. I think I like geography better than any of my other lessons. I have gone through the four quarters of the globe with Miss Willis, and I begin again on Monday at the map of Europe and through each country, beginning at England. . . .

Annabella's father died when she was thirteen and for a time she went to school in Parramatta. Then with her mother and sister Margaret she went to live with her uncle, Major Innes of Lake Innes, where she had already stayed several months. Mrs Innes, her aunt, had several children and taught them herself. Margaret and Annabella joined them in their lessons.

The day began when the Highland piper employed by Major Innes sounded a tune on his bagpipes to wake the household. 'School' started at 10 o'clock with reading and recitations from the Bible. Then came half an hour of arithmetic and some dictation. Afterwards they went on with the lessons each had prepared as 'homework'. Annabella wrote:

> I said my lessons and did sums and translations in good old-fashioned style for four years.

The two-wheeled cart was used around the settlers' farm or to carry goods to market. Piled high with mattresses and pillows it was comfortable for the ladies.

Picnic at Mrs Macquarie's Chair painted by an unknown artist in the mid 1850's.

The sign on the rock reads:

BE IT THUS RECORDED THAT THE ROAD
Round the rock and a G[ ] Person Called
D[r] MACQU[ ] ROAD
So named by the Governor La[ ] [ ]here being Originally,
named L.M. [ ] [ ] 37½ Yards
[ ] [ ] on the 13 Day of June 18[ ].

(By courtesy of the Dixson Galleries, The Mitchell Library, Sydney).

An early reading light. As the candle burnt it was pushed up by a spring in the base of the lamp.

Butter was made by hand in this old churn and shaped with the wooden paddles.

An Australian kitchen 150 years ago. In the fireplace is a collection of old cooking utensils. To the left is the bread oven.

She was nearly twenty when she said goodbye to the school-room.

Although Annabella wrote about many parts of her growing years, she mentions very few toys, but we can be sure she had some. Toys began coming into Australia in the early years. They were part of the cargo which captains of the sailing ships bought and sold for their own profit. Advertisements in the *Sydney Gazette* often mentioned Children's Toys and Amusements in the For Sale notices. They included tambourines and music boxes, puppet shows, battledore and shuttlecock sets, toy animals and soldiers and figures dressed in the costumes of other lands. One shopkeeper wrote his advertisement in rhyme:

> Drums and trumpets, harps and fiddles,
> Mystic cards for solving riddles;
> Coaches, curricles and horses,
> Infant dolls for infant nurses.
> Guns assorted, swords and lances,
> Music set to country dances;
> Owls and geese and Dutch dragoons,
> Tygers, Frenchmen and baboons. . . .

There were books for children, but these would have been of the 'preachy' kind. Adventures and stories written just to be enjoyed were not known in those days, and stories about families were usually full of warnings to children that they had better be good or dreadful things would happen to them.

Annabella doesn't mention her early books. She began to read adult books when she was fairly young and such writers as Walter Scott and Charles Dickens. But her mother would not allow her to read all the books in the library, and Shakespeare for one was forbidden. It was considered most unsuitable for a young lady to read Shakespeare.

Another thing which girls were not supposed to do was whistle. Once Annabella and her cousins had a girl guest who was a first-class whistler. They could not let their mothers hear her so they always closed the doors or went outside before they asked her to perform.

But in spite of restrictions like that, and although Lake Innes was several hundred miles from Sydney, Annabella never complained that life was dull or even quiet. The family spent a good deal of time at the beach, taking their bathing dresses as

Annabella called them, but she does not say how they were made.

The young people galloped their horses along the beach and rode everywhere. The girls rode side saddle, of course, at first in habits made of brown holland, and later in blue ones.

They went visiting a great deal, and many guests stayed at the house. At night they sang round the piano, or played games, or danced: reels, waltzes and quadrilles. Annabella mentions an occasion when her uncle was supporting a relative at the elections. He invited a large party to Lake Innes to meet the candidate. Followed a busy few days decorating the house, arranging flowers and helping to entertain the guests. It came to an end in a lively fashion:

> Lunch in both rooms went off with great eclat, and then the whole party went out on the lawn . . . we found about twenty natives assembled there and dancing vigorously, while Bruce (the household piper) played. When they had finished, Dido proposed that we should dance a reel, and at once the whole party seemed inspired with a wish to join, and really there could not have been a gayer scene; we four girls in white frocks and pink sashes and bows flying through the dance pursued by nimble partners . . . occupied one end of the veranda, the rest being crowded with onlookers who had not been happy enough to find partners while another party, all gentlemen, danced upon the lawn (while) Bruce marched about in his Highland dress, his bagpipes decorated with a pink scarf besides the tartan ribbons. . . .

When Annabella was twenty the family became devoted to the polka, the romping dance which swept into favour in the days of bustles and many stiffened petticoats. Said Annabella:

> Fashionable people seem now to think they cannot put on too many, and some wear hair cloth bustles. They say the proper criterion is to see your bustle when you look over your shoulder.

The occasion which made Annabella write about the fashions was when the Governor, Sir Charles Fitzroy, was a guest at Lake Innes, and a dance was given in his honour with the ladies in the latest gowns.

Even at this time, Major Innes' affairs were causing worry, and in the next few years he left his lakeside house forever.

Annabella had already gone when this happened. She went back only once to the house where she had spent the last happy days of her girlhood. It was not until she had children of her own that she wrote down for them what life had been like when she was growing up.

Today only a few ruins mark where the fine house stood at Lake Innes, and the bush grows where Annabella planted seeds in the garden and gathered roses. But the beach where she rode her horse, the town where she went to church and the church itself are still there to remind us of days gone by, and of girls and boys who lived when Australia was younger and much different from the land we know today.

Life's Treasurings

These are life's treasurings:
The sudden sun through rain;
Stars on a frosty night;
Grass rippling o'er the plain;
Tempest grown still;
Hearth-fires when the long roads end;
Candlelight in a quiet room;
And the still silence of a friend.

MARY GILMORE

The Technical Age

FROM *The Bulletin* NEWSPAPER

Illustrations by Will Mahoney

The Overland Telegraph line between Adelaide and Darwin is copper nowadays. But I can show spears I collected after we had been attacked by Aborigines in the Territory in 1886, and most of them have points made by doubling a two-foot piece of No. 8 fencing wire, stolen from the telegraph line.

A linesman told me that the natives shinned up the poles like monkeys and hung on to the wires like flying foxes until there were enough to bring the wire (and themselves) down in a heap. Then they bent it about at the other end till it broke, and bolted away with about a chain length of Government property, and the line went dead. "And," he concluded, "we poor blokes have to go out and fix it."

Pieces of that No. 8 wire were traded right up into the Cape York Peninsula and over into the Kimberley country in West Australia by the Aborigines long before 1890.

'Larrapinta'
15 January 1930

The frogs round Lismore have a sense of rhythm. When the train from Sydney puffs laboriously on the upgrade, the frogs seem to hear it about a mile away. Every frog in the roofs and gutters bursts into chorus and keeps time with the train till the sound dies away in the distance. After that there is a pause and then they resume their croaking—but not in rhythmic unison.

'Kianga'
5 March 1930

The Darwin–Brisbane 'air' mail does a good bit of its travelling in the good old way. During the dry season (April to November) it is scheduled to leave Darwin for Daly Waters per rail at 8 a.m. on Wednesday. On the Friday it lights out per motor waggon for Camooweal, and there it is transferred to the plane which departs for Brisbane on Saturday morning and completes the journey on Monday.

In the wet season the itinerary is somewhat different: the mail leaves Darwin at 8 a.m. for Birdum where, all being well on the following Monday, it is transferred to packhorses and shoo-ed along to Daly Waters. Weather and other circumstances permitting, it arrives at that interesting spot early on Friday, to depart by plane for Camooweal which is reached on the same day. Leaving Camooweal on the Saturday, it is delivered in Brisbane on the Monday—almost a fortnight after leaving Darwin. The northbound mail is handled on similar lines.

'Bad Australian'
19 March 1930

... and the Bush at Night

How many bushmen have seen a rainbow by moonlight? While I was prospecting east of Karnalpi (West Australia) years ago, a sharp shower of rain fell at night. Going out to gather water from the pools I found a beautiful rainbow showing right across the sky. It was less distinct than a daylight rainbow, but the spectrum colours were there quite distinguishably.

'Billy See'
19 March 1930

The Old People

Illustrations by Joyce Abbott

THE CICADAS

THERE was once an old woman named Dirrangun. When the tribe used to go out hunting and gathering food, they used to leave all the children with this old woman.

While they were away, this old woman used to dig a big hole inside the camp. She used to dig it deeper and deeper every day while the mothers and fathers of the children were out hunting.

Once, while all the mothers and fathers were away, the old woman put all the children down into this hole.

When the tribe came home they saw no children playing around the camp. She was there, that old woman Dirrangun, she was sitting on top of that hole. She was waiting for the tribe to return.

The mothers and fathers asked the old woman where the children were. "Ah," said Dirrangun, "I don't know where they've gone. Maybe they have wandered somewhere away out of the camp." She was pretending to cry for them. She said that she'd been looking for them, but couldn't find them.

The children in the hole were digging a passage. They were trying to get out. When the old woman put the children into the hole she put bark and grass, her own bed, over the hole and sat on it.

The oldest children inside the hole dug and dug other passages so that they could come out. When the children came out of the ground they turned into cicadas.

Many of the little children in the hole died. When the *wee-uns*, the clever-men of the tribe, found this out they killed the old woman Dirrangun.

The *jurraveel*, the spirit-place, of the cicadas is at Back Creek. We call that place Irring. There is a hole there, with a vine growing in it. When the old people wanted a lot of cicadas to eat, they would go to this place and pull the vine and call out, "*Bunjarrbar irrimbarmo!*" This means, "Cover this place all over with cicadas!"

Told to Roland Robinson by Julia Charles of the Githavul Tribe.

THE SPINY ANT-EATER AND THE BUTTERFLY-PEOPLE

MY OLD mother told me this story. There was one old man, a grandfather, and he had two little grandsons. This old man, he'd kill an ant-eater. He'd send the two poor little fellers out to get some leaves, coolibah leaves, to cook in a ground-oven with the ant-eater.

The two little grandsons would set out. They'd call out, "*Nguga, Thaththa?*" That means, "Here, Grandfather?" But the grandfather would tell them to run further on.

And while those two poor little fellers were right away, hunting for those leaves, that old grandfather, I suppose, would eat nearly all that ant-eater.

Just the same, if that old grandfather had emu, or kangaroo, he'd do the same thing: send them poor little fellers out after the leaves while he ate up all the tucker.

So anyway, one day all the people from round about found out what this old feller was doing.

And these two little boys, they seen all these butterflies coming. You know how they go past, all drifting past. The two little boys would see that the butterflies were people with spears coming after that old grandfather.

The two little boys would call out, "*Thaththa!* You see all the people coming?"

And that old grandfather, he would say, "O, they're not people, they're butterflies."

They come then. Them butterfly-people got to that old grandfather because he was cruel to the boys. They got to him with their spears. All those spears been stick into that old grandfather. That old grandfather, he become spiny ant-eater. He been spiny ant-eater ever since.

And I suppose that all the butterfly-people took them two little boys away with them and reared them up.

Told to Roland Robinson by Maria Boney, Yoalarai Tribe.

JABBOR THE NATIVE CAT

WHEN Koopoo the red plain-kangaroo was travelling from Arnhem Land towards the eastern sea, he met Jabbor the native cat. Jabbor asked Koopoo to give him half of the big business which was all the secret rites, ceremonies and corroborees called Jaboordoorawa, belonging to Koopoo.

And Koopoo said, "No! This big business is all mine."

Jabbor then said he would fight Koopoo for it, but Koopoo called up all the blackfellows. And the blackfellows speared Jabbor with a flight of many spears. And this is why Jabbor comes to have spots all over him, for these spots are the holes that the spears made.

And as Jabbor lay dying, Deert the moon came along and said to him, "If you will drink this water of mine you will always be able to come back to life."

But there were many other native cats there who heard Deert the moon say this, and they would not let Jabbor drink.

"Very well, then," said Deert the moon. "Now you must all die. Animals, blackfellows, everybody must die forever. If you had drunk my water, you would all have been able to come back to life. I shall die, but you will see me return again. I am Deert the moon."

A legend from the Djauan Tribe.

ERNEST O'FERRALL

The Lobster and The Lioness

Illustrations by Will Mahoney

AT eleven o'clock Thomson, who had broken his glasses during a last whirling argument re the chances of the Liberal candidate, was pushed gently out of the side door and told to go home. Instead, he sat on the horse-trough and held an indignation meeting with himself until Sergeant Jones happened along.

"Good night Mr Thomson," said the sergeant kindly.

Thomson pushed his boxer hat to the back of his head. "Good evenin'," he returned sulkily.

"Are ye comin' down the street?" ventured the sergeant.

"Cert'nly not!" said Thomson. "I've lost me glasses, an' me eyesight's 'stremely bad. I can't see what I'm doin'!"

"Well, come along and walk with me. I'll see ye as far as the gate."

Thomson rose unsteadily. "Do you mean to 'sinuate I'm *drunk?*"

"I do not!" said the Sergeant. "I never saw a soberer man in my life. But come along now, an' I'll tell ye something I heerd today about Prince Foote f'r the Cup. I'm goin' your way."

On those honourable terms, Thomson consented to take up his lobster and allow Jones to pilot him.

According to Thomson's reckoning they had trudged through 283 deserted streets, and turned 1834 corners, when he found they were both standing still on a vacant piece of land.

"Whasser matter?"

"I heerd a strange sound," answered the sergeant. "Be quiet a minit. Maybe we'll hear it again."

They waited breathlessly. . . .

A deep, muffled grunt arose close by.

"That's it!" said the sergeant excitedly.

"Somebody's drunk," sighed Thomson. "Sailor prob'ly."

The sergeant snorted. "No sailor ever made a sound like that! Look, it's gettin' up! Is it a dog? . . . *Run, man! Run for your life!*" he yelled, and ran heavily up the dark lane.

Thomson, swaying on his feet, patted his leg and called to the approaching thing, "Goo' dog!"

Two yellow eyes glowed in the darkness.

"Goo' dog!" cooed Thomson, and patted his leg again. A deep, hungry growl. "Come on, ole feller. I won't hurt yer!"

The thing with the smouldering eyes came a step nearer, and Thomson cried out in delight. "By George, that's the finest mastiff I've ever seen! I'll get him to foller me back to the boarding-house!" He staggered off sideways, stopping every few yards to flick his fingers or pat his leg. And the escaped circus lioness followed him.

They went slowly up the long, flat street that stretched away to a plain of burnished silver—the sea. Thomson staggered on, hugging his lobster, till he reached a lamp-post. Then he sat down and, calling affectionately to the lioness, started to eat. "Here ye are, ole boy," he cooed. A claw hit the lioness on the nose and dropped to the pavement. The beast growled, but ate the fragment and licked her chops with pleasure.

Thomson dissected the food with his hands and chewed stolidly, occasionally throwing a bit over his shoulder. The lioness sat on her haunches and growled between courses, but accepted the scraps. This went on till the lobster was no more. Thomson then wiped his mouth with the back of his hand, leant against the lamp-post, and closed his eyes. In a minute he was asleep. In another thirty seconds he gave a long, whistling snore like the wail of a distant siren.

The wild beast, sitting erect like a thing of stone, growled nervously.

Thomson snored again.

The lioness growled angrily.

Thomson awoke with a start. "Who said that?" he demanded. He turned slightly and beheld the enormous beast. "Goo' dog," he cooed. "Goo' dog!"

Faintly, from the distant sea of lights, came the clear chimes of a clock, followed by twelve deep, solemn notes. Thomson rose slowly and flicked his fingers. "Come on, ole boy! Mus' be gettin' home!" He staggered along for about twenty yards, and the lioness, her head down and her tail straight out, tracked him step by step. Thomson didn't notice her; his mind was grappling with some problem. "Where did I leave it? . . . I'll go back and look." He steered a wavering course back to the

lamp-post, moored himself to it, and peered all round the circle
of light. "I wonder where I left that lobster? . . . I'm certain
I had it—an' I can *smell* it now! . . . Somebody's done me for it!"

Far up the street, approaching boot-heels made a clear,
crisp clatter in the still night. "I'll ask this chap if he's seen it,"
murmured Thomson, and took a firmer grip of the post.

The lonely pedestrian came up, and proved to be a young
man in evening dress.

Thomson raised his hat. "'Scuse me, did you notice a
'stremely large lobster as you came 'long?"

The stranger stopped dead, stared past Thomson into the
gloom beyond, and with a muffled cry of horror turned in his
tracks. He ran with amazing swiftness into the night.

"Hol' on!" yelled Thomson after him, but there was no
answer—merely the sound of a man running. The lobster-loser
turned, and found the lioness looking intently after the stranger.
"Serve him right if I sooled the dog on him!" he reflected
bitterly. "Come on, Carlo ole boy, if coffee-stall's open I'll get
a pie." Once more he set sail, and the lioness followed stealthily
in his footsteps at a distance of three paces.

Down the road they went, round two corners, then along a dark, shop-lined street. At the far end, near the kerb, gleamed the headlights of a coffee-stall. As Thomson drew near, the proprietor was seen leaning on the counter absorbed in reading the account of the previous night's fight.

Out of the darkness a command came to him: "Hey! Give's a pie an' 'nother f'r the dog."

The proprietor looked up cheerily. "Right-oh!" He put down his paper and turned to fill the order. As he opened his oven door a delicious whiff of hot meat perfumed the frosty air. The lioness in the shadow growled loudly.

"'Oo did that?" the hot-pie man asked suspiciously.

"Sorright," Thomson assured him, "the dog won't hurt yer."

"Wot sort dog *is* it?" persisted the pieman, vainly trying to see beyond the light.

"Mastiff," explained the amateur lion-tamer wearily. "Prize mastiff—mos' 'fectionate beast. Gimme two pies."

The pie artist took two of his finest works from the oven, and placed them on the counter just as the lioness growled hungrily again.

"Better give us another pie f'r the dog," said Thomson, putting a shilling down on the counter.

The coffee-stall man ignored the order and, leaning far over the counter, looked into the shadows. His eyes bulged. "*That* ain't no mastiff," he breathed at last. "It looks more like a— GORSTRUTH!" With one mad bound he was over the counter and away. Thomson howled after him indignantly, and waited for five minutes to see if he would come back. He didn't. At last Thomson climbed carefully over the counter, threw two sizzling pies at the lioness, and commenced on his own. Fortunately, the lioness's share fell into the gutter, and was thereby cooled, otherwise tragedy would probably have happened then and there.

After the light refreshments, Thomson climbed down and invited Carlo to follow him again. Some blind instinct guiding his feet, he at last came to the terrace house where he wasn't a star boarder.

Hanging on to the frost-cold railings in the moonlight, he communed with himself thus: "If I take the dog roun' back, I'll wake up all th' dogs in th' place and fall over dust-bin. . . . Yes, I better take ole Carlo in fron' door and go through house. That's it! That's what'll do. Come on, ole chap!"

With extra care and patience he at last found the keyhole and flung wide the door. Then he lit a match and cooed encouragingly, but in vain, until the match burnt his fingers. "*I'll* get him in!" he muttered, and, stumbling through to the kitchen, he found a large piece of raw steak. After opening the back door, he returned to the front and waved it at the lioness. "Come on, Carlo," he commanded. The beast, growling slightly, started to follow him. He backed into the hall, intending to lure his prey right through, but she was too quick for him. At the foot of the stairs she darted forward and snatched the steak from his hand.

"Give it here," he hissed, and made a wild grab at the goods.

The brute snarled horribly, and thumped the floor with her heavy tail. Thomson staggered back and his match went out.

A door on the first landing opened, a wavering light shone on the staircase, and a quavering soprano voice cried, "Is anyone there?"

"Sorright. It's only me," replied Thomson irritably. "I've gotter dog."

The candle, a wrapped-up head, and a long thin arm appeared over the banisters. "Do you mean to say you are bringing a dog through the *house*, Mr Thomson?"

"It won't hurt the d—n house!" retorted Thomson, staring upward defiantly.

"Mr Thomson," chattered the landlady, "you are not in a fit state to argue. I will speak to you in the morning." The hand that held the candle shook with rage, and the light wavered.

"I *am* fit to argue, and I *will* argue 'slong as I please. Come on, Carlo, ole chap!" He made a grab at the lioness's head, but missed. The brute snarled again, louder than the largest-sized dog.

"If you have any respect for yourself," wailed the landlady, "you will take that bloodthirsty brute out of the house!"

"Gorrer bed!" shouted Thomson. "Gorrer bed, you—you *ole meddler!*"

"How *dare* you!" shrieked the landlady, and fled to her room.

Then, alone and unseen in the hall, Thomson performed a really fine taming feat. Lighting the second last match to see what he was doing, he walked behind the lioness and gave her a hearty kick. "*Gerrout!*" he yelled, and the lioness, with an ugly shriek, ran lightly down the hall and into the yard. Thomson then shut both doors and stumbled upstairs to his room where, without troubling to undress, he climbed into bed.

On the stroke of three he awoke and muttered, "Warrer!" He struggled out of bed and blinked at the washstand. He could not make out a water-jug, and started to fumble for matches. He persevered until the water-jug meanly bumped against his elbow and smashed with a terrific sound on the floor.

"That settles it!" he said, and plumped down on the bed. For five wrathful minutes he sat and savagely wondered how best to avenge himself. Finally he opened his door and bawled: "Where's my shavin' water?"

The house remained asleep.

"Where's my *shavin' water?*" he howled again.

The walls flung the echoes back, and outside in the yard the dust-bin rolled to and fro.

Something hungry was ransacking it.

"D'ye think I'm goin' t' wait all day f'r my *shavin' water?*" roared the mastiff-finder for the third time.

The landlady's door flung open. "How *dare* you?" she cried. "How dare you make such a noise at this hour? What do you *mean* by asking for shaving water at this hour?"

Thomson lurched to the lobby railings and leant over. "I'll tell you why! *I want t' drink it!*"

"This is too much," wailed the wretched landlady. She rapped sharply with her bony knuckles on the door of the next room, and a sleepy male voice said, "All right. Be there directly."

Thomson leaned far over the railings and sniffed. His nose wrinkled in disgust, and he said something in an undertone about the place smelling like the Zoo. "Who's keepin' bears?" he demanded out loud. "I'm not goin' t' stay in place if you're goin' t' take in bears!"

"You are drunk," chattered the landlady furiously.

Thomson sniffed again. "The house stinks like a circus! It's bears, or tigers, or somethin'."

The door of the other room opened, and a tall, thin, spectacled man in a purple dressing-gown stepped out. "What is all the noise about?" he asked bitterly, holding his candle on high like the Torch of Liberty.

"I say there's bears in the house," repeated Thomson.

The tall man inhaled deeply. "There certainly is a strong odour of animals," he remarked acidly.

"What did I tell yer?" cried Thomson. His voice rang through the house, and two more doors were heard to open.

The tall, bitter man turned to the landlady. "I suppose, Mrs Tribbens, Mr Thomson has brought home a monkey or something of the kind. He seems to be able to do just as he pleases in this house; but I really must object to being called up in the middle of the night to talk about it. Surely it would have done in the morning."

"You don't understand, Mr Pyppe," retorted the landlady.

"No, I'm afraid I don't," said Pyppe irritably.

Crash! The tinkle of glass told the landlady that the kitchen window had broken. "What's that?" she gasped. Down in the pitch-dark hall they heard sounds which suggested a burglar in stockinged feet dragging the body of a murdered boarder over the linoleum.

"I will see what it is," Pyppe announced, and went

cautiously downstairs, a step at a time. Thomson and the landlady stared after him.

"Who is there?" cried the brave man, holding his candle far out over the railings. There was no answer.

"Who is there?" he snapped. His candle tilted, and a drop of hot wax fell into the well of gloom. A grating, bestial roar of rage rang through the place, and a lithe yellow animal sprang into the lighted radius and stood lashing its tail.

"*My God, it's a lioness!*" shrieked Pyppe, really shaken for the first time in his life. His candle clattered from his hand.

"I *tol'* yer so!" shouted Thomson outside the landlady's door, from behind which came hysterical sobs.

"The police!" wailed the distracted woman. "The telephone! Ring for the police!"

"I give you notice now," continued Thomson. "I think it's disgustin'. Why, your d—d lion might have eaten my dog! I'm goin' t' leave t'morrer. I'm not goin' t' live with lions."

A deep menacing growl floated up the staircase.

Thomson sprawled over the rails. "*Shurrup!*" he commanded, and the lioness, absurdly enough, was still. Without the slightest sign of fear, he made for the telephone on the landing.

"That the p'leece station? Yesh. Well, this is Thomson speakin'. Yesh, Thomson. Of Gladstone Manshuns. . . . I say, there's a lion in the hall here, waitin' to be fed. . . . Yes, a lion. . . . No, I'm wrong, ole chap—it's th' lion's wife. . . . Well, it's waitin' to be fed. I don't know who it b'longs to, but I'm leavin' in the mornin'. It's stinkin' th' place out. . . . Yesh, Gladstone Manshuns—you know th' place near th' Town Hall. . . . No, nobody's killed. There's nothin' here to eat but boarders—never is. Are you comin' along? . . . Right-oh." The bell tinkled in the darkness. Thomson fumbled his way to his room and shut the door.

It was a lovely, peaceful morning. There wasn't a sound until two policemen, and a little man in the ring-costume of a tamer, trotted round the corner. Thomson waved to them from his window.

"Go roun' side an' get in th' scullery winder!" he howled. "Look out f'r my dog in th' back yard—he's a big mastiff, but he won't hurt yer. If he growls, give him a bit o' lobster!"

Miss Laura Wellborn's Song

Amaranth lived in a Hansel house
with a groundsel bell with a tinsel chime
in grassful fields by the shadeful trees
and she sang *Blue Gentians* all the time.

Amaranth lived with a prideful cat
with a mouthful smile and a wrathful tail.
Amaranth made her restful bed
and she fetched the milk in a brimful pail.

Amaranth lived with a bloomful spring,
with the hazeful summer and shootful fall;
the dashful winter cried her by,
and she sang *Blue Gentians* through it all.

She sang, she sang, to her soulful cow
in the dewful grass at the songful dawn,
and again by night to her purrful cat,
who heard her out with a stretchful yawn.

RANDOLPH STOW

(These two songs are taken from unpublished
extracts of *The Midnite Papers*)

Trooper O'Grady's Song

A boot-faced wife sat on the quay
fishing like mad for kedgeree

She fished and fished, from dawn till night.
She did not get a single bite.

The more she fished, the more she sat,
the more she wished she'd worn her hat.

She fished for forty-eleven years.
For bait she used goannas' ears.

(There's nothing, as you may have guessed,
that kedgeree so much detest.)

When I am tired and sick of life,
I think about that boot-faced wife.

The more I think, the worse I seem.
Some people make me want to scream.

RANDOLPH STOW

Illustrations by Edwina Bell

BILL BEATTY

Here Comes The Tram !

A WOMAN approaches a tram terminus in Sydney. A conductor steps down from his tram to meet her and, with courtly grace, shakes hands with the woman and helps her aboard.

"Thank you, conductor."

"Please take a seat, madam. But first let me dust it."

"Thank you. And would you tell the driver to be very careful. I just can't abide this newfangled craze for fast travelling.'

"Leave it to me, madam. Now are all passengers comfortably seated?" There is a chorus of assent. "Very good. Then off we go!"

Believe it or not, that was a typical scene in the days of Sydney's steam trams during the late 1880s. If you are sceptical, here are some of the rules from the list of official regulations laid down for conductors:

The tram conductor must welcome and shake hands with all passengers, and conduct ladies to their seats.

He should dust each seat before the passenger sits on it.

The conductor must next inquire if everyone is comfortably seated. Then he should look right and left before signalling the driver to start.

On the route he must call out the names of all intersections, junctions, and the various stores.

Should the conductor notice any strangers in the tram, he should direct the attention of such passengers to places of scientific or historical interest.

At crossings the conductor must walk ahead of the tram with a red flag by day and a red lamp by night. He must also hold up cross traffic with a red flag and signal the tram to proceed by waving a green flag.

With the advent of the double-decker trams the conductors always carried string for the needs of the ladies. Southerly busters blew up ladies' skirts on the top of trams, and the string was a first-aid measure.

In the 1890s Sydney had the finest steam-tram system in the world. You could post your letters on the trams and be assured of an express mail delivery. The express trams from such out-lying places as Bondi, Coogee, and La Perouse whisked you to work at fifty miles an hour non-stop! Slow, local steam trams were backed into sidings to let the express trams through. First- and second-class accommodation were provided on the express trams. Their crews were proud of their reputation for speed and schedule. Passengers stop-watched the drivers and laid bets on the morning race, such as the Bondi express beating the Woollahra one, or the La Perouse tram licking the Botany tram.

Taylor Square, Darlinghurst, and Mark Foy's corner were winning-posts. The pointsmen were exceedingly worried men when the express mails came hurtling from different directions to the intersection. Luckily there was never a dead heat.

It was during this period that Fishing Specials were intro-duced. These took fishermen by express steam tram to the old Bondi terminus near the top of Tamarama. Fishermen boarded the trams with their gear and spent a day on the rocks with rod and line. Kegs of beer were placed in a special truck attached to the tram. Beer and bait were bought from the drivers and conductors, who were keen fishermen themselves. Those unlucky enough not to catch any fish did not need to go home in disgrace; there was always plenty to buy from those who did make hauls, and you could buy a basket of mixed fish for a shilling.

Many of the drivers of the ordinary local steam trams had pets that accompanied them on their daily runs. Best known was Teddy, the two-up cockatoo who was an expert at heading the pennies with his beak. He was much in demand at the trammies' two-up school in the rocks at the foot of Waverley Bay.

Another of the pets was a hen who, on the daily run, rarely missed laying an egg for the heavily moustached driver. Then there was the rooster who always crowed when the tram reached the top of a hill. Possums, too, rode on the steam trams and in winter would huddle near the engine or even drape themselves on the drivers' necks. And many fine tom-cats were drivers' pets. They were sudden death to rats at Darlinghurst water siding.

On Sundays the trams always stopped for the church hour. Many a Sunday's dinner was warmed in front of the fire on the engine, and picknickers could get plenty of hot water—given with the best of goodwill—for their billy tea. Such was the friendliness and community spirit of those days that the drivers would often wash the children's dirty faces with warm engine water and a clean rag. And there was never a tram strike or stop-work meeting of protest.

When the tramway authorities in Sydney tried out an electric tram for the first time, there were no overhead wires; the power was in a storage battery on the tram. Also the lines were the ordinary ones on which the old steam trams ran. The experiment was unsuccessful, and after a trial of about two weeks the electric tram was taken off. However, a most interesting fact was the official reason for its discontinuance; the tramway department stated that the tram had proved a failure because the electricity affected the watches of passengers!

Trams have now vanished from the streets of Sydney, and buses have taken their place. The modern-day busman is of another race and, for that matter, so is the modern-day passenger.

Acknowledgments

Every effort has been made to trace the ownership of copyright on material used in this book. We believe the necessary permissions have been obtained, but in the event of any question arising as to the use of material we, the publisher, will be pleased to make the necessary correction in future editions and we express regret for any error unconsciously made.

Acknowledgements are due to the following for permission to reprint copyright material:

Angus and Robertson, Sydney, for the poems 'Winter Stock Route' by *David Campbell* from SPEAK WITH THE SUN, 'The Bunyip' by *Douglas Stewart*, 'The Snow Gum' by *Douglas Stewart*, 'Life's Treasurings' by *Mary Gilmore*; Wentworth Books, Sydney, for the poem 'Two Thoughts about Waves' by *Lydia Pender* from BROWN PAPER LEAVES, published by Wentworth Books, 1971; Mrs I. M. Hall for the poems 'Autumn Wind' and 'No Night' by *Irene Gough*; Clive Sansom for the poem 'Close Your Book' by *Clive Sansom* from THE GOLDEN UNICORN, published by Methuen, 1965; Jack Pollard for the extract 'The Great Australian Game' by *Bob Skilton* from HOW TO PLAY AUSSIE RULES, published by The Pollard Publishing Company.

Ure Smith, Sydney, for the extract 'Tramway Topics' by *Bill Beatty* from TALES OF AN OLD AUSTRALIA, published by Ure Smith; Roland Robinson for six aboriginal tales collected by *Roland Robinson* from THE MAN WHO SOLD HIS DREAMING, ABORIGINAL MYTHS AND LEGENDS, and LEGEND AND DREAMING.

Rigby Ltd., Adelaide, for an extract from MAD AS RABBITS by *Elizabeth Lane*, published by Rigby Ltd;

N. L. Ray for the following stories: 'A Promise is a Promise', 'Gumboil and the Golden Belt', 'Where's Charlie?', first published in the New South Wales Department of Education's School Magazine;

Richard Parker for the story 'The Fire Curse';

The Bulletin Newspaper for the following extracts: 'Cap This', 'Outback Tales', 'Told in Town', 'The Technical Age', taken from columns in *The Bulletin*;

The Dixson Galleries for permission to reproduce the painting 'Picnic at Mrs Macquarie's Chair', artist unknown;

The Age Newspaper, Melbourne, for permission to use three photographs facing pages 80 and 81;

The Sydney Morning Herald Newspaper, Sydney, for permission to use three photographs facing pages 160 and 161;

Densey Clyne for permission to use four photographs for 'Cicadas' facing pages 96 and 97;

Ella McFadyen for permission to use three photographs for 'Lizards' facing pages 64 and 65;

256

H. J. King Tasmania, for permission to use two photographs and Keith Gillett, for permission to use five photographs for 'The Sea, the Shore and the Pool', between pages 16 and 17;

Jack Butters for permission to use six photographs for 'Flight to Fiji' between pages 120 and 121;

Jo Dearnley for permission to use three photographs for 'Bushman' facing pages 128 and 129, and for the photographs facing pages 48, 49, 112, 113, 176 and 177;

Hambledon Cottage, Parramatta, The Hawkesbury Msueum, Windsor and The Australian Village, Wilberforce, for permission to photograph historical objects for 'The Younger Land';

The Newcastle City Art Gallery, Newcastle, for permission to reproduce the painting 'Portrait of a Strapper' by Sir William Dobell;

John Brackenreg, Sydney, and the artist, for permission to reproduce the painting 'Mother and Child' by Michael Kmit;

Sali Herman, Sydney, for permission to reproduce his painting 'Ming 1963'.